MENTOR
and
MONITOR

First published in 2024 by
John Samuels, in partnership with Whitefox Publishing

www.wearewhitefox.com

Copyright © John Samuels, 2024

ISBN 9781916797543
Also available as an eBook
ISBN 9781916797550

Designed and typeset by Karen Lilje
Cover design by Dan Mogford
Project management by Whitefox
Printed and bound by CPI Group (UK) Ltd, Croydon CR0 4YY

HIS HONOUR JOHN SAMUELS KC

MENTOR
and
MONITOR

A ROLE FOR THE JUDGE

JS (John Samuels) by Michael Noakes (2000/2001): Past President of the Royal Society of Portrait Painters. Also living in Reigate, we became friends with a shared interest in Samuel Palmer, the Victorian artist who lived for 20 years in the house in which I grew up. Having painted the official portrait of my father when Chairman of the LCC (1959), he agreed to paint me at a similar age. At my request I dressed informally – not like his famous sitters: sovereigns, academics and dignitaries. Michael hated painting my jacket and shirt, destroyed his initial version, and wreaked his revenge by painting my tie crooked, which he knew would vex me.

*To Maxine; my immediate family members; my friends;
and my mentees: you know who you are!*

CONTENTS

PREFACE

It was only after many years in the law that I realised I had become a mentor. Equally serendipitously, I stumbled into judicial monitoring. This book describes my unexpected journey.

Definitions usually help:

- A 'mentor' is an experienced and trusted adviser, who also assists and befriends.
- A 'monitor' maintains regular and/or effective supervision over others.

I have spent my life in the law, so the book touches on its developments and relevant changes in judicial thinking and attitudes. Inevitably, it includes something of a personal biography.

I had never written a book. Essays, formal opinions, judgments and rulings, occasional speeches, lectures and articles, responses to government consultation papers and the production of the odd poem had been my limit. In my ninth decade, I found that I have something more to say. Paradoxically, its inspiration was *Prisongate*, also a first book, written by my friend General Lord Ramsbotham, whom I first met in his first month as Chief Inspector of Prisons. His inspiration had been the speech of Winston Churchill when Home Secretary in 1910:

> '*The mood and temper of the public in regard to the treatment of crime and criminals is one of the most unfailing tests of the civilisation of any country ... a desire and eagerness to rehabilitate in the world of industry all those who have paid their dues in the hard coinage of punishment ... and an unfaltering faith that there is a treasure, if you can only find it, in*

the heart of every man – these are the symbols which in the treatment of crime and criminals mark and measure the stored-up strength of a nation, and are the sign and proof of the living virtue in it.'

My enthusiasm for judicial monitoring came to an unexpected climax when the group of life-sentenced prisoners whom I had been visiting routinely for eight years gave me a retirement party on 18 April 2024. This book explains why.

I must abandon my preferred understated style of advocacy – *let the dog see the rabbit* – and be direct. I have been besotted with the law for more than sixty years. The hallmark of civilisation is the rule of law. In 2024, much is amiss with civilisation and the rule of law. The book does not, save in passing, highlight what are the most obvious examples – such as the Post Office scandal, and other notorious miscarriages of justice – but sketches, selectively, the sea changes that have so altered the legal profession, and particularly the approach of its judiciary, since I became a student member of Lincoln's Inn in 1960.

I see this book as a toastie, one of my favourite lunchtime snacks. The butter on the outside of the first slice of multi-seed bread represents my background: parents, school, university life and growing up generally, including early experiences in soldiering and in politics. That holds together the first slice: the Unexpected Mentor. The sandwich filling – Lincoln's Inn, a lifetime in the law and how it has changed over more than sixty years – is enclosed by the second slice: Judicial Monitoring. Within that metaphorical sandwich filling is a slice of pickle, representing not only a personal pickle in which I became embroiled, but also its rehabilitative outcome. That experience, as well as a personal involvement with many individuals who have endured far worse, has helped me to empathise with others, which underpins what mentoring and monitoring is all about.

Remarkably, it was only in 2003 that the purpose of sentencing was identified in a statute, and that purpose includes 'the reform and rehabilitation of offenders'. Unexpectedly, I became aware of an ability to assist others through mentoring, and discovered that this might be focused, through judicial monitoring and supervision, on those who genuinely wish to turn their lives around. That experience convinced me that the judiciary has a critical role to play. With prisons overflowing and social and psychiatric problems exponentially increasing, all who are alive to these demands cannot assume that hard-pressed prison and probation officers can provide everything that those who genuinely wish to improve may crave. It is for each judicial officer to decide how best to assist. This book will have achieved its aim if it provides some suggestions that strike a chord.

I have raided my contemporary diaries. When aged fourteen, I wrote: 'A person who writes an autobiography about himself, wholly and fully, cannot be left afterwards with anything more valuable than an empty chrysalis.' While I believe that this was an original thought, it should not discourage you from continuing to explore. I have always maintained a good filing system, and have retained some of the more interesting bits and pieces. My personal correspondence with the two outstanding judges of my generation, Lord Denning and Lord Bingham, will interest a wider audience. Some of my cases at the Bar are included, although I have tried to limit the detail, to maintain the interest of the general reader.

I practised as a barrister for thirty-three years; was a judge, both part-time and full-time, for thirty-two years (my part-time role obviously overlapping with my time as a barrister); and I continued as a Parole Board member when my age ended my sitting in the Crown Court. Anyone who seeks details of the cases that I conducted in these capacities will be disappointed. There will inevitably be some vignettes, either sanitised with changes of name or repeating what is already in the public domain; but my primary purpose is to focus on judicial monitoring, which I discovered by chance, and which I believe needs to be more widely known and enthusiastically adopted if rehabilitation is genuinely sought as a primary purpose of sentencing.[1]

---

1   Section 57(2) Sentencing Act 2020 provides:

*The court **must** have regard to the following purposes of sentencing:*

   a.   *the punishment of offenders,*

   b.   *the reduction of crime (including its reduction by deterrence),*

   c.   *the reform and rehabilitation of offenders,*

   d.   *the protection of the public,*

   e.   *the making of reparation by offenders to persons affected by their offences.*

If offenders are effectively rehabilitated so that they commit no further offences, the reduction of crime is achieved and the protection of the public is secured. Over a quarter of a century's experience of the practical operation of judicial monitoring and supervision, both as a Crown Court judge and as a judicial member of the Parole Board, and in a voluntary role in my retirement, has convinced me that judicial monitoring is the best hope of securing what are the proper objectives of good sentencing practice.

I have borrowed from Shakespeare's 'Seven Ages of Man' in some chapter headings. This reflects my enthusiasm for the apt quotation. However, for the time being I reject any analogy with the description of Shakespeare's sixth age, 'the lean and slipper'd pantaloon'. While I accept that in the fullness of time I shall, inevitably, face the seventh age, 'mere oblivion', I hope to survive that fate for a little while.

BEGINNINGS

At first the infant,
Mewling and puking in the nurse's arms
Shakespeare, *As You Like It*: Act II, Scene 7

'Mr Briggs, what are all those flying things?'

'They're called doodlebugs, John, and they're going to land on London.'

The sky was black with them. It was early summer 1944, just before my fourth birthday; and we stood in the back garden as they flew on, over Reigate, on their deadly mission. It seemed as unreal then as now, eighty years on. Where they landed, I never knew; but wherever they landed, at least one home was destroyed: at least one family eliminated. Why was it Mr Briggs, my mother's gardener, and not my parents, who had to explain all this to me?

The trick is to decant the reality of those early memories. More than thirty years later, I was trying to persuade the Court of Appeal that a five-year-old child propelled through the plate-glass window of a shop by a car that had been stolen by a fourteen-year-old, and whose mother was cut to pieces by the glass, was likely to have lifelong memories of this terrifying event. The child, mercifully, was unharmed physically: the issue was the extent, if any, of his psychological injury. The presiding Lord Justice, whose career at the Bar had specialised in personal injury litigation, was genuinely bemused to be told that a child of five would retain such a memory. 'I have no recollection of anything at all', he pronounced to this surprised advocate, 'before being sent away to boarding school at the age of seven.'

So, with a respectful bow to his Lordship, my more vivid wartime memories remain just that: vivid. One of the first: looking up at the arch

1

of summer jasmine between the back door and the lawn of my first remembered home in Reigate. I am sure I saw this, lying in my pram, and since the jasmine would have been in flower in July/August, it must have been in 1941. The following year I would have been too old, approaching my second birthday. Another – more prosaic: sitting on my potty. This could have been at any stage up to the age of three or so, because it was forbidden to get off that enamelled object until success was achieved with the appropriate waste product in its bowl. Boredom encouraged long voyages of discovery across the herringbone parquet-pattern linoleum. Sometimes, to my delight, the whole caboodle tipped up, which usually meant no more than some pee on the floor. On one of these journeys, I saw something flash past the window. It was followed by a huge bang – a shell, which exploded opposite a house at the end of our road. It blew all the windows out. The house was that of my first girlfriend, Susan. I was hugely relieved, because I knew there was a crack in my playroom window, not yet discovered by higher authority, that could henceforth be confidently attributed to enemy action.

I made a poor impression on Susan. We were supposedly matched by our mothers, being of a similar age; but Susan's main interest (for me) was that she had an absentee dad in – I think – the Merchant Navy. Ultimately, he returned to Smoke Lane; but by that stage there was a cooling of the lukewarm relationship between Susan and me, because her mother objected vociferously (and, in the circumstances, not unreasonably) to the fact that I had discovered that yew berries squashed in Susan's hair were a cast-iron way of getting attention – albeit of the wrong kind.

I can picture, vaguely, a dogfight between aircraft, high in a cloudless bright-blue sky; vapour trails; and then, fascinated, my neck creaking with the strain of looking up, the billowing out of white parachutes, floating slowly and sedately downwards. Of this last memory, I have no doubt. Another: standing at the level crossing at Reigate station, as a freight train tugged slowly at its long burden of dismembered aircraft on their way to assembly or repair. My contribution was to keep counting the wagons and giving up, somewhere in the hundreds. But there was nothing frightening; no shortage of which I was aware – even sweet rationing, which persisted until well after the war was over, had no significance, because my personal sweet ration was one sweet a week. This was one of my father's inflexible rules.

Perhaps the closest I came to wartime excitement was when I was being ferried to nursery school by Miss Lloyd, the intrepid headmistress, in her van. She had removed the front passenger seat and replaced it with a wooden bench, which we called the motorbike. A dozen tiny tots scrambled on to this, clasping each other round the waist, as Miss Lloyd imposed her idiosyncratic driving discipline. One day, probably in late 1944 (my assumption, as I started nursery school in September 1944, and daylight bombing raids on the Home Counties petered out by the end of that year), the air-raid sirens – that familiar wailing double note, only modified by the more cheering single note of the all-clear – sounded, and Miss Lloyd decided her charges had to de-bus instantly and take shelter. While she knew the house into which we all crammed, it was new to us, as we squashed into the unfamiliar air-raid shelter. This was a big adventure! Nights in our own Morrison shelter, which was under the sideboard in the dining room, are only a vague memory. I do clearly remember the steel mesh on the side. Peering through the holes remains part of the texture of those nights; and the occasional repetition of the all-clear siren still makes the hair on the back of my neck prick up.

The coalition Home Secretary, Herbert Morrison (who gave his name to the shelter), contributed vividly to my wartime, as well as to later, memories. Morrison was the first of a series of outstanding Labour leaders of the London County Council, all of whom played some part in my early years. Labour came to power in London in 1934; and Dad, who had been active in Labour politics in Battersea as a teenager and was first elected to Battersea Borough Council aged just twenty-one, was one of Morrison's lieutenants. Dad was first elected to the old London County Council in 1928, and in 1934 he became one of the Morrison cabal of committee chairmen. One Sunday, not later than the early spring of 1945, Morrison spent the day with my father. I never knew why, but I vividly remember that after Sunday lunch, Morrison and Dad went for a postprandial walk. At the corner of Smoke Lane there was a refuse bin, strategically placed to collect pig swill – part of the wartime effort to boost food production.

This had been pushed over by a greedy dog. Its lid was lying some way away, and the dog was enjoying its Sunday lunch. Morrison, Home Secretary, was appalled by this undermining of the war effort. He righted the bin, collected the lid, which he jammed back on, and strode purposefully away, picking up his conversation with Dad. Toddling along in the rear, I glanced back, and was delighted to see the bin, again lying on its side, with the dog resuming its interrupted meal. The symbolism of that moment remains an example of political power meeting its nemesis.

What of other wartime memories? One comes unbidden: bathtime in the duck-egg-blue bath. Under the wooden tray at the tap end, I crouched spellbound as my mother pretended we were in the French resistance. I was Jean; and we always outwitted the Germans, and ended up singing the Marseillaise, which I had word perfect before I went to nursery school.

My mum's enthusiasm for teaching me to learn poetry by heart was evidenced at this early stage. My first 'party piece' was 'Overheard on a Saltmarsh' by Harold Monro.

Nymph, nymph, what are your beads?
Green glass, goblin. Why do you stare at them?
Give them me.
    No.
Give them me. Give them me.
    No.

My mother had a sense of the dramatic, and took some pride in having played the part of Elizabeth I in an amateur production before her marriage. I remember her recreation of Elizabeth's speech to the troops at Tilbury before the Armada. The timbre of her voice rising musically from the bottom of the register to a contralto – 'and of a King of England, too!' – echoes, with total recollection, today. This vocal quality enabled my mother to speak with mesmerising authority in later life, and to encourage her audience to believe they had heard something of real profundity, whereas the written word could not objectively justify such a compliment. My father, by contrast, was the master of the short speech. He took immense care over the preparation of whatever he was going to say; and his notes on how to do so, 'The impromptu speech', were influenced, as he told me, by Lord Birkett. While inevitably they have a dated quality, there are some timeless lessons there for anyone who addresses an audience. Curiously, while Dad was an authoritative and persuasive speaker, it was far easier to listen to my mother, and to be beguiled more by how she sounded than what she said.

Two memories stand out. The first is being prompted to recite the Harold Monro poem one day, aged just four. It was before I went to nursery school. Among the admiring relatives present was my Aunt Katie, my gran's sister, a former schoolteacher, who pronounced majestically at the end of the performance: 'That is cruel!' The fact that I have an abiding love of poetry, can still recite vast chunks of what I once learned and loved, and have spent much of my adult life speaking to audiences must owe something to these early lessons.

The vivid recollection of 1945 was VJ Day: 15 August, my fifth birthday. We were on holiday on the Isle of Wight. I cannot forget the 9 o'clock morning news: the announcement that the war with Japan was over; and just as I had taken that on board, the bell rang, the postman arrived, and it was a parcel for me! My first Meccano set. A present from Uncle Joe (an important person in my life, for he was in the Home Guard) and Aunt Mary. They continued for many years a happy tradition of finding the best and most unexpected Christmas and birthday presents. It made me feel disloyal to acknowledge even privately that the excitement of opening their carefully selected Christmas parcel was greater than that of my parents' more predictable presents. As a childless couple – by choice, according to my gran, but how should I know? – they were always first in line for spoiling their only nephew.

Family photographs trigger memories. Seated on a pony, I was encouraged to learn to ride. This was a disaster. I was tipped, head-first, into a patch of brambles and stinging nettles under which, for good measure, there was a pile of broken bricks. I was bleeding, scratched, bruised and understandably in tears, but the formidable Miss Lloyd pronounced: 'You will never be able to ride, John, until you have had at least half a dozen bad falls.' With impeccable if immature logic, my conclusion was that if this is what it took to be able to ride, it was not for me.

Other memories are rooted in Isle of Wight holidays. Just down the road from the B&B where we stayed was an abattoir, and my father thought it would be educational to take me there. I vividly recall the squeals of the pigs as they were driven into the abattoir; and, after an appropriate interval, their corpses, covered with blood, were secured to a slowly progressing conveyor belt. Dad adopted a similar approach when I was just nine. We went to Barcelona, and he took me to my first and only bullfight. To ensure that the lesson was not forgotten, we subsequently read, together, Hemingway's *Death in the Afternoon*.

Another memory. My father had borrowed a car, and an educational trip was arranged to Carisbrooke Castle, in which Charles I had been imprisoned by the Parliamentary forces. I was told, in graphic detail, about the decapitation of Charles I. On the return journey, Dad was stopped by a policeman because the car was not displaying one of its rear lights. The policeman poked his head through the window of the driver's door; and I, sitting in the back seat, promptly burst into tears. Sobbing, I asked the policeman: 'Is my daddy going to have his head cut off?' My first successful plea in mitigation.

In 1945, I had my first experience of surgery. I needed to have my tonsils removed, a procedure that was then far from straightforward. This was the first occasion on which I had *ever* been exposed to sharing a bedroom with another child. To ease the unwelcome experience, with an unknown boy in the next bed, I was presented with a new toy. It was a cardboard sailor, who rocked convincingly on a shaped wooden base. New toys were rare, and they were unsophisticated. I can remember clutching the toy, possessively, just before I became unconscious. Later, as I fought through the waves of nausea and was violently sick, I stretched out a hand for my sailor – but he had gone! The floods of tears, mixed with a raging sore throat, combined to sear the experience in my mental commonplace book. The promise of ice cream, for the sore throat, was of no more than minimal solace: I had been robbed. The other boy had woken far earlier from his operation; he had pinched my sailor from the bedside locker that separated our beds, and had, at a stroke, determined my future career as a cross-examiner, and a judge.

———

It is hard to determine when I first appreciated the qualities of my parents, or that the nature of their attraction was similarly unique. My father was the clever elder son of an established Jewish family, who had settled in Battersea before he was born. My paternal grandfather was a kindly man, who owned a men's outfitters in Battersea Park Road. My paternal grandmother, Stella, to whom I remained very close, and who died just as I left school in 1959, plainly adored her Jack, and described a man who never knew an enemy. Short, prematurely bald – he was bald when Dad was a toddler – he was described as a tailor, but, unlike my other grandfather, he appears to have had no tailoring skills.

I know so little of my grandfather's family, and its roots, that I wonder whether this was either of no interest to my father or simply that he regarded the route he had followed to his own career as so much more distinguished than his immediate family that the latter was not worth passing on. Despite my closeness to Dad – and until my mid-twenties we remained very close indeed – I cannot remember him speaking of his father as an individual; and this now seems more than strange.

Jack's father had, like so many Polish Jews, arrived in the East End of London as refugees in the 1870s. Jack was the fifth child of Morris and Millie Samuels, one of eleven siblings, at least two of whom – females, who never married – were deaf-mute, a genetic condition that caused my father to investigate the possibility that it might be passed on to his own offspring. Dad told me his father was born in London; but this, with other family information, is belied by the 1881 census, which records his place of birth as Poland. Jack married my grandmother Esther (Stella) Woolf on 7 June 1899, and my father was born on 12 May 1900 – describing himself, quaintly, as a Victorian.

My father was named Albert Edward, after the Prince of Wales, who gave his name to the Edwardian era. The emphatically English names given to their firstborn son were because Jack and Stella were determined to integrate into the society in which their only grandson became, at least superficially, entirely assimilated.

What of my mother, formerly Sadie Beatrice Isaacs? The complexity of her character baffles me, her only child, whose genetic composition must largely have been based on hers. The dynamics of her own family throw some light on this, but she remains, for me, 'most near, most dear, most loved and most far' (from George Barker's poem 'To My Mother': who could not, based on the rest of that poem, have been more different).

Born in relatively straitened circumstances in Camberwell, of which she rarely spoke, by the time she was seventeen her parents had moved to Cricklewood, and she was able to go to St Paul's Girls' School. There she blossomed, was taught the piano by Gustav Holst, and made close friends. She was able to run, and did so very fast. She matriculated in July 1919, before going to the relatively newly founded London School of Economics. My mother was hardly a blue stocking; her appreciation of economics was limited, albeit she presented herself as having a degree in economics and public administration, and she graduated in 1923 with third-class honours. At LSE, she made many friends; she was a lively and certainly charismatic young woman, of markedly striking appearance. She met my father while he was at King's College, reading for his LLB, which he completed in 1921, the year he also qualified as a solicitor. My father was one of four close friends: all qualified as solicitors together in 1921. Each of the other three (Dingwall Bateson, Edwin Herbert and Arthur Driver) became President of the Law Society. Edwin Herbert was the architect of the report that led to the creation of the Greater London Council and the end of the LCC. He and my father went on walking holidays in Switzerland. He was elevated to the House of Lords as Baron Tangley.

Dad was articled for five years to Sir Thomas Cato Worsfold, who was elected to Parliament for Mitcham in 1918. The articles cost his father £150, plus £80 in stamp duty: a huge sum. Its payment probably saved Dad's life. Inevitably, he tried to enlist, albeit underage (he once told me that most of his school class had died in training for the Royal Flying Corps), and Worsfold told him that if he enlisted, his father would forfeit the money paid for his articles. Stella played a similar part in dissuading

Dad from going to France. She told me that she found the Sam Browne belt my father had surreptitiously bought – as a former cadet in his school cadet force, he had assumed he would be commissioned – and threw it in the dustbin. Dad never spoke about this.

I was vaguely aware that my father had pursued my mother for some ten years. In my mother's autograph album, which is remarkably empty (although clearly acquired while at St Paul's Girls' School), the following anonymous note appears in Dad's handwriting: *I saw a lady at the top of a staircase and said, 'There is my mate'. I spoke with the vanity of youth but a quarter of a century later found that Providence had smiled on me and had made me prematurely wise.*

My mother's father, Albert Isaacs, was the seventh son of a seventh son: a feature that in Jewish folklore proclaims extreme good fortune. With one exception, so far as I know, the totality of his extensive family perished in the Holocaust. I have gleaned little about it in my own research. Maybe it was thought I needed to be protected. The sole exception was a cousin of my mother's, who was living in Israel in 1960. I was put in touch with him by Moshe Sharett, former prime minister of Israel, a friend of Mum's at LSE. I telephoned and asked to meet. He brusquely refused: 'Why should I have any interest in meeting you?' That hurt, at the time. Over sixty-four years later, I understand: he had coped by refusing to look back.

Albert was born in 1873. He was due to be called up into the Russian army, which he did not want to join. Aged fourteen, he walked from Poland and ended up in the East End of London. He spoke no English; but, as other desperate immigrants found, the immigrant community welcomed him, and gave him all the support he needed. He was soon an apprentice tailor; and the skills he learned in that profession remained useful, despite his subsequent career as a diamond merchant. During the First World War, he had a Home Office role in overseeing the control of diamond smuggling. Shortly after the war ended, Grandpa took my mother with him to Poland and introduced her to her cousins. On the night before they left, he asked her to give him her jacket. When they returned to London, he took it from her, and removed the buttons. They were full of uncut diamonds.

When my mother married in 1934, Grandpa lived at a smart Kensington address. Like many immigrants of his generation, he dressed fastidiously. Relatively tall, my family photographs show him in an impeccably cut suit and a perfectly knotted tie. He had a goatee beard, which he rubbed against my cheek when he kissed me. How I hated that! My grandparents' flat in Hove was dark and gloomy. I remember a couple of Rembrandtesque portraits of Grandpa's parents and a large sofa, behind which I played with a set of Bakelite ashtrays for what seemed like a *very* long afternoon. There was nothing else to do. Children should be seen and not heard.

Grandma was someone whom it was difficult to love. While I imagine she took some pride in her only grandson, not only was she an inveterate troublemaker between my parents, but her behaviour towards me as a small boy was hurtful. I remember with painful clarity asking her in the gloomy Hove flat, when aged no more than five:

'Don't you think I'm clever, Grandma?'

To which I received the crushing response: 'Certainly not! You are a horrid, conceited little boy! Go and stand behind the door until you learn what a stupid, silly boy you are.'

I can still feel the slow deflation of that prematurely pricked ego.

She would often say, when in one of her not infrequent depressed moods: 'I shall turn my face to the wall and die.' In 1958, following a distressing schism between my mother and her siblings, for which I am sure my mother was not to blame, that is what Grandma did. A horrific aspect of the dispute between my mother and her brother and sister was that she only learned of her mother's death by reading the announcement in *The Times*. This described Grandma as 'mother of Sidney and Lily'. Sadie, my mother, was simply not mentioned.

My parents devoted most of their lives to what can properly be described as public service. My mother became chair of the management committee of a large mental hospital, and remained in that post, by all accounts a distinguished as well as a highly respected chairman, for some twenty-one years between 1948 and 1969. She was subsequently chair of a local boys' school for nine years. My father had been involved in Battersea politics since he was a teenager, and was first elected to the London County Council in 1928. He later served as a member until the abolition of that council in 1965, and thereafter became a member of the new Greater London Council. He had served as chairman of major committees of both councils; served as chairman of the London County Council itself in 1958–9, a particularly memorable year; and retired as 'Father of the Council' in 1967. He was a Justice of the Peace for forty years: by coincidence, he was presiding in Battersea Magistrates' Court when I accepted my first brief in a criminal court in 1964, a fact unknown to both of us beforehand; and served as chairman of a hospital management committee, a valuation court and rent assessment committees.

Despite this joint record of service, neither of them received any award from the Queen, save for the Coronation Medal in 1953, which Mum wore with what seemed to me immoderate pride. By paradox, the only formal honours bestowed on my father came from the Italian and German governments, whose insignia, broadly equivalent to an English knighthood, were only worn by him at the state banquets at Buckingham Palace when their presidents visited the United Kingdom in 1958. I believe that the satisfaction they achieved from doing what they did, and doing it well, sufficed.

Each of them had a complex personality, and their relationship was correspondingly complex. Each of them wound up the other, in little as well as major ways. During my father's year as chairman of the LCC, no one could have had a more loyal and supportive consort, and my father paid an appropriately fulsome tribute to my mother at the conclusion of that year. However, there were tears and much frustration from time to time; and it was obvious to me, even as a small child, when my mother disappeared for a few hours from the house, that all was far from well. Superficially, though, and to everyone outside the immediate family circle, everything was fine, even though my father used to go for a constitutional walk, on his own, virtually every evening after supper if I was not available to accompany him, and in later life developed a chronic and painful skin condition, about which he rarely complained.

For many years, my father's preferred holidays were taken either on his own, usually to the South of France, or with his lifelong friend Howard

11

Morbey, although Dad and I took several memorable holidays together. I remember with nostalgia trips to North Wales and the west coast of Scotland, and even as an adult I accompanied him to Antibes, shortly before going up to Cambridge. Such letters as have survived from him to my mother, specifically when Dad was in Yugoslavia in 1958, reveal a warm and supportive relationship.

Despite his wide-ranging professional and political experience, Dad used me as a sounding board in relation to his campaigns, his ambitions, and his political and professional setbacks. He seemed to value my input and advice, although he must have realised how limited was my practical experience. After a lifetime of thinking about it, I believe he was using these opportunities to educate his son, in whom he had invested all his residual ambition.

A feature of my mother's personality that continued to puzzle me was that she told me she was ten years younger than her chronological age, and persisted in that deception at a time when I was likely to discover it. In 1950 I had made her a birthday card, which referred to her thirty-ninth birthday (she was born on 3 December 1901); and I then discovered – as children do! – a silver cup, from her family, dated 1910. I demanded to know how this could be correct, given that she was not born until 1911. Against floods of tears on her side, coupled with the quiet feeling that I had conducted rather an effective cross-examination, Mum confessed. It certainly taught me a lesson in questioning the reliability of every parental utterance.

After they had both died, and each was cremated, I installed a small garden where their ashes are scattered, and paid for a plot to be inscribed with their names, dates and the epitaph *Gratulere conspectis*. This would be described by purists as 'dog Latin'; but I regarded it as both apt and a double entendre, so both aspects attracted me. It was my own composition, which I translate as 'Give thanks to those on whom you look down' and 'Be grateful for what these distinguished persons have achieved'.

THE UNEXPECTED MENTOR

'Tis education forms the common mind:
Just as the twig is bent, the tree's inclined.
Alexander Pope (1688–1744)

Had anyone suggested, when I left school at the age of eighteen, that the pattern of my later life would be impacted by a broad enthusiasm for mentoring, the broadest aspect of education, I should have dismissed the notion out of hand. *Those who can, do; those who can't, teach.*

I never aspired to be a teacher. Since I knew I was to be a lawyer, and prospectively an advocate, the idea of teaching others never entered my head. However, in my last term, when I had secured my A levels and my Cambridge entry, with the brief authority vested in me as acting head of the school, the headmaster allowed me to teach Latin to a class in the lower school. I had forgotten this until, in 1981, I arranged a consultation with my junior. We were both briefed in an appeal to the House of Lords, and met at my home. When he came through the door he said, accurately: 'You don't remember me, but you taught me at Charterhouse.' I denied all knowledge of teaching anyone, ever. Curious, I asked if I was any good? Reassuringly, he told me that he had won an exhibition in Classics to Worcester College, Oxford.

The perspective of time lets you see the larger picture. As a young TA infantry officer, I accepted that my soldiers considered me a 'Rupert' (a derogatory term, applied to an apparently posh young officer); but, with hindsight, I can appreciate that to some of the younger members of my platoon I gradually became a bit of a role model. I accepted the shy invitation of one of them to teach him to read and write, and I enjoyed staying

13

behind on drill evenings for an hour or so to do so. Some years later, when recruiting in Dorking High Street, I was warmly greeted. I asked him what he was now doing. 'I joined the Metropolitan Police,' he said. 'It was all down to you, sir.'

It was in 1969 that I agreed to accept my first pupil, a Ghanaian. He seemed devoted to me. Following his return to Ghana, where he launched what turned out to be a successful banking career, we lost touch. My redis-covery is fleshed out in my diary of a visit to Ghana in 2007. This visit was the happy result of my placement at a dinner after her Call to the Bar with one of my many subsequent Lincoln's Inn mentees, a determined Ghanaian who was focused on succeeding as a barrister. She asked me if I would help her to create a Lincoln's Inn/Ghana Alumni Association. Despite believing the project to be impossible, I readily agreed. Supported by the president of Ghana (an honorary Bencher of Lincoln's Inn), a party from the Inn undertook a memorable week-long visit to Ghana, and I delivered the inaugural Lord Denning lecture to mark its launch. I was reunited with my first pupil, whom I had assumed had died following a military coup. He was delighted to see me, and presented me with an inscribed copy of the book on banking law in Ghana that he had written. As the primary purpose of the visit was to train the local Bar in advocacy, it clearly qualified as educational.

He was but the first of a succession of some twenty-five pupils. I actively enjoyed trying to pass on what I had learned to each of them, whether this was the technique of pleading, the mystery of successful negotiation, or the art of advocacy. It was a wrench to discontinue the pleasure of such a relationship when I took Silk in 1981. I invariably learned from my pupils, as well as trying to pass on something valuable to them – if only some war stories. Many of them have remained close friends.

I had taken several pupils following my first from Ghana, but these had been suggested by the Education Department of Lincoln's Inn. Once I arrived at 4 Paper Buildings, I became a little more selective, and not only the quality but the longevity of my relationship with my pupils reflected that approach. My first memorable pupil at 4 Paper Buildings was Nich-olas Davidson. In conversation with David Neuberger, then President of the Supreme Court and the Treasurer of Lincoln's Inn, David commented that Nicholas was the cleverest of his contemporaries and had beaten him in the Bar exam.

Nicholas, who took Silk in 1993, has remained a good friend. By coincidence, he subsequently left 4 Paper Buildings at a similar time in his career as a Silk to my departure; and similarly, I believe, came to regret doing so. He remains in successful practice (having returned to Hailsham Chambers) as one of the leading lights in professional negligence, and played a prominent role as my junior throughout the twelve years of the Sunday trading saga between 1982 and 1994.

Nicholas was followed by Angus Glennie, a refugee from shipping chambers. Extraordinarily able intellectually, Angus had an abrasive quality that brought him into conflict with Douglas Hogg, then an aspiring politician, who could be equally astringent. The difference was that Douglas was the established tenant, and Angus was the pupil. The particular *casus belli* related to voting in the then forthcoming first Common Market referendum. Douglas asked brusquely how Angus intended to vote. The languid reply was: 'I am unsure, but I shall adopt whatever is the Communist line.' That went down like a ton of bricks. Shortly afterwards, I had to spend a day in a distant county court, leaving Angus in chambers to draft an urgent affidavit. On my return, I was pleased to find the draft sitting on my desk – until, turning over the last page, I read the unwelcome note: *Now 6.00. Finish it off yourself.* A few weeks later, with the end of pupillage in sight, Angus asked whether his prospects of a tenancy were good, as he was reluctant to return to the shipping chambers, which had already offered him a provisional place. I had to explain, with some disappointment, that a formal application for a tenancy was unlikely to succeed. So back he went to shipping, got his tenancy, and swiftly transferred his practice to Scotland, where he could indulge his primary passion as a sheep farmer. He became a High Court judge in Scotland as Lord Glennie, in charge of the commercial list in the Court of Session.

My next memorable pupil was John Paynter. He could have had an excellent common law practice, but following a further pupillage he left the Bar for the City. A highly successful career developed. City success took him away from London, and funded the acquisition of a country estate near Bath; he died prematurely in July 2016, having retired on health grounds from the chairmanship or non-executive directorships of a host of well-known institutions. At his crowded memorial service on 13 September 2016 – he was the first of my twenty-five pupils to die – it was reassuring to learn how fond he was of me.

John Stevenson, son of Mr Justice Melford Stevenson, was my next pupil. He had been destined for a tenancy at the highly successful chambers established after the war by his father. Placed with the completely brilliant Christopher Bathurst, he was at first simply out of his depth. Tom Bingham, by then my favourite leader in commercial cases, rang me up and explained John's need to be taken on by a good all-rounder, rather than exposure to the esoteric practice, which he had hated. I was happy to oblige. When John arrived, he appeared shell-shocked by being out of his depth at 2 Crown Office Row (now Fountain Court); but he thawed out well. He had some memorable idiosyncrasies. Piloting his own aircraft seemed a little sophisticated in a pupil; and when I said that I was apprehensive about my forthcoming appearance before Mr Justice Bagnall, it was disarming to be told, 'He'll be fine'. On going into court and receiving a warm greeting (directed, obviously, at the pupil rather than to me) from a usually cantankerous judge, I was suspicious. On leaving court, I demanded an explanation. 'I won £400 at cards from him at the Travellers last night.'

Christopher Baillieu was a joy. He had been president of the Cambridge University Boat Club and went on to win a silver medal in the Olympics and a gold medal in the World Rowing Championships. To my regret, he abandoned the Bar in favour of a career in sports administration.

Another memorable pupil was Francis Maude. Son of a well-known politician, it was clear that Francis was likely to follow in his father's footsteps. I enjoyed the six months he spent with me, but could not persuade him to remain. He had already booked a second six-month pupillage in the chambers of Michael Havers QC, MP (later Attorney General and briefly Lord Chancellor), and that experience did not tempt him to remain at the Bar. He went into the City, made a good deal of money before entering Parliament, and ended up in the Cabinet. He is now Lord Maude of Horsham. Long after I had retired, I went to an event addressed by Lord Maude. He caught sight of me in the audience and announced to general amazement (including my own): 'There is John Samuels: he taught me everything I know!'

Morag Alexander was not the first of my female pupils. She was, however, by far the most personable. She had no particular wish to be a barrister, and certainly no desire to practise. I clearly remember that on the only occasion she went to court to advance a plea in mitigation, which I was persuaded to write out for her in full, she returned and said firmly: 'Now I have done that, and I shall never do it again!' Morag's father had been in the Welsh Guards with Hugh Griffiths during the war, and the Bar seemed like a good idea. She was no doubt a far more attractive marshal to Hugh Griffiths than I had been to Fred Lawton (see chapter 7, 'First Steps in the Law'; and predictably, with 20/20 hindsight, returned from that spell as the intended bride of the other marshal. I was able to write, tongue in cheek, to Hugh, complaining of his breach of trust: I had lent him my pupil on the basis that he would take all due care of her. Hugh subsequently made the best speech at a wedding that I have ever been privileged to hear. Morag had become the inadvertent owner of a black-and-white kitten – Charlie. Somehow, we inherited Charlie; and Charlie and her daughter Sooty (named by my son Adam) became fixtures with us for the next twenty-two years. Their respective progeny were shared among members of chambers, including the clerk.

My next pupil, Michael Pooles, is the antithesis of Morag, save that he has equal charisma. It was a personal pleasure that, when I took Silk, not only was he able to inherit much of my junior practice, but we did a great deal in harness, long after my departure from 4 Paper Buildings. Michael remained a loyal junior, encouraging his solicitors to continue to use me as a Silk right up to the time when I went on the Bench in 1997. Michael took Silk in 1999; and, having served his term as Head of Chambers at 4 Paper Buildings, has become the doyen of Silks specialising in solicitor negligence.

It was with regret that I could no longer take pupils once I took Silk in April 1981, a state of affairs that no longer persists. The importance of pleading, previously the exclusive province of the junior, has declined; and the gulf between the practices of the junior and the Silk have narrowed across the board.

Thanks to Malcolm Carver, Under Treasurer of Lincoln's Inn, in 1983 I became a Hall representative of the Inn, initially on the Senate, and later the Bar Council. I had been co-opted to the Bar Representation Committee in the Inn shortly after taking Silk. My card as a potential volunteer was marked. This led to a six-year term as a governor of the Council of Legal Education, brilliantly chaired by Tom Bingham. Its high point was my role on a three-member panel chaired by the vice-chairman, John Hobhouse, whose task was to identify a suitable destination for the then Dean, who had lost the confidence of both governors and staff.

The third member was Donald Nicholls QC. Flatteringly, Tom asked me again.

'One of the topics in the context of Rawlinson [the committee that recommended the future governance of the Bar] is the future membership of the CLE ... At the Council meeting yesterday, it was resolved that there should be a (very small) subcommittee to review this question and make proposals to the Senate drafting committee. Nicholas Phillips [later Master of the Rolls, Lord Chief Justice, and Senior Law Lord] has been asked by the Senate to look into the matter, and as a member of the Council also he seems a very suitable person. I wonder if you would be willing to act as the other half of a subcommittee with him and make recommendations? I do not think the task is very onerous ... One always feels guilty at making requests of hard-pressed practitioners...'

I was happy to agree; and the fact that my three colleagues all became so eminent, and I became nothing at all, is just one of those things.

More pertinently, this opportunity to represent the Inn in the broader educational field enabled me to develop my thoughts about what the profession needed to equip its pupils, as well as the membership generally, with the experience necessary for contemporary practice. The clear-mindedness of the 1986 chairman of the Bar, Bob Alexander QC, gave me my head. Bob encouraged me to create a practice management course for pupils. This covered a variety of topics, including accountancy advice for the pupil; how to read a balance sheet; professional conduct; relations with a pupil master and with the clerks; first days in court; and so on. This course filled a real need, and for over thirty years it remained a compulsory component of every pupil's calendar. Similarly educational was the little pamphlet '*Advice to Counsel: Counsel's Guide to Chambers' Administration*', which, following the distillation of the advice from a working group that I chaired, went through three well-received editions.

In 1999 I was introduced to Prisoners' Education Trust (PET) by their patron, Harry Woolf. They wished to recruit a trustee. As a judge by then exercising an exclusively criminal jurisdiction, this actively interested me. I was duly appointed; I declined an invitation to become chair of the Trust in 2001 (because I regarded fundraising as inconsistent with a full-time judicial role), but succumbed in 2006. I remained chairman for over six years, before securing the succession of the new chair, and subsequently remained actively involved with PET as its president. While I was a trustee of PET, I arranged a succession of visits by London judges to education departments within London prisons, and these were educational too: most judges had no idea that those whom they met were interested in education as a key to their personal rehabilitation.

I had stumbled into prison education just as, shortly afterwards, I stumbled into the concept of judicial monitoring and sentencer supervision. In July 2004 I was nominated by the Judicial Studies Board to attend a two-week criminology course at Robinson College, Cambridge. This proved a revelation. The more enlightened, and less cash-strapped, Home Office of the time sponsored the course, which brought together senior police officers, prison officers, Home Office officials and a smattering of magistrates to dip a toe into the water of issues affecting the criminal justice system. Quite apart from an introduction to those who subsequently became friends and colleagues, I was enabled formally to develop my burgeoning thoughts about sentencer supervision by the carefully focused idealism of Alison Liebling (now Professor of Criminology and Criminal Justice at the

Cambridge Institute of Criminology) and Nicola Padfield (now Emeritus Professor, and former Master of Fitzwilliam College).

Another event occurred adventitiously, as a result of one of my educational visits to Strasbourg and Luxembourg with Paul Heim. Paul became a Bencher of Lincoln's Inn when he retired as a senior European civil servant. His career had culminated as Registrar of the European Court of Justice. He then introduced generations of Lincoln's Inn members to European law and the important courts of Luxembourg, Strasbourg and the International Court in The Hague. Musing, as we did, on the unfairness visited on young members of the Inn, who were being called in ever-increasing numbers as the providers of the Bar vocational course recognised the financial advantages of running such a professional qualification as a postgraduate course, but which – due to the reductions in pupillage available at the self-employed Bar – meant that for many the cost of the course was worthless, we decided to address the problem. Our joint concern was that the Inn, which we both cherished, would be seen as an irrelevance by its increasingly disillusioned members. The upshot of our conversation was the creation of what became the Inn's Pupillage Foundation Scheme.

The scheme launched in 2003, and has recently completed its thirty-fifth iteration. In essence, the scheme matches individual mentors, who are mostly members of their chambers' pupillage committees, with each mentee. The mentors then individually review the written applications for pupillage provided by participants. At subsequent events, they provide interview practice and feedback. Detailed guidance is offered in relation to how to structure pupillage applications, and how to cope with the difficult questions, such as 'Why do you wish to be a barrister?' Key to the success of the scheme is not only the enthusiasm and competitiveness of independent mentors to ensure the success of their mentees, but the informal party at the end of each session, at which mentors and mentees chat in a supportive atmosphere. Opportunities for mini-pupillage and the availability of openings that potentially lead on to pupillage emerge from these gatherings. At every opening of the scheme, I have emphasised that we do not aim to achieve pupillage for everyone. On the contrary, each member of the Inn who takes part is encouraged to believe that membership of the Inn is important; and the scheme enables each member to secure their career potential, while retaining appropriate links with the Inn. That so many of those who have passed through the scheme regularly tell me of their gratitude is an inspirational tribute to something that now works so well; and, as a by-product, statistics show that some 40 per cent of those who have passed through the scheme have secured pupillage in independent practice, some doing so several years after their Call. It has been a joy when I was subsequently teaching or acting as a senior Rover at a Pupils' Advocacy or New Practitioners residential weekend, and those whom I have supported on the Pupillage Foundation Scheme are there.

More actively concerned with 'hands-on' education has been my engagement as an Inn advocacy tutor since 1997. For many years I was categorised as a lead tutor and tutor trainer, and in that capacity have chaired the Grading Sub-Committee of the Inn, which assessed the relative roles and responsibility of the teaching faculty of the Inn, now extending to some one hundred members. I completely revamped the structure of that committee in 2014, and it now insists on evidence-based recommendations for promotion or otherwise of individual tutors. I also identified, in a document provided to every tutor, what the Inn expects of them, whether brand-new or experienced tutors. For many years I routinely either taught or acted as course director, or senior Rover, on the Inn's compulsory Pupils' Advocacy residential weekends, the New Practitioners' Programme, or both.

In July 2016, I agreed to undertake the chairmanship of the Inn's Euro Group, founded by Paul Heim, which, in addition to arranging prestigious lectures on topics of European and Human Rights law, facilitates placements for appropriately qualified students in The Hague, Brussels, Strasbourg and Luxembourg through Inn scholarships and grants.

———

Following my full-time appointment to the Bench, I welcomed the opportunities for marshals, or those who hoped to be appointed as Recorders, to spend a week or so with me, observing the routine of the Crown Court.

These visits were on top of the visits I encouraged those interested in my sentencer reviews to make on Fridays, when I routinely reviewed those who were the subject of my monthly Drug Treatment and Testing Order and Suspended Sentence Order reviews.

One of these marshals was a lecturer from Nottingham Law School, whom I met at a dinner for law tutors held by the Inn. She asked to be my marshal. That was the beginning of a warm friendship. Fast-forward to 2011: Becky, by then promoted to Reader (and shortly to be further promoted to Professor), introduced me to the Dean; I agreed to become a Visiting Professor at Nottingham Law School, and in February 2012, to my amazement, I found myself addressed by a respectful receptionist as 'Professor Samuels'.

At that stage, I had not the faintest idea how I could contribute to this new role. As time went by, I was asked to deliver a few set-piece talks on soft topics such as 'How to please the judge' and 'Why do we send people to prison?' These seemed to be well received, but I questioned their value. In time, I grew in confidence – more particularly when a third-year student quoted back to me, with flattering accuracy, what I had said in the lecture during her first year.

A more objectively useful role developed incrementally. My visits to Nottingham included individual advice sessions for those pursuing a legal qualification. They focused on the pursuit of pupillage and scholarship applications and seemed to address an unmet need. Similar advice was dispensed in seminars. I expanded this role by inviting those who wanted a more sustained mentoring relationship to become my mentee for the year. Over the years some of my mentees have, to my great pleasure, remained in contact.

My mentees received focused feedback on their individual pupillage applications, as well as learning of specific educational opportunities available in their Inn of choice. More recently, I expanded my role by giving informal talks to criminology students, as well as those within the Law School; and, through Socratic dialogue, tested whether my theories of sentencing reform are too radical for general consumption.

In October 2016, it was an unexpected pleasure to be provided with feedback from two of my mentees at Nottingham Law School. These were couched in the kind of glowing terms that I should find embarrassing were I to be standing at the pearly gates – which I have no expectation of doing in any event. By June 2018, I was tired of the bureaucracy of claiming expenses, and decided to retire gently from the role. Following a generous retirement lunch hosted by the Dean, I thought that was that. To my surprise, I was offered a similar role at the local Roehampton University.

From about 2016 I accidentally became involved with a reading group at HMP Coldingley. All the prisoners are life sentenced, and most of them have multiple university degrees. They have expressed enthusiastic interest in my contributions, which have extended, through the Learning Together programme operating out of Cambridge University, to HMP Warren Hill, HMP Send and other prison establishments.

My involvement with the Learning Together programme had a very sad and unexpected outcome. On 29 November 2019, I was a guest at Fishmongers' Hall at what was intended as a celebration of five years' success.

In due course, I was a witness at the inquest. The morning session had ended about 1.45 p.m., and so far as I was aware I was the first person to use the toilet. Usman Khan emerged from the toilet at 1.56 p.m. It is likely that he had preceded me, and was in a cubicle, strapping on his knives, while I was there. A 'sliding doors' moment. Jack Merritt, a charismatic mentor, and full-time manager of Learning Together, was the next person to enter the toilet. He remains deeply mourned. Both John Crilly and Steve Gallant, each mentees of mine, received gallantry awards to reflect their outstanding bravery in confronting Khan, whom they believed was about to detonate a suicide vest.

To my disappointment, the Learning Together initiative could not survive the criticism generated at the inquest into the deaths of Jack Merritt and Saskia Jones. While the crux of that criticism focused on the lack of information-sharing between the agencies intended to supervise Khan while on licence, Learning Together could not avoid the conclusion that their invitation to Khan to attend this event was imprudent; and the consequential lack of support that the organisation received from the university authorities led to the termination of this otherwise imaginative initiative.

———

Was my interest in mentoring foreshadowed in early school reports?

I was of little distinction at Charterhouse until I found my niche as an organiser. While I played indifferent football, the attraction of a soccer ball was that it was larger and moved more slowly than a cricket ball. My short sight meant that I never saw a cricket ball in flight. The object of compulsory cricket – I played in a team known variously as First Tics and Second Tics – was to be all out in the fastest possible time.

By the end of July 1958 I had grasped, with both hands, the leadership opportunities presented to me. I steered the house to victory in the inter-house athletics competition ('Ladies Cup'), in which participation by everyone was essential for ultimate success; and, very much to my surprise, I won the inter-house cadet force competition (Arthur Webster trophy).

My housemaster, Percy Chapman, commented approvingly: 'He has shown considerable gifts of leadership and his results in the Arthur Webster and the Ladies Cup speak for themselves. He should do well in charge of the House in these next two quarters.' At Christmas 1958, he wrote: 'He has been an outstanding Head Monitor, and has taken infinite trouble. He is more human and sympathetic than most, and as well as running the House most efficiently has also regarded the office as a pastoral one. I was very pleased that he won the Cyril Maude prize...' This was for public speaking. I had also won the Thackeray Prize for English literature. This was a direct result of Owen Rowe, Head of Classics and of the school cadet force, using his considerable persuasive powers to good effect. He had asked me what book I proposed to read before this voluntary competition. I had chosen *A Passage to India*, on the basis that it was the easiest. He told me to read Milton's *Paradise Lost*. I adopted the advice, read all twelve books over the summer holiday, learned much of it by heart, and won the prize.

My success in the Arthur Webster and Ladies Cup competitions stimulated my ambition. I aspired to become head boy, but I belatedly came to recognise that Charterhouse was not a school that would have accepted a Jew, even a less than observant one, as its head of the school. I was head of my house, and automatically a school monitor, from September 1958. Paradoxically, the appointee, in my final term, fell ill after a fortnight, and I took over for the rest of the term.

My final school report rounds things off, rather like a judgment.

Percy Chapman wrote:

'He has been a very good Head Monitor, thoughtful, sincere and effective. He has thought of his job in the widest terms. He has been full of ideas, most of them, I thought, good ones. He has been a vigorous person and has made his mark in many ways. I shall miss him and wish him every good fortune in the future.'

Owen Rowe wrote:

'His strength lies in the wider aspects of the classics and in general argument, but the linguistic work has forced on his attention the importance of detail and accuracy. I am grateful to him for his help in the CCF and for all the suggestions he has made to me. We shall miss him.'

In my CCF (Combined Cadet Force) record of service, he marked my character as 'Outstanding'. Unusually, I had been promoted to Senior Under Officer, the only such promotion of my generation.

Brian Young, the headmaster, wrote:

'There is a maturity and a weight about everything he does which is unusual in one of his age, and he has used and developed his powers admirably during his time here. I am grateful for all he did as Acting Head of the School, and I wish him all success in the future.'

I was lucky to be the secretary of the school Poetry Society. One of my contributions was an introduction to T.S. Eliot's *Four Quartets*. It resulted in the most genuine compliment I have ever received. After I left school, the secretary of the society wrote in the school magazine:

'The Society, whose brows are perhaps the highest and whose member-ship the lowest in the school, has had another successful year, marred only by the loss of J.E.A. Samuels: his sensitive commentary on Eliot's Four Quartets *will be remembered with gratitude by those who heard it. When the Marshal Duke of Luxembourg died, Louis XIV created eleven new marshals to replace him. We have done the same on a smaller scale and hope to tap the new sources in the near future.'*

My subsequent enthusiasm as an educationalist and mentor owes much to some inspirational teachers.

———

When my ten-year maximum term as a Parole Board member was concluding, I was offered – with others who had joined the Board with me – a two-year membership extension, to mentor new members. I was then the elected chairman of the newly created members' organisation, repre-senting all members of the Parole Board, and was the first judicial member to have been appointed to its Standards Committee. I had recently received a glowing annual appraisal from a long-serving independent member. To secure an extension, we all had to take a psychological test. Alone of my cohort, I failed. My feedback included that my approach was 'more suitable to a teacher-child relationship than a mentoring relationship. Appeared wedded to doing things the way that he was told. Closed to new ideas.' I found this puzzling. I asked a psychologist member, who had been present at my test, to explain. The response was: 'You should have googled "How to be a mentor".' My preference has been experience.

———

In 2017, I was asked to assist the Worshipful Company of Educators to establish an award for those involved in the provision of education in prison. When their first award was presented in 2018, they kindly invited me to dinner: more pleasantly, I did not have to make a speech. The following year, I was asked again. During that event I was asked to consider joining the Company. I made the expected excuses: too old to join a livery company, what can I contribute, etc. I succumbed, and just before Covid struck in 2020 I was installed as a Freeman. I was required to give an account of myself, which included:

> '*An educationalist for almost 60 years, only recognising the description recently! Ad hoc teacher; College Governor; Educational grant maker; pupil master; judicial tutor; Trustee, Chair (now President) Prisoners' Education Trust; advocacy tutor and tutor trainer; Visiting Professor, Nottingham Law School; and more recently Roehampton University; prisoner discussion group leader; and homework supervisor to my grandchildren.*'

At my first post-installation dinner, I was pressed to assist in the creation of a Special Interest Group of the Company, devoted to the criminal justice system. Again, I succumbed, and the group became one of its most active. Once Covid restrictions were over, I became a Freeman of the City of London: the necessary preliminary to becoming a Liveryman. In September 2022, I progressed to the Livery. In 2023, I was invited to be a judge for the awards offered by the Educators' Trust to inspirational educators. For someone who once sneered at education, the wheel has come full circle.

GROWING UP

Topsy, asked how she grew up, replied: '*I 'spect I just grow'd.*'
Harriet Beecher Stowe (1811–1896)

Self-doubt never entered the head of this eighteen-year-old school leaver. Had anyone suggested that he had some growing up to do, the very notion would have been scorned. The banalities recorded as his final entry in the leather-bound House Annals (confidential to successive generations of head monitors) show, with embarrassing hindsight, some insufferable self-satisfaction.

Within days of my departure from Charterhouse, my gran died on 7 April. I collected Dad at Redhill station, and he looked ashen. He insisted that I continue with my plan to leave for Italy, although that coincided with the funeral; and my instinct was, of course, to postpone the journey. In the early autumn of 1959, I went with Dad and Joe to a ceremony in which Gran's ashes were interred. Dad was quite cross about this. Gran had asked Dad to modify her will in some way, and, as he was otherwise occupied, he passed this easy task to his assistant solicitor, Bill van Straubenzee (who subsequently became a well-known Conservative MP, was knighted, and became a Church Commissioner). Bill strongly disapproved of anything other than conventional burial, and inserted a provision in Gran's will that her ashes should be buried – the next best thing to a conventional burial. Dad felt he had to comply with this, although he knew perfectly well that they were not his mother's wishes. I know nothing of the funeral, who attended, or where it was. Instead, I took myself to Victoria, and got on the boat train to Paris.

Of the journey to Perugia, one memory clearly stands out. I had nodded off somewhere under the Alps, and woke to find two princes of the church, bishops in full canonical purple, in animated conversation. As there had been no one in my carriage when I nodded off, I thought I must be dreaming. I changed trains for the branch line to Perugia; and at the station, with my suitcase becoming heavier with every stride, discovered that the station was in the valley at the foot of the mountain, and the city of Perugia was at its summit. The only pre-planning I had undertaken was to book into a small hotel.

Somehow, the monoglot Englishman and his suitcase got to the hotel at the mountaintop. Registration at the Italian University for Foreigners was a relative doddle: it was established to welcome students from all over the world. Issued with my student identification card, I was licensed for free entry into all museums, art galleries and historical sites for the duration of my stay. The next task was to find somewhere to live. I struck lucky: seren-dipity, as ever, being my constant companion. My landlady only spoke Italian, which meant that, until my vocabulary improved, our communi-cation was limited to sign language. She offered me a comfortable room, with shared use of the bathroom. There was a collection of sticks placed under the bathtub. If you wanted hot water in the bath, you first had to light the fire, and wait.

The house was just outside the city walls. In time, I was joined by another English student. He had not only money, but a Morgan motor car. This might have made exploration throughout Umbria, and indeed farther afield, more comfortable than my traditional hitchhiking: but his arrival was only a couple of weeks before my planned departure, and there were few joint expeditions.

What are the stand-out memories of that magical era? Walking past the pizzeria: those great slabs of pizza in the shop window. As I rationed my daily expenditure strictly and was determined to repay Dad the £75 he had lent me for the four months of my course – and duly did – temptation was hard to withstand. The *passeggiata*: everyone who was anyone in Perugia perambulated up and down the Corso in the evening, making neighbourly conversation. A budding friendship with the daughter of the Prefect, with whom I travelled memorably to the Spoleto Festival, to the first performance of a brand-new work; and an even more memorable meeting with its composer, Gian Carlo Menotti. Trying to look appropriately soigné for the occasion, I commissioned the creation of a tailor-made linen suit, which cost the princely sum of 3,500 lire (£2).

The celebrations on 1 May 1959: the hundredth anniversary of Garibaldi's Risorgimento. Being presented, by an exceptionally pretty girl, with a red carnation. For many years afterwards, on May Day I chose a red carnation for a buttonhole – in memory of the original donor. Gubbio, the fairy-tale hilltop town, for the Festa dei Ceri, when huge wooden statues (the *Ceri*) were carried in a race to the mountain peak behind the town by the men of Gubbio, and the subsequent feast in the town hall at which I was welcomed, so warmly, as a gratuitous participant. Combining my Italian language studies with a determination to make sense of the Italian Renaissance, by creating my own timeline of what was happening elsewhere in Europe. Visits – assiduously pursued – throughout Umbria and Tuscany; to Rome; and once, particularly memorably, to Naples and Paestum. These geographic memories have been blurred, not least because I returned with Maxine, in 1970 and again in 1988, when (without, so far as I remember, any parental influence to do so) our son David chose to come to the same city of Perugia for his gap year before Oxford.

The expedition to Paestum started as a routine hitchhike to Rome. Picked up by a schoolmaster, he pointed didactically to Mount Soracte. Both of us were surprised when I responded with the appropriate line in Horace's Ode, in Latin. Even today, a few lines linger. South of Rome I was picked up by a couple of young men in a lorry, en route to Sicily. Their purpose, quickly explained, was to develop their knowledge of English. As a recently retired Latin teacher, this posed little challenge until it became equally clear that their plan was to polish the most appropriate chat-up lines in English to such young ladies as might come their way. Chat-up lines in English were not yet within my own vocabulary, in any language. They were both charming and persistent; and this continued until we were in a suburb of Naples. There, I was introduced to the most wonderful meal:

broad beans, straight from the pod; fried chicken in a basket of chips; and fresh oranges as dessert. There was also, inevitably, a great deal of wine. Despite entreaties to stay with them, and to drive on to Sicily, I left them at the crossroads to Paestum and began to walk to the village, a few kilometres away.

As I rounded a corner, the moon suddenly appeared from behind the clouds, brilliantly illuminating the three temples, which had hitherto been cloaked in darkness. Simply unforgettable! I plodded on, arriving in the village about midnight. All was in darkness. I knocked on a door, and by chance had found a guesthouse. Up early the next morning, I was off to the modern museum adjoining the three temples. That is when the first wave of nausea hit me! Violent sickness and diarrhoea, fortunately contained within a modern lavatory block. As I sat miserably wondering what the diagnosis was, I remembered, with some anguish, that my guidebook said that the temples of Paestum had survived intact for so long because they lay in the middle of a malarial swamp. Clearly, I had contracted malaria.

Throwing economy to the wind, I took the train to Naples, and caught a taxi. I muttered something about a hotel and was awake enough to recognise the hotel to which I was driven: the rather superior one in which, in 1958, Dad and Mum (with me) had been installed as guests of the city of Naples. Dad was there as the chairman of the London County Council. The city was not expecting me. I was placed at a table a very long way away from my parents, the guests of honour. My companions were an admiral and a general, neither of whom spoke any English. Our dinnertime conversation was conducted *exclusively* in Latin (I had just completed my A levels in Classics). I quickly asked for a less prestigious hotel. I ordered copious quantities of mineral water, and somehow San Pellegrino did the trick.

All too soon, the love affair with Italy had run its course. I describe it as a 'love affair', but this is a mis-description. Yes, I learned – remarkably swiftly, in retrospect – to speak good conversational Italian. Yes, I became a devotee of Italian paintings, and still remember my scorn when a party of American tourists arrived ten minutes before closing time in the Uffizi in Florence and aspired to 'do it all'. Yes, I had a good collection of postcards to prove where I had been. But in love? Possibly in love with the concept of love, but at no stage was I prepared to let the mask slip, or to extend the hand that leads to a warmer friendship.

———

By August 1959 I was being actively pursued to join the TA, but some full-time paid employment was necessary. Serendipity, my guardian angel, helped again, and I became the first management trainee of Hall & Co, an established sand and gravel company. This company started in the pre-Victorian era. The Hall family retained control. Joseph Hall, its then president, was the grandson of the Hall who founded the firm when William IV was on the throne; and the chairman, who appointed me in 1959, was one of at least two directors named Hall. The company remained a supportive family firm, with a quarterly house magazine and a staff dinner dance at the Connaught Rooms. My contract confirmed a salary of £500 per annum, well more than I deserved.

The supportive employers organised a week-long residential training course for the younger recruits; and I was a rather bashful participant. All the trainees were male, and most had just completed their National Service. I was moved rapidly round the company. A spell in the vehicle repair depot was memorable for my supervision by a lovely chap who had been a glider pilot at Arnhem. The noise in his unprotected glider had left him profoundly deaf, but his enthusiasm for life remained infectious. My next move was to Purley, where I became the coal delivery manager. Here is my contemporary record (written just after I arrived in Cambridge in October 1960, under the less than catchy title of 'It happened to me').

'It all started when I proposed to my beneficent employer that February was an ideal time for a holiday. There are trades which sleep peacefully through the long winter months, awakening joyously for the summer season; but the coal trade in the respectable London dormitory in which I served the great god Mammon has a winter gaiety and liveliness all its own.

Nor were circumstances backward in making life too easy for the coal delivery manager – my grandiloquent title, which in fact meant answering

3 telephones simultaneously, separating and removing to hospital the remains of our two boxing coalmen brothers-in-law, composing strong replies to Head Office to complaints of 'non-conciliatory telephonic language' to customers, and in final desperation personally loading the coal. Never in so small an area have there been so many new-born babies, chronic invalids and directors' friends; never has the rain fallen for so long so incessantly; and never has the NUR in its wisdom chosen a happier moment to announce a national rail strike.

Deaf to all pleas, I fled for a break to Holland, and returned to find a happy state of chaos: a glorious week in which we provoked every customer to apoplexy, as he spluttered over the scandal of his two-month empty cellar. But as warmer days returned, so did our coalmen, who had migrated en masse to the shed at the end of the yard in December, only emerging to collect more fuel to feed their roaring stove – the only coal for miles. Order was gradually restored, and with it came the depressing realisation that I had only 6 more days' holiday before October. In vain the branch manager urged me to think of the easy days of summer, in vain did the Chairman plead to prevent his first trainee escaping from the fold. Like the bull in the Plaza de Toros, the trainee should not escape alive to warn prospective victims of his plight. But the wanderlust whetted last year was upon me again, and I went.'

In April 1960 the Paris summit conference, convened by President de Gaulle, was imminent. I decided to go. This is my contemporary account:

'The Summit Conference was at hand; it was to take place in Paris; and it was Spring. Such a cogent coincidence compelled me to begin in Paris, and I was soon well installed and strolling down the Faubourg St-Honoré in search of the great or bizarre. A gendarme stopped me. 'You are a journalist?' 'Yes.' 'Your pass?' 'Oh – I have left it behind.' 'I am sorry, sir.' Checked, but not vanquished, I sought inspiration (liquid); in the café I joined a group of Germans and Americans, slightly the worse for wear. It was not too late in the evening before I had an invitation to Cologne,

and, more important, an identity card from an unpronounceable Bonn newspaper.

Better armed, I hurried Chaillot-wards the next morning, and successfully evaded several suspicious gendarmes. A few yards from the Palace someone hailed me in German. For the second time this year, I fled. I saw the Big Four and listened to the hourly bulletins on the breakdown of negotiations, but as a spectator.'

What I did not further describe is being in the Conference Hall and having an unobstructed view of the Big Four: de Gaulle, Eisenhower, Macmillan and Khrushchev. The latter, incandescent with rage (probably histrionic), was complaining of American duplicity: the US pilot Gary Powers had just been shot down when engaged in an aerial reconnaissance mission deep over Soviet territory. This was my first experience of witnessing a historic event.

———

It was probably more in hope than expectation that the Borchard family in Reigate offered me a chance, as the single passenger on their chartered German cargo vessel, to go to Israel in the early summer of 1960. The hope related to Kate, the elder daughter of the family, already an undergraduate at Newnham. Kate married a slightly older and far cleverer version of me: a commercial practitioner, who subsequently became a commercial judge in Central London County Court when I also sat there. By then, his marriage to Kate had long since ended.

The reality was a remarkable journey, calling in at Gibraltar, Malta and Cyprus (both Larnaca and Famagusta) before arriving in Haifa. Apart from the captain, no crew members spoke English; and the captain's wife decided it was her vocation to teach me German. I embarked at Tilbury, and soon learned how quickly the crew anticipated the delights of the next port – I was genuinely surprised to learn that even though the cook had only just been married, that event did not curb his adventurous spirit. I spent my twentieth birthday in a force 10 gale in the Bay of Biscay and remember praying fervently to die.

Gibraltar was touristic – Barbary apes and the fortifications were duly admired; and it was a pleasure to launch into the relative calm of the Mediterranean. Malta was spectacular as we entered the Grand Harbour at Valletta; and the two Wyllie etchings of Gibraltar and Malta in my study serve as daily reminders of each. Cyprus was different. The struggle for independence was ongoing, and at one port I was at a large public gathering addressed by the striking figure of Archbishop Makarios. The archbishop was more impressive than the Cypriot brothel to which I was escorted by crew members anxious to complete my education. The madam of the establishment paraded her silent and uniformly ugly girls for inspection, and all of us turned tail and fled.

Mum had written to her old LSE friend Moshe Sharett to let him know of my arrival, and he arranged some interesting introductions. One, a native-born Israeli of my own age, encouraged me to go out into No Man's Land in Jerusalem. I describe this incident, and a few similarly hair-raising excursions, in the next chapter. I was surprised by my sense of detachment from the Israeli cause. This was, of course, only twelve years after the foundation of the State of Israel, and well before the military successes of the Six-Day War in 1967, or the subsequent Yom Kippur War of 1973. The horrific events of 7 October 2023, and their dreadful aftermath, were simply unimaginable.

To the Israeli, all was black or white: either you were with them, or against them. As I was not 100 per cent committed to what they regarded as their personal struggle for survival, I was deemed to be no more than a tourist. With time, I accepted this dismissive status: but I did so with a sense of dismay. A bit of what I then wrote, with strong flavours of Eliot, follows:

> I have sat in the synagogue at Capernaum;
> and the merciful shade of a fallen pillar of a falling faith
> showed me the hope that I did not wish to grasp
> gave me the help that I did not wish to use
> told me the half that I did not wish to learn.
> Three pillars remain, a testament to the anguish of Jairus.

The Lion and the lizard – yes, the same
repetitious clangour at each succeeding schism
of stone and stone, of heart and hearth: only the lion
is never there: dignity dies with the present.
There goes the lizard! Quick, catch him, catch him!
Too late: into the vaginal arch of the scorched, bewildered
Mother, he flees and finds a haven from himself.
The reptile cannot know himself or know he knows not.
Yet he flees.

I do not think the lion would run away:
The lion stands on the frontier with a rifle;
his only gambit in death's grim life-game
while the blue shield blows bravely on deep Galilee.
I cannot bear this searchlight of conscience, this
same sun smiling, bullying, searing five thousand years of my heritage.
I drink from an iron cup,
chained to the wall of the Dominican convent.
The water is sour, the cup is cracked, but it will not pass from me.

I left Israel by ferry for Greece; and on the way called in at Rhodes. Of Rhodes I remember nothing, save for wearing a Panama hat, which belonged to my paternal grandfather. That hat accompanied me not only through the ports of the Mediterranean, but into a slit trench facing Syria on the Golan Heights: another episode in the next chapter.

In Greece, various highlights stand out. I retain a little pottery vase that I acquired at Mycenae: probably the oldest item in my collection of interesting bits and pieces. Money changed hands for this: and, but for a benevolent statute of limitations, my acquisition of my little scent pot would fall foul of modern export embargoes. However, I acquired entirely openly in an Athens souvenir shop a clay votive dove and a pottery oil lamp. They are of no value, but the fact that they relate to the period of my Athenian studies gives them personal interest. The Mycenaean pot is far older: it is probably 1000 BC.

I must have spent some time in Athens on arrival because I have a crop of photographs of the Acropolis generally, the Parthenon and the other temples. Before taking off on foot for Olympia, Delphi and the theatre of Epidaurus, I was at Cape Colonna (the Temple of Poseidon at Sunium) and have an evocative sunset photograph to prove it. At Epidaurus, the most stunning of all amphitheatres, with legendary acoustics, I went to the centre of the stage early one morning and declaimed from Euripides' *Medea* (my Greek A-level text, much of which I had learned by heart) the speech that Medea made when she decided to murder her children. Out of the wings stepped a Greek tour guide: 'That was magnificent: but what language were you speaking?' A vivid recollection remains of Delphi. I had a room in the village and was woken at sunrise by the braying of an ass just outside my window. I was up quickly, and captured the sublime beauty of the Tholos before anyone else arrived.

I must have been hitchhiking to all these destinations, because I was picked up by an American of my own age in a bright red sports car. Unlike most of my lifts, this one developed into at least a temporary friendship, because we stayed together for several days, culminating in our return to Athens, where we shared a room. That evening, we decided to go to a wine festival on the outskirts of the city. That was another rash decision, to add to the collection of stupid things in 1960. Initially, all went well; and after paying a modest entry fee, the wine was free. At about midnight, Braynard (he had this ridiculously poncy name – he was in fact Braynard III) and I were sharing a fountain. Braynard announced 'I can't move', and tossed me the car keys. There were many sensible reasons why I should not and could not drive his car back to Athens, not least of which was that I was also very drunk; and had never driven the car (or indeed a left-hand-drive car); and had no idea of the way back. Wisdom went out of the window; I drove, and somehow we returned to our destination both unscathed and unscraped. Braynard was noisily ill during the night, but had recovered sufficiently the next morning to show me the letter he had just received from his mother. In it she warned him, magisterially if not maternally, of the dangers that might befall him were he to succumb to the temptation to pick up any hitchhiker! We laughed about that, parted with promises to keep in touch (swiftly broken), and I made for the airport to fly home.

Incidents were not quite over. At about 30,000 feet I looked out of my window, to see something break away from an engine cowling. A stewardess was passing my seat, and I drew her attention to it. She went white, and rushed up to the flight deck. We made an unscheduled landing in Rome.

My contemporary diary gives away nothing significant. I returned home on 24 September. The following week could hardly have been more humdrum: and on 2 October I presented myself at Queens' College Cambridge.

While Day 1 is otherwise a bit of a blur, of one fact I am certain: it was my first memorable meeting with Peter Abbott and Richard Rumary, both of whom became my lifelong friends, and the three of us seemed to bond immediately. Superficially, each of us had much in common. Each of us had been head of his house at our respective schools, but the similarity probably stopped there. As soon as I spotted Peter in the crowd of freshmen, I was sure that we had met before; and many years later we identified precisely where this had been: near Milford, where Peter then lived with his parents. More significant, but not clocked at the time, was that he was then accompanied by Maxine, who had started her nursing training at St Thomas's in January 1960, and often visited the Abbotts. Denny Abbott had been at Sandhurst with her dad, and we later realised that Peter and Maxine had shared a playpen in India.

My first lodgings were rather remote from the college, in a pleasant house in a cul-de-sac off Huntingdon Road, so much of that first term involved cycling in and out of the city several times a day. The Crown Princess of Holland was in the house next door. While we spoke politely to one another, nothing akin to friendship developed, robbing me of the later prospect of being a welcome visitor to Queen Beatrix of the Netherlands.

My early ambition was to shine in the Union and develop my political interests generally. With hindsight, I made a mess of both ambitions. Although I was quite assiduous in my attendance at the Union – I joined as a life member and spoke in a debate on the motion 'Britain should now join the Common Market' – I was insufficiently focused, amusing, or identifiable as a Union hack to rise up the ranks. I received a generous letter from the president (Leon Brittan) after my first speech; and having now reread it, I was amazed to discover that I then opposed the motion. I had always believed that I was an ardent European.

It is rather depressing when the realisation gradually kicks in that you can no longer remember when a seminal event occurred. There is absolutely no doubt about the event; and it continues to resonate as an important memory. However, when and in what circumstances it occurred has become less clear. The event is the visit I made to the concentration camp at Dachau. The camp was totally deserted.

Today, Dachau is a place of formal pilgrimage; but when I arrived it was abandoned. A series of empty, rotting huts stood in rows. There was nothing to prevent my access to the site. I vividly remember finding a hut that contained thousands of pairs of abandoned spectacles; and looking down, through broken floorboards, at piles of rubbish. But what shocked me to my core was peering down through the broken floorboards and seeing piles of sheet music. That, in the silence and desolation of the spot, could not have been more unexpected, nor more poignant.

I had left Reigate in my Armstrong Siddeley Typhoon – a splendid vehicle that I purchased for £50. The plan, in August 1961, was to meet up with a fellow Queensman in Vienna; to drive through Yugoslavia to Dubrovnik; and ultimately to return together. Unbeknown to me at the time, I entered Czechoslovakia at the commencement of the building of the Berlin Wall. When I crossed from Germany on 23 August, I was casually aware that there were no other vehicles on the road travelling east, but that there was a constant stream of military vehicles travelling west. A misplaced sense of TA-inspired duty encouraged me to press on, if only to obtain information that, in my opinionated belief, would be of immense value back in England in the event, as looked increasingly probable, of a new European war breaking out.

I pressed on to Prague: nothing of significance to report back, or to record. My journal focused on distances travelled and times. I was a tourist in Prague for two days, before turning south to Brno. There I found a pleasant hotel, and a particularly pleasant hotel receptionist. She told me that her husband was a political prisoner. She had two daughters, who were desperate to learn English. Could I possibly send her, from England, some English-language magazines, which were unobtainable behind the Iron Curtain? I was invited to visit her home. I did so; it was sparsely furnished. I agreed to send her a batch of women's magazines, and did so, on my return. To thank me I received a postcard that, when placed on the turntable of a gramophone, played the opening bars of Smetana's *Má Vlast*. It was only after the next chapter of my introduction to the world of spooks that I began to wonder whether I was being softened up.

That began with an invitation to Dad to a cocktail party in London. Dad had suggested that I should accompany him, and I was curious enough to do so. Dad was in conversation with an urbane Romanian military attaché, to whom I was introduced as a TA officer. That was, of course, strictly correct; but at the height of the Cold War it was inappropriate, if not unwise. I thought very little of the conversation until, wholly unexpectedly, the colonel turned up in my room in Queens' one lunchtime and was already sitting on my sofa. He asked me out to lunch; and, out of curiosity, I accepted. I had sufficient savvy to report the approach, and discussed it with the regular training officer of my TA battalion. He had an intelligence background. He arranged for me to go to see an anonymous character in the War Office, which the passing of time enables me to identify as MI6. Here, I got a briefing. I was required to acquiesce in everything and anything I was asked to do, but must report it all in detail. My reports were to be in my own handwriting, and I must use a blue Basildon Bond envelope and place a mauve 3d stamp on it.

The colonel was a suave and pleasant lunchtime companion. He took me to some nice London restaurants, following the first lunch in Cambridge. The final lunch was strikingly memorable. The colonel had to cancel at the last minute, leaving his air attaché to keep the appointment. The air attaché spoke little English, and was painfully lacking in conversation. His instructions were to order the most expensive items on the menu; and so it was that at a restaurant in Leicester Square I was treated to steak tartare, which, second only to oysters, I cannot stand; accompanied by a ludicrously expensive and, in other circumstances, luscious bottle of Château d'Yquem. I faithfully recorded all this in the requested report. After a decent interval, with no further requests for lunchtime meetings, I asked my War Office contact what was happening. The response was: 'We are extremely grateful. As a result of your reports we have had both Colonel Dinculescu and his air attaché expelled. There were, of course, tit-for-tat expulsions: but we thought it was all worth it. He was someone we had had under observation for a long time.' I waited, in vain, for my medal, or even a casual mention in dispatches, but neither ever came.

———

The two Queensmen met up satisfactorily in Vienna on 26 August; and left two days later, travelling into what is now Slovenia, before moving on effortlessly to Zagreb. There was a single motorway in the former Yugoslavia, running from Zagreb to Belgrade; but our route lay through Bosnia-Herzegovina, and there were no discernible roads. I have traced our subsequent route on the map, via Banja Luka, Jajce, Sarajevo and Mostar, before returning to Dubrovnik, the southernmost city of Croatia, on the coast. The totality of that route, approximately 440 miles, was on unmade tracks or dried-up riverbeds.

Dubrovnik, where we stayed for three days, was a pleasure, after which we pushed north up the coast road bordering the Adriatic. Somewhere close to Split, and still on unmade roads, the car ground to a shuddering halt. One rear wheel was detached from its axle. The driver of a passing oxcart, laden with hay, responded very favourably to my then far more fluent Italian than any Serbo-Croat I had picked up en route and volunteered to tow us into Split, where he was sure that repairs would quickly be effected. The 'repairer' had a cycle shop, and I was not sure that a motor vehicle, albeit of a certain age, would come within the expertise of a bicycle repairer. My concerns were brushed away, with the less than logical observation that the primary occupation of the cycle repairer was in the shipyard in Split.

The next morning, we returned, to check on progress. The Armstrong was, literally, in bits: festooned across the road, in front of the shop. My companion went white, anticipating not only being marooned in Split for weeks, but – more important – being asked to contribute to the potentially massive cost of the repair. Without further discussion, he took off for the railway station and caught the next train travelling north-west. It was my first experience of being dumped; and our friendship suffered as a result.

———

My notes from some of my Union speeches survive; and I was sufficiently involved to be awarded the opportunity to make a 'paper speech' in Michaelmas 1961. The names of the proposers and opposers of the motion were printed on the paper identifying the topic for debate. This was on the light-hearted topic of 'This House would rather be a Stately Home'. By then, I had ceased to be an aspiring Cambridge politician. While I had joined each of the political associations, and attended those events that interested me, I was aligned to none of them, nor to the Union; and found an appropriately welcoming home in the Cambridge University United Nations Association.

This was numerically by far the largest of all the undergraduate societies. No doubt those who joined during the annual freshers' week felt a warm glow of internationalism, without committing to any specific political path; and the size of the membership enabled me, as chairman from the summer of 1962, to operate on a wider stage.

In July 1962 I was invited as CUUNA chairman to a lunch at The Dorchester in honour of the Acting Secretary-General of the UN, U Thant, addressed by Harold Macmillan as Prime Minister and Hugh Gaitskell as Leader of the Opposition. A few days later I attended the General Council of the UNA and was introduced to U Thant as chair of 'the largest branch of the UNA in the world'. While this puff owed more to the enthusiasm of Cambridge freshmen than to an active membership, the Secretary-General pressed me to consider a career with the UN, and specifically invited me to go to Geneva, where there was a vacancy with the International Labour Organization (ILO). My response makes me shudder: 'Thank you, but I'm committed to a career at the Bar.'

During my time as chairman, CUUNA meetings were addressed by a variety of well-known speakers of eminence, and we nearly managed to persuade the Duke of Edinburgh to come too. One of the perks of my role was that throughout my term I kept my car in college, on the spurious grounds that I needed it to ferry visiting speakers to the venue. The senior tutor asked whether I knew whose car it was outside my room. I confessed that it was mine.

'This is a newly created car park for Fellows,' he pointed out.

'I thought that it had been generously provided for me,' I cheekily replied.

Absent a direction, I continued to park there.

During this term the Cuban missile crisis dominated not only newspaper headlines, but undergraduate thought. There was a mass meeting on Parker's Piece when hysteria developed, and most were convinced they would be annihilated by the next morning. My response was uncharacteristically blasé. 'If I'm going to be part of a mushroom cloud tomorrow, I'm off to bed now.' CUUNA held a special meeting to discuss the aftermath of the crisis, and the local press declared it as 'a loose victory for the Russians'.

I engineered Peter Abbott to succeed me as the chair of CUUNA for the last term of our undergraduate year. As such, he was one of my early mentees. My involvement in CUUNA faded away; but not before the Valentine Ball in February 1963. My partner, Micaela, a Finn who was in Cambridge to improve her English, had lodgings with Major Kenneth Scott, the leader of the visit to Germany described in the next chapter. During the ball, our party was encouraged to return to the home of Eli Lauterpacht, the distinguished international lawyer (I was in no doubt that his focus was on Micaela). I tagged along, determined to prevent the premature rupture of a happily developing relationship. At about 3 a.m., I managed to extract Micaela. As we reached my car, snow began to fall; and it is that magical memory, watching the snowflakes drifting down and covering the elegant bonnet before we returned to her lodgings at a disgracefully late hour, that lingers happily.

What other activities and memories persist from those three golden years at Queens'? While I had no serious ambition to be a sportsman, I had a fleeting ambition to be a university athlete. At school, I had run very fast over a limited distance and had been in the athletics team for the previous three years. At Cambridge, I learned to my horror that athletics was a winter and not a summer sport. On a particularly wet October afternoon, I located the athletics ground. Understandably, no one was there. In desperation, I began to jog round the track. After a bit I was joined by a friendly Australian, and we chatted sociably as we jogged a couple of laps. Suddenly, he took off: and it was only when he was on the far side of the track that I recognised Herb Elliott, then the world record holder in the mile. Having run with him I decided, then and there, to retire from athletics. My principal subsequent activity, albeit only in a gentlemanly form, was rowing. Queens' was particularly successful at this time, being Head of the River throughout my three years; so it was not so very undistinguished to be a member of Queens' IVth boat, which included Peter Abbott and John Groves. In the Lent races in 1963, I made history by being the only oarsman who had ever taken part in both gloves and trousers: it was snowing and absolutely freezing!

I must have been a normally social undergraduate, as in addition to CUUNA I was the president of the College Law Society (I enjoyed the title of 'President of the Queens' Bench'). Less can be said about my academic progress. The indolence that marked my early school years was back with a vengeance. My first year was a compromise choice of subject: I had hoped to read history, at which I should have been enthusiastic; but Dad said I would find it 'too easy'. He wanted me to continue with Classics; and Economics (in which I could in part indulge my enthusiasm for economic history) was the middle way. Economics is a subject that never began to engage me; and I switched somewhat lazily to law in the summer of 1961.

Involvement in lectures was minimal. I had a friend who loved going to lectures, and if supplied with carbon paper would provide copious and legible notes, some of which I subsequently read. More persuasive, in terms of lecture attendance, was the presence of the stunningly beautiful Elizabeth Bagaaya, Princess of Toro. She came to the Bar, undertook a pupillage in defamation chambers, and successfully made a fortune when the world's press accused her of an improper assignment in Orly Airport with the Ugandan foreign minister. 'Ugandan conversations' entered the vocabulary. The nearest I got to such a get-together was to sit, puppy-like, next to her at the few lectures I attended.

After graduating in 1963, I was on my way to 'First Steps in the Law' (chapter 7). Bridging that development was the creation of a joint household with Peter Abbott. We arranged to share a ground-floor flat in Wandsworth. Peter had been a natural scientist; and, after a post-graduate flirtation with accountancy, decided on a career in the Royal Navy. A wise decision, as he ended up as the hugely admired Admiral Sir Peter Abbott GBE, KCB, and Vice-Chief of the Defence Staff.

We had a flat-warming party in December 1963. It was a great success. Peter invited Maxine. Late in the evening I walked her across the road to the bus stop, from which she could catch one bus directly to her shared flat in Southampton Row. Being a diffident young man, there was little contact; but I was encouraged to believe that this was something special. Periodically thereafter, Maxine telephoned; and if I answered it, my first enquiry was: 'Do you want to speak to Peter?' Our paths diverged for nearly two years.

Peter married Sue on 7 August 1965. As the principal usher, I was looking out for Maxine, who arrived – unusually late – just as the bride was expected (she had borrowed a car, and had a puncture). As I escorted her to her seat, I placed a hopefully reassuring hand on her waist. During the subsequent reception, Peter's father (whom I had grown to know well) muttered, perhaps in jest, 'I always wanted Peter to marry Maxine; but she's available'! (Months later, Maxine admitted that Denny Abbott had said virtually the same to her, on the same occasion, and then steered her in my direction.) Some of those who had been at the wedding went out together.

At the end of what was a gloriously happy evening, I asked Maxine when we should meet again. 'Never' was the unexpected and crushing reply. She was going home to Canada that week and did not expect to return. Fortunately, her plans changed. On 8 November, she sent me a postcard of Niagara Falls. It is preserved with other priceless keepsakes. She wrote:

> *'I think I said I would send you a p.c. or something – well here it is! Will be back in London on 15th Nov & hope to hear from you sometime. Just in case you haven't the phone no its HOL 5061 – very forward of me! Maxine.'*

In pencil, and in large capitals, she added: AIR MAIL. The diligent, but unromantic, post office clerk had stamped the card 'Short paid for air conveyance'. The card reached me on 28 November. I rang Maxine on its arrival. We went out for dinner the following night. Remarkably, there is nothing in my diary; but there is, in Maxine's 1965 diary! Dinner with me is underlined, twice. Nuff said. For practical purposes, with the usual ups and downs of life, we have been together ever since.

'THEN A SOLDIER'?

Then a soldier,
Full of strange oaths, and bearded like the pard,
Jealous in honour, sudden and quick in quarrel,
Seeking the bubble reputation
Even in the cannon's mouth.
Shakespeare, *As You Like It*: Act II, Scene 7

In November 1956 the entire country was split in its views. The cause of this division was the aggression by British and French military forces, following a clandestine agreement with Israel, to launch extensive hostile operations against Egypt. This followed the nationalisation of the Suez Canal by President Nasser of Egypt; and the belief by Sir Anthony Eden, then prime minister, that unless decisive action were taken to topple Nasser, the whole of the Middle and Near East would be vulnerable to a hostile takeover by the USSR. The legality of the Anglo-French action, and its apparent breach of the United Nations Charter, not only created a rift in the alliance between the United States and Great Britain, but launched a precocious sixteen-year-old schoolboy on a course that saw him proclaim, to anyone who would listen, that he was a pacifist.

In 1956 I knew that I was liable for National Service, and that if I refused to do so, I should face not only a tribunal as a conscientious objector, but also the obloquy of my contemporaries at school, all of whom jingo-istically supported the invasion. Peter Wainwright – head of my house, victor in the recent inter-house drill competition, CSM in the Corps – was scathing. 'What is all this nonsense about you being a pacifist, John? Don't you realise that you are going to be next year's platoon commander? Surely you wouldn't want to let the house down?' What later happened to that master of psychology? The appeal to put house interests before the dictates of conscience was bound to succeed.

The following year I was, indeed, a rather wobbly platoon commander; and to my amazement, and that of the platoon generally, the Daviesites house platoon won the inter-house CCF competition. As with all successful infantry actions, more was due to luck than skill. The rain on my glasses made it hard to spot where we were being fired on. My runner thought it came from one location, and I believed it was another. My orders were a mess: the platoon was divided into two sections, each of which charged the distinct points from which the enemy fire had apparently come; and, alone of the attacking forces, we had luckily destroyed our enemy, who had unsportingly based themselves in two different spots. The outcome was that Corporal Samuels was instantly promoted to Sergeant; and a transformation occurred. Next term, after a summer CCF camp at which he tasted the sweetness of a little brief authority, CSM Samuels led his house in the drill competition; and the following term he achieved the ultimate promotion, as head of the CCF, to Senior Under Officer.

When I left Charterhouse, I was approached by two territorial units: 5th Battalion the Queen's Royal Regiment, the local Surrey infantry regiment, to which Charterhouse CCF was affiliated – we wore the cap badge of the Queen's (the Paschal lamb); and a cavalry regiment, the Westminster Dragoons. My flirtation with the latter was brief. I was told that I would be commissioned once I could take an armoured car to pieces and reassemble it. Recognising that this was unlikely ever to happen, I chose the infantry. So it was that on 7 November 1959 I received a commission in the Territorial Army and 2/Lieutenant Samuels emerged from the chrysalis.

I retain much affection for the Queen's. On my desk there is a Queen's silver mounted swagger stick, part of the furniture of my house at school. Might that have been carried into No Man's Land on 1 July 2016? I wrote an early draft of this chapter in July 2016, a hundred years after the Battle of the Somme. This is not the place to elaborate on that senseless slaughter. Two footnotes suffice. First, when I was about nine, Mum had a gardener named Mr Wilden. He was built like an ox. He was one of six brothers, he told me; all of whom served in the Royal Sussex Regiment. He was the only survivor: the rest perished on the Somme. I do not know if what he told me is true. If it is, it makes the storyline of *Saving Private Ryan* rather tame.

My second note concerns an oil painting that I bought about forty-five years ago. It is of a cornfield being harvested on the slopes of the North Downs. I have identified its location as Reigate Hill. It is by Horace Mann Livens, a most unusual subject for him. Livens trained in Belgium as a pupil of Verlat, and his fellow pupils were Vincent van Gogh and Frederick John Widgery (the watercolours of the latter being much collected by me). Livens aspired to be a barrister – he executed some self-portrait etchings wearing a barrister's wig and gown – and his normal oeuvre was gloomy. This work is joyous, an impressionist idyll. The date on the stretcher is 1 July 1916. What a striking coincidence; and what a contrast to what was happening just across the Channel.

In 1961 the Queen's merged with the East Surrey Regiment, to form the Queen's Royal Surrey Regiment; and two territorial battalions emerged. The old 5th Battalion Queen's Royal Regiment metamorphosed into 3rd Battalion the Queen's Royal Surrey Regiment. Despite these changes, I remained throughout – until the TA underwent a further radical reduction in 1967 – an officer in 'A' Company: initially a platoon commander in Reigate, and latterly as the lieutenant in charge of the platoon at Dorking.

Detailed instructions for completing the paperwork followed from the training major, Paul Swanson, who took a paternal interest in my progress. That included details of my pay and emoluments: 25/- (£1.25) per day, plus 5/- (25p) for evening training; a bounty of £7 per training year; plus an annual uniform allowance of £4.

Early in January 1960, there was a battalion live firing exercise. Although I had previously taken part in various live firing exercises, this was my first experience of a full-scale battalion attack, in which I was in charge of a platoon, advancing as part of a full company formation, in extended line abreast. I can remember with crystal clarity enjoining everyone to 'keep the line' – I was not in favour of being fired on.

In March 1960 there was a combined operation involving the Royal Navy and a number of TA units. As a junior subaltern I embarked on HMS *Plover*, the only mine layer in the fleet, at Portsmouth. Our target was Dungeness (albeit we had no idea where we were going until we arrived). We stormed ashore in the dawn – the first successful invasion of England since 1066. Other memories: an injunction to consume only pink gin, as tonic water cost more than the gin; and overwhelming the defending forces of the Buffs. A photograph of JS on HMS *Plover* survives; as does the ship's tie, which marks me as an honorary member of the wardroom.

My next commitment was the two-week TA probationary officers' course at Mons Officer Cadet School. I remember some ribald activity in the barrack room that involved the decoration of one of the participants' beds with a collection of water-filled condoms. Fortunately, I was neither on the receiving end of this attention, nor part of the raiding group. Our section sergeant was entirely pleasant, but the young captain commanding our group was someone from whom I instinctively recoiled. He stood out, since he had just won an MC in Borneo: a rare feat in that period, when for practical purposes there were no hostile activities worldwide on which the British Army was engaged; and his distaste when I delivered my lecturette – on the technique of etching – was palpable. Anyone who had an interest in anything vaguely artistic was necessarily suspect. Paradoxically, I had chosen the topic because, apart from my then active interest in Samuel Palmer and his etchings, I thought it was helpful to describe how to do something. The confidential report at the end of the course included the following: 'He is too quiet at present, and fails to convey any sense of enthusiasm or dominance to those under him. This is particularly bad when lecturing...' My CO, who knew me quite well, on receipt of this report said he could not understand it. He added: 'You are going to the Bar, aren't you, John?'

I was appropriately terrified of the RSM, Noddy Lynch. It was his job to make us feel humiliated. 'I call you Sir; you call me Sir; and you ******* mean it!' Fast-forward a couple of years: I was at annual camp, and had volunteered to stay behind, to earn some extra pounds. There was a tentative tap on the door. When I encouraged entry, I was delighted to see the newly commissioned Lieutenant Noddy Lynch on the threshold. He needed my permission to do something. While I graciously granted it, revenge (eaten cold) was extremely sweet.

I attended my first annual camp with 5 Queen's in the Lake District. Islands of memory pop up in a general haze. They include a four-day night exercise in the Langdale Pikes: de-bussing from a 10-ton truck in the dark, and enthusiastically encouraging my platoon to 'follow me', only to find myself waist-deep in water. When I ultimately removed my boots, four days later, my feet were unrecognisable. Driving up and down the Hard-knott and Wrynose passes without lights, hoping the moon would emerge from the clouds. The glorious summer weather of 1960: days of unbroken sun. Burgeoning friendships with fellow officers, and growing respect from my platoon. No other camp was quite like that at Millom.

It was at this camp that I had my first experience of driving a 10-ton truck. Paul Swanson merrily gestured to me and told me to follow the departing convoy. I sat in the driving seat ... and could not find the starter button. I expected an ignition key, or at least something broadly equivalent. Embarrassed, I confessed that starting the engine had defeated me. The button was pointed out on the floor, beneath my feet: no vehicle I had ever previously driven, and there were many of them, had this peculiarity. The obstacle once overcome, I roared off in pursuit of the convoy. All went remarkably well. By the time I drove back into camp, I felt like an old hand. I drove back to my hut, forgetting that the canopy of the truck was far higher than that of the saloon car I usually drove. At 30mph, I collided with the overhead water pipes. The frame of the truck canopy was bent back to a crazy obtuse angle, and a cascade of water flooded in all directions. The colonel was shaving in his hut. He emerged with shaving foam all over his face. I was helpless with laughter. As there was no court-martial, he must ultimately have seen the funny side.

In Israel I had met David, a Sabra: Hebrew for 'prickly pear'; prickly on the outside, but sweet inside. There was an instant attraction. He had recently completed his military training. With my own TA experiences, we seemed to have much in common. He proposed that I should accompany him on an unauthorised night patrol into the No Man's Land area of the then divided city of Jerusalem. Why I agreed is unfathomable. Equally foolish was my volunteering, a week later, to man a slit trench in a kibbutz facing the Syrian Golan Heights when an attack was threatened. Armed with a Lee Enfield .303 and my grandfather's Panama hat, I echoed the experience of every infantryman: long hours of boredom, punctuated by a few seconds of terror. Had things turned out differently, dear reader, you would not be ploughing on.

In Cambridge I was seconded to Cambridge University Officers' Training Corps (OTC). In my file there is a reference to an exercise in May 1963 about which I remember nothing. Why I was spending a Saturday shortly before the final Law Tripos playing soldiers near Duxford is odd, but may explain my subsequent poor exam results. The highlight of my Cambridge OTC experience was a week-long visit to Germany, led by Major Kenneth Scott, the landlord of my then Finnish girlfriend Micaela. I wrote a contemporary report of this experience, which survives, including a flight into the then newly divided city of Berlin, and a sober description of Checkpoint Charlie, as well as of the many who had died while attempting to cross the wall into West Berlin.

More vivid is my memory of how close to death Ken Scott came because of my inept hurling of a grenade into a puddle during a live firing exercise. In circumstances that leave me, more than sixty years later, terrified by the recollection, he went fishing with his hands for the grenade. While I and the rest of the group cowered behind a brick wall, he located the grenade, tossed it out, and saw it explode in mid-air.

During the Easter vacation in 1963, I devised a night training exercise for my Dorking platoon. This terrified a retired group captain, who wrote a lengthy letter of complaint to the War Office. My company commander backed me to the hilt. His letter included:

'You will be pleased to learn that the poor Group Captain nearly had hysterics in 6 pages to the War Office. You received an honourable mention as being courteous but firm – "completely disregarding the nerves of his frightened, high rateable value, CBE, household". John Burgess [the

training major] *was inclined to offer panic apologies and swear we would never go there again. However, I persuaded him to see our point of view – we had permission – we cleared with the police and we did nothing wrong – in addition we will most certainly need that, or other nearby land, again. All appears to be quiet at the moment. He is probably boiling up for the second round. (We must earmark his house for requisition!)'*

I much enjoyed my role as the platoon commander at Dorking. Nominally responsible for the entire Drill Hall complex, loosely under my auspices were an army cadet unit and a unit of air force cadets. The latter had the good fortune to have as its president Sir Barnes Wallis, the inventor of the bouncing bomb. He routinely attended each annual showing of *The Dam Busters*. He was a delightful, modest man, much interested in the welfare of each of the cadets, and always happy to answer any questions. I had a very varied platoon. Sgt Ernie Clamp, the signaller, joined the TA in 1938. He had been at Arnhem in 1944; and said that his limited height (he was less than five feet tall) saved his life. Sgt Mick Brady was loyal and dependable. Cpl Kane was an extrovert: he was my first client at quarter sessions.

Social events oiled the wheels of training. Dinners in the mess at Sandfield Terrace, Guildford, were far too well lubricated with alcohol. Returning home along the A25 in the early hours of the morning, and striking the offside kerb, woke me up with a jolt that, after more than half a century, I still remember. Boisterous games at camp – such as 'High Cockelorum'; the ever-exuberant Major Dick Asser launching himself, horizontally, on to a table filled with glassware, smashing the lot, and emerging unscathed – are still evergreen. In June 1964, while at camp, I crept out of bed after a heavy previous night to procure a copy of *The Times* to learn whether I had passed the Bar exam. Relieved to find that my name was there, I said nothing. That evening, there was a formal guest night. The mess president, a solicitor, had spotted my little triumph. He begged the loan of a wig and gown from the local town clerk. Before all the assembled guests and my brother officers, I was duly called to the Bar: but not in the time-honoured ways of Lincoln's Inn. Unforgettable.

By the summer of 1966, it was clear that the TA as we knew it was being slimmed down drastically. A list of personnel identified for future service omitted my name, and that of my fellow platoon commander Jon Pullinger, with whom I continued to share the Wandsworth flat when Peter Abbott joined the navy in June 1964. The news came at an excellent time because my career at the Bar was just taking off. Most of my spare time was being spent with Maxine. On 1 November 1967 I received a formal letter from the Ministry of Defence, informing me that I had been transferred to the Regular Army Reserve of Officers. I was informed that I would cease to do so on my fiftieth birthday. My chest remains devoid of medals.

POLITICS

It happened to Lord Lundy then
As happens to so many men:
Towards the age of twenty-six
They shoved him into politics ...
Hilaire Belloc (1870–1953), *Cautionary Verses*

My father was undoubtedly frustrated in his political ambitions. In 1934 he was poised for a successful career as a Labour politician, not only on the London County Council, where Labour had for the first time come to power under Herbert Morrison, but in all probability on the national stage. He was the youngest and probably the most able of Morrison's group of committee chairmen. Many of them, including Lewis Silkin and George Strauss, became members of the Attlee Cabinet in 1945. My father shortened his honeymoon in 1934 to a four-day break in order not to interrupt his campaign for re-election to the LCC. By 1937, my mother had other ideas. She pointed out that my father, a sole practitioner, needed to build up his practice; and whether or not the darkening political situation in Germany was part of their thinking, he chose not to offer himself for re-election in 1937. The consequence was that for nine years he was for practical purposes out of politics: a frustration of his career ambition of which he never spoke, but which with hindsight moulded his tenacious insistence that his only son should pursue the career path that had been snatched from him.

To a ten-year-old, Dad seemed to know everyone, particularly prominent politicians. He introduced me to Clement Attlee, then prime minister, who asked me what I wanted to be when I grew up. 'Prime minister,' I precociously replied, 'so that I can make things better for everyone.' I still cringe at the memory. Jim Callaghan was another. 'He is going to the top,' Dad told me. However, it was Herbert Samuel, the pre-war leader of the Liberal Party, who made the deepest impression. He spoke directly to me and was a quiet inspiration.

My earliest memories of politics include canvassing with my mother in the 1946 LCC election, when I was aged five. She was moved to tears by the squalor in which so many of my father's constituents were forced to live: a combination of bomb damage, housing scarcity at the end of the war, and the fact that no resources had been allocated to house building for ten years. My father lost his LCC seat in 1949; but to my huge delight, as recorded in my contemporary diary, he was re-elected in 1952 for the relatively safe seat of Stoke Newington and Hackney North. His fellow candidates could not have been more different: George Hayes, a retired firefighter, who became mayor of Stoke Newington and took an avuncular interest in me; and Neville Sandelson, a young barrister who was responsible for securing my first tenancy in the chambers in which he was a member.

I joined the Reigate and Redhill Labour Party at the age of fifteen. I diligently attended local ward meetings. This activity sat uneasily with my role as a Carthusian. In broad terms, I compartmentalised things quite well; although in school debates, and in some of my essays, I clearly demonstrated an active interest in the origins of the Labour Party, as well as contemporary Labour Party politics, and probably stuck out as unlike most of my peers.

At Cambridge I was not aligned with any political party, and joined each of the Conservative, Labour and Liberal clubs. In the Cambridge Union I pursued an internationalist approach, which explains both my lack of success in achieving a Union following, and my emergence as chair of the Cambridge University United Nations Association.

My involvement in Labour politics was sealed in November 1963, when I should have focused on my forthcoming Bar exams. I accepted an invitation from the Greater London Coordinating Committee of the Labour Party (its chairman, Bob Mellish MP, knew me since he was MP for Bermondsey, my father's LCC constituency); and, no doubt on Dad's initiative, he had agreed to support me as a candidate for the new GLC. However, as he candidly admitted, he forgot to do so; but since he thought I showed promise, he asked me to lead the campaign team for the election for the new GLC. The election was on 9 April 1964.

This experience exposed me to frontline politics. I arranged for teams of Labour MPs to canvass across Greater London; and I accompanied Harold Wilson and George Brown, then leader and deputy leader of the Labour Party, as they addressed multiple meetings in cavalcades across the capital. I retain Harold Wilson's speaking notes, which he presented to me at the end of the day, with some encouraging and appreciative noises for my role as the coordinator. I was struck by the way in which he composed them and stuck faithfully to them throughout the day.

Against the odds, the election result was a clear win for the London Labour Party. While the authority then elected was a 'shadow' body – the LCC continued in office until 31 March 1965 – my role in its creation was acknowledged when I was elected as a co-opted member of the new Education Committee of the Inner London Education Authority. Under the new arrangements, this authority continued the responsibility of the Education Committee of the LCC for education in Inner London. Success in the GLC election was the springboard for the success of the Labour Party in the subsequent general election of 1964.

The fact that Dad and Uncle Joe were also members of the Education Committee, as existing members of the London County Council and new members of the shadow Greater London Council, provoked some noisy hilarity (if three Samuels were present) whenever votes were called at committee meetings; but, save for a minor role as a governor of two Colleges of Further Education, I cannot claim that my membership brought many benefits to education in London. The role was, however, memorable in several ways. First, I was wise enough to realise that it would be imprudent to speak on any topic before I was ready to do so: I had learned that lesson in debates at the Cambridge Union and in the Queens' College debating society. My chosen target was to intervene in the sub-committee of which I was a member, the Further and Higher Education Sub-committee. This committee was chaired by Mrs Margaret Cole (a leading Fabian thinker, who later became a Dame). She looked like the cartoon character in the *Sunday Express* produced by Giles, known as 'Grandma', with a squashed face; and appeared to me to be aged about 101. I prepared my intervention with care. Mrs Cole, from the end of the table, was underwhelmed. 'Young man,' she interrupted, 'when you have something worthwhile to say, you may say it. Until then, shut up.' Crushed, I retreated into silence.

Equally memorable, but a role by which I am now rather embarrassed, was the small but not insignificant part that I played in the destruction of London grammar schools. It was the policy of the ILEA in 1964–7 to develop the comprehensive school; and my task was to chair a succession of public meetings. The theory was that by achieving excellence across the board, educational standards would rise for all. We now know, with the hindsight of experience, what actually happened. However, it was not all gloom and doom when chairing large public meetings in the educational world. I remember a prize-giving in a vast all-female school (Mayfield) in Wandsworth, at which the prizes were presented by Shirley Williams (later Baroness Williams of Crosby). I was the only male person among about 2,000 girls: and, as I took my seat, the cheers and wolf-whistles – I then had a full head of hair – provided me with my nearest experience to being on stage at a pop concert.

———

Within the Reigate and Redhill Labour Party, I prospered. I was selected to fight a local seat for the new Surrey County Council (its boundaries had been modified to reflect the creation of the new GLC). This election took place in March 1965. While I was predictably unsuccessful, objectively I put up a good showing. I was asked to become the secretary of the Surrey Federation of Labour Parties. While this was not a role for which there was a huge amount of competition, it had a surprising amount of patronage attached to it. In those days, appointment to the local Bench was organised on party political lines, the new recruits to the ranks of JP broadly reflecting the proportion of local seats held on the Surrey County Council. I had the last word in the nomination of party members as magistrates.

This created a problem when I declined to support the nomination of the chairman of my own constituency Labour Party, on the grounds that in my view he simply lacked judicial quality.

I was formally nominated as Labour Party Parliamentary candidate for the Reigate constituency. There was a final selection meeting in July 1965. My speech for that meeting owes much to Dad's influence. However, I concluded with a passage that was not only my own, but accurately represented my then beliefs:

'Labour is more than a political party. It is a faith and a positive force for good in the world. Constantly it campaigns for social justice throughout the whole range of human affairs. Its deeds are as impressive as its words – an unusual quality in these days of high-pressure economic and political propaganda. Labour's strength and power and purpose is no accident: it comes from the people who make up the Party. People from all walks of life, of all ages, and from every social group. Men and women and young people who see wrongs around them and are determined that society shall put them right. They are people with consciences, with ideas, with zeal. Down at the heart of things we regard all men as being born equal. Abilities obviously differ, as do aptitudes and needs. But these can only be properly discovered and assessed where there is political and economic freedom, and they can only be satisfactorily developed where every child is given the fullest opportunity in education and employment. Society must be organised, not to give the biggest profit to the few, but to produce the greatest benefit for all. Today our claim to office is not just that we can manage things better than the Tories: we aim to create – and we are creating – a different and a better society.'

I was duly selected. Over the next eight months or so I was assiduous in building up the strength of the local party. I reduced what had hitherto been my regular attendance for TA purposes in Dorking; and my personal life was subordinated to political activity. While I was then formally a pupil, I was able to balance the demands of pupillage with these political activities, which of course included continuing involvement in meetings of the Education Committee of the ILEA, and governors' meetings of the two Colleges of Further Education to which I had been appointed.

My Tory opponent, Sir John Vaughan-Morgan, lived locally, and in 1966 had represented the constituency for sixteen years. Vaughan-Morgan retired from the House of Commons in 1970, to become Lord Reigate of Outwood. In 1966, Vaughan-Morgan's election address included a Freudian slip: 'Living here I know the local followers...' A correction slip had to be inserted into each address, to my huge amusement: For *'followers'* read *'problems'*. This gave my own election address an unexpected boost, for under my photograph with the Market Hall, Reigate, in the background, and speaking to a lady who posed as a housewife, the slogan *John Samuels knows the housewife's problems* gained greater resonance. The results of the election were that Vaughan-Morgan obtained 24,163 votes; I gained 16,649; and the Liberal candidate 10,197. The Tory majority fell from 9,389 in 1964 to 7,514. A reduction in the Tory vote, coupled with an increase in the Labour vote of almost 3 per cent, was something of which I felt justifiably proud. I returned to chambers on 1 April 1966 (a significant date) to have that pride duly pricked: see 'First Steps in the Law', chapter 7.

―――――――

While I have disposed of most of the letters I received from the electorate, all of which I faithfully answered, one had asked for my views on the relaxation of the Sunday trading laws. My tactful response was 'at the moment I am not in favour of any relaxation of the present law with regard to the opening of shops on Sundays', and it is noteworthy that, with a greater appreciation of the issues, less than twenty years later I was leading the campaign to introduce Sunday trading (see 'Never on Sunday', chapter 14).

Maxine was playing an increasing role in my life from December 1965 onwards, and diligently helped out by canvassing on my behalf. However, with the perceptiveness that is her speciality, she made it clear that while she would continue to support me in my pursuit of a political career, I was unlikely to be a success: I was simply too sensitive to do so. As I had entered politics to achieve change, there was only one legitimate aim: to become a minister. I realised that the task of persuading others to support me in the rise up the greasy pole was anathema, and my enthusiasm rapidly waned. By the summer of 1966 I had fallen out of love with politics, but fortunately a greater interest, closer to home, was actively developing. I had been warned, by one of my most loyal party supporters:

> *'I think I should tell you that many party members regret the fact that they have seen so little of you since the election. If you think of standing again for this constituency, I think it would be wise to take a more active part. I hope you will accept this in the spirit in which it is written!'*

Following the GLC election in 1967, Tory control of the council was achieved; and my membership of the Education Committee of the ILEA came to an end. Although I remained the secretary of the Surrey Federation of Labour Parties until sometime in 1968, for practical purposes my involvement in politics ended after Maxine and I married in 1967. I was hardly encouraged to remain in Reigate politics when I was told in a curt two-line letter from my former constituency secretary and agent that I was no longer wanted as the local Parliamentary candidate. It was modestly reassuring to be told by the regional organiser, in his subsequent letter:

> *'I am like you completely mystified on the Reigate business ... so far as I am concerned we would be very happy to see you as a prospective candidate in any constituency in the region, and we would be very sorry to lose you from the Regional Executive Committee.'*

I allowed my Labour Party membership to lapse, and never subsequently joined a political party.

There was a sequel to my involvement in the ILEA Education Committee. In 1974, when we had been living in Richmond for seven years, the Richmond Council Education Committee decided to co-opt persons of 'special experience in education' to their committee. Richmond was a council with an overwhelming Conservative majority, so the impact of a few co-options was unlikely to shift the balance of power. I was duly nominated, and my appointment was announced in the local press. Late in the day, the leader of the council wrote to ask me which political party I supported. I replied that I was no longer a member of any political party, and had no intention of becoming one. 'In those circumstances,' he responded, 'your appointment cannot proceed: we first need to know how you would vote on any contested issue.'

In the result, the four co-options were filled by the appointment of three former Tory councillors and the former Labour leader on the council. Gracious in defeat, I offered to serve the community in the education field without accepting membership of any political party. After a couple of months' delay, I was told: 'Occasions do arise when fundamental political policy divides the committee.' I was clearly not wanted.

Nevertheless, on 29 June 1982, out of filial loyalty, I attended the meeting of the GLC following Dad's death and sat on the dais in the Council Chamber. I had last done so in 1958, when he had become the chairman of the London County Council. The minutes of that meeting include:

'Finally, I have the sad duty to inform the Council of the passing on Saturday 19 June of Mr A.E. Samuels. Ted Samuels served on the London County Council for 36 years. He was Chairman of the Council from 1958 to 1959 as well as Chairman of the Public Control Committee and of the Establishment Committee continuously over a period of 30 years. Whilst on the Council he represented Southwark from 1964 to 1967. His son, John Samuels QC, who served as a member of the Education Committee of the ILEA from 1964 to 1967, is however present with us today and I know that I speak for all members in expressing to him our deep respect for Ted and the many years of service he gave to the people of London through his work in this building. We salute his memory and we send our very sincere sympathy and condolences to his family.'

The detail of the record is wrong. Dad served on the LCC for twenty-two years, concluding with the dissolution of that council on 31 March 1965.

He was chairman of the Public Control Committee between 1934 and 1937, and again between 1946 and 1949; and chairman of the Establishment Committee between 1952 and 1965. On the GLC he chaired the Public Works Committee, responsible inter alia for the design of the Thames Barrier at Woolwich. Despite these inaccuracies, I was glad I was there; although the formality of proceedings swiftly broke down, with Labour members clambering on to their chairs and shouting at the tops of their voices. That was when I made my dignified withdrawal from the Council Chamber.

Despite the disillusionment I felt when I last sat on the dais at County Hall in 1982, I retained an active affection for the building that had been the centre of my father's life for so long. Stung by the political posturing of the GLC and its leader, Ken Livingstone – placards had been strung across the facade of County Hall opposite the terrace of the House of Commons, mischievously proclaiming 'London isn't working' – the government of Margaret Thatcher resolved to abolish the GLC; and did so.

Power was devolved to thirty-two local boroughs, a decision that in the aftermath of the Grenfell Tower disaster in 2017 now looks particularly unwise; and the seat of London government was devolved to an expensive and architecturally questionable new building on the South Bank of the Thames.

On 6 October 1986, I wrote to *The Times*:

'*The appearance of the first advertisement for the sale of County Hall should send a shudder of shame through every Londoner. The building, whose foundation stone was so proudly laid by King George V, is not only an architectural monument to the best of early 20th-century public works but, on its dramatic and historic site, has been a focus for Londoners and visitors alike in the capital city. Few buildings of its scale are of such immense cultural and historic importance. For whatever silly policies and facile placards may recently have defamed its reputation, defaced its facade and irritated its political opponents across the Thames, this noble structure is not to blame: and future generations of Londoners may well consider themselves to have been cheated if its continued use does not lie within the public domain. The public sector is crying out for new museums, art galleries, courts and public buildings of many kinds: cannot all those concerned for our architectural heritage and environment assemble, now, a committee to find a continuing role for County Hall, and then to preserve this national resource for what is still one of the most important capital cities in the world?*

———

The attraction of politics did not totally disappear. For sixteen years or so, as an appellate advocate, the enthusiasm with which I mounted the stone staircase leading from the robing room in the House of Lords to the Committee corridor, where Lords' appeals were then held, owed something to the glamour of the red benches in the Lords' chamber, on which it had once been my probably vain ambition to perch. In 2002, as chairman of the Criminal Committee of the Council of Circuit Judges, I attended the Lords' debate on the then Criminal Justice Bill and sat in the gallery reserved for authorised visitors. Lord Renton, who had become a good friend on the Bench of the Inn (he made his disapproval of Ian Percival, and Percival's conduct towards me, as detailed in chapters 12 and 13, very clear when I first sat next to him at lunch at the Bench table in 1990), had spoken twice in the debate when he caught sight of me. David Renton was then aged ninety-three. His cheery hailing of me boomed across all the microphones. 'What are you doing, John? Come and have a drink!' Two gin and tonics later we had put the whole of the bill, as well as politics generally, to rights. Since then, I have been a regular visitor to the Committee corridor in the House of Lords, but rarely fail to remember David; and a nagging sensation of envy sometimes creeps in.

That tiny sensation of envy was fanned in 2009/10. In no way inspired by me, Keith Cutler – then Secretary of the Council of Circuit Judges, and later its President – decided that the judiciary needed a more prominent spokesman to fight their corner in the legislature, and to act as a voice of experience when commenting on the detail of legislation. Rather to my surprise, two sitting members of the House of Lords actively supported my nomination: Lord Ramsbotham, former Chief Inspector of Prisons; and Baroness Linklater, a Liberal Democrat peer, on whose advisory board of her programme for Rethinking Crime and Punishment I had served. Initially, I was only prepared to agree to this nomination as a 'People's Peer' if it received the support of my friend Lord Woolf. He told Keith that he would support me; but subsequently, in some embarrassment, telephoned me to say that he had been persuaded to support a retired member of the Court of Appeal (who, in the result, was not appointed). Keith secured support for my nomination from three other peers as well as others of varied eminence; but – as I had anticipated – the attraction of the retired Circuit Judge when contrasted with a household name was likely to be an unequal contest.

LINCOLN'S INN

No man is an Island,
Entire of itself;
Every man is a piece of the continent,
A part of the main.

...

Any man's death diminishes me,
Because I am involved in mankind;
And therefore never send to know for whom the bell tolls;
It tolls for thee.

John Donne, Preacher to Lincoln's Inn (1572–1631)

To encapsulate any kind of history of an organisation whose origins lie in the mists of time – its known records, the Black Books, date from 1422, but Lincoln's Inn is believed to have far older roots – is hopeless, particularly as my involvement within the Inn occurred so casually. However, almost sixty-four years after becoming a student member of the Inn, some perspective is achievable. In my relatively brief membership – about one-tenth of its recorded history – the Inn has been transformed. From a remote institution, focused on seniority, arcane tradition and the importance of precedent, the Inn has become a collegiate body, with education of its members at its heart. By good luck, I ended up in the middle of this quiet revolution; and, without realising what was happening at the time, became a mentor to many. This role encouraged the judicial monitoring that developed from it.

The educational role of the Inn was minimal: appropriately promising students were encouraged with a scholarship or a prize, following distinction in the Bar exam. Little else was on offer. The social outlook of the Inn shortly before my admission is encapsulated in a report in January 1956.

'Would the Inn benefit from a reduction in the number of students of non-European origin (below referred to, for brevity, as "coloured students")? ... The feeling that led to our appointment was, we think, not so much that the Inn was admitting too many coloured students as that their disproportionate numbers made the Inn less attractive to "white" students, in particular to those from Oxford and Cambridge.'

Reading those words today makes me shudder.

In 1959, Lincoln's Inn societies were formed at Oxford and Cambridge respectively. Council noted that 'there are not more than fourteen members of Lincoln's Inn resident at Cambridge, of whom only eight are undergraduates'.

This was the background to the Inn to which I was admitted on 25 July 1960. The Inn moved slowly towards what might be viewed as a contemporary institution. In May 1961, Council approved with obvious reluctance the recommendation that 'compulsory Latin should be abandoned'; but added that 'if Latin is not to be compulsory, neither should Roman law be compulsory'. I had a weekend's grounding in Roman law in 1963.

A lack of academic application did not preclude the pursuit of my chosen career. I was summoned to an interview for a scholarship. A month later, I was informed by the Under Treasurer that I had been awarded a Mansfield scholarship: one of the Inn's major scholarships, payable at £400 per year over a three-year term. The interview had been striking. The Scholarships Committee was chaired by Lord Parker of Waddington, Lord Chief Justice of England. On his right sat Lord Evershed, until 1962 Master of the Rolls; and on his left Lord Denning, who had succeeded him. At least twenty other Benchers were present in the drawing room of the Inn, filling the room-length tables. I was ushered in, to perch at a chair (the only one without arms) at the end of the table. I cannot remember any of the interview, save that I spoke up clearly, and spoke slowly. I am convinced that this was what achieved my success. I suspect that a favourable reference from my college helped.

Shortly after my Call in 1964 I took root on the lunch table, located next to Norman Hepple's celebrated group portrait *The Short Adjournment*. This portrayed the nine members of the Court of Appeal in 1958 who were members of Lincoln's Inn. As there were eleven members in all, the Inn was well represented. Lord Denning, standing close to the door, was about to be appointed to the House of Lords. Rupert Evans and Donald Rattee, the junior members of my pupillage chambers at 7 New Square, regularly lunched there. Gavin Lightman, Peter Rawson, Martin Buckley, Roger Cooke, Freddie Marr-Johnson and Geoffrey Jacques were my initial regular companions, and all of them remained faithful to it until, in due course, we each joined the Bench.

Lunches apart, my involvement with the affairs of the Inn was minimal until I took Silk in 1981. Malcolm Carver, the Under Treasurer, suggested that as I was likely to have plenty of free time (a proposition that I readily agreed, although fortunately the forecast was wrong), I should be co-opted to the Bar Representation Committee. This proved a revelation. The primary function of the committee was, as its name implied, to enable those members of Hall who were not Benchers to sit on committees of the Bench, where their contributions, advanced with appropriate diffidence, were rare and usually non-controversial. The Bencher who presided at these committee meetings was styled Vice-Chairman, a nod to the fact that the Treasurer nominally chaired each committee of the Bench. Appointment to committee membership was in the exclusive gift of the Treasurer.

The Kitchen Committee was the preserve of a senior Bencher, John Monckton, who presided over its formal deliberations with a funereal solemnity. Monckton, as the senior Bencher in practice, was also Vice-Chairman of the Benchers in Practice Committee, a body of which all Benchers still in practice at the Bar were *ex officio* members. Its role was to select those practising members of the Bar who might be considered for election to the Bench to replace those who had died or accepted a judicial appointment. This committee met once each year; and with few exceptions its preferred Silk candidates were chosen by reference to their seniority, while those who were Chancery juniors were selected by reference to whether they were 'good eggs' and would provide stimulating conversation over dinner.

As Benchers at that time routinely sat at dinner in strict order of seniority, you got to know the characteristics of your immediate group of Benchers particularly well. The Bencher immediately senior to me was Helen Grindrod QC; and next after me was Peter Rawson. We enjoyed many well-lubricated dinners. When I was elected a Bencher in July 1990, it was regarded as your duty to dine on the Bench after every meeting of Council, an obligation I maintained regularly for more than twenty years.

I joined the Admissions and Call Committee in 1982; and I remained a member of that committee (latterly its chairman, with widened responsibility for pupillage matters, for ten years) continuously until I ceased to be an ordinary member of the Bench in 2010, following my retirement as a Circuit Judge. The then Standing Orders of the Inn required any ordinary Bencher who had retired to become an Emeritus Bencher on attaining the age of seventy. The downside was that an Emeritus Bencher had no vote; but the advantage was that you were no longer obliged to keep terms and pay term commons. In 2014, when a topic of some sensitivity divided the Bench, my little note on 'Voteless Benchers' persuaded Council to restore voting rights to any Bencher requesting them; and the status of 'Emeritus Bencher' has become voluntary.

Malcolm Carver recognised my gratitude to the Inn, following the successful lifeboat service launched in my direction in the summer of 1987 (this is explained in chapter 12, 'Temptation'). He correctly identified that, following my election to the Bench, I should demonstrate that gratitude by becoming one of the Inn's representatives on the Bar Council, as well as taking an active part as a member of Bench committees. I had already represented the Inn as a Hall member, successively on the Senate of the Inns of Court and the Bar, and then the Bar Council, between 1983 and 1986; I had chaired the Joint Regulations Committee of the Council of the Inns of Court (COIC) and the Bar for three years between 1987 and 1990; and in that role I was routinely invited to attend meetings of the

COIC. I also represented the Inn on the Estate Management Advisory Committee of the four Inns; and chaired several inter-Inn initiatives, such as investigating whether – and if so, on what terms – solicitors with higher rights of audience might enjoy a measure of social membership of the Inns.

I have mentioned, in chapter 2 ('The Unexpected Mentor'), the warm friendship that developed between Paul Heim and me, which resulted in multiple visits, with receptive and enthusiastic Inn students and young barristers, to European institutions over the years: to the European Court of Justice in Luxembourg; the European Court of Human Rights in Strasbourg; the International Criminal Tribunal for the former Yugoslavia, the International Criminal Court and the International Court of Justice, all in The Hague; and to the European Commission in Brussels. Paul, as a former European senior civil servant, had established a Euro Group to facilitate knowledge not only of European law generally, but also the career opportunities available in Europe. Scholarships to develop these opportunities have been created by the Inn; and these have enabled a succession of able students to undertake internships. Extensive international friendships were created. Following the appointment of Tim Eicke as the UK judge in Strasbourg, in 2016 I became the chairman of the Euro Group that Paul had founded. With no pretensions to be a mainstream European lawyer, I had easily sidestepped this role in the past, when successively Tom Sharpe and Tim Eicke had discharged it with distinction. During my subsequent term I secured the attendance of very distinguished lecturers to present the Sir Thomas More lecture, the jewel in the crown of the Group's annual activity, as well as a series of updating lectures in human rights, which have placed the Inn in the forefront of European law.

Two other initiatives within the Inn following my appointment to the Circuit Bench in 1997 deserve a mention. First, in 1998 I inaugurated the Lincoln's Inn Circuit Judges' dinner, an annual event that has recently celebrated its twenty-fifth anniversary. The driver for this was to bridge the social gap that then existed between those members of the Inn who had been appointed to the Circuit Bench but who, following that appointment, had become ineligible to be elected to the Bench of the Inn. Second, and as a consequence of the first, when Sir Martin Nourse was Treasurer of the Inn in 2001, he appointed me as a member of the Advisory (Benchers) Committee, specifically in order to promote the candidature of otherwise eligible and involved Circuit Judges as Benchers. While I remained a member of that committee, I achieved the election of at least two Circuit Judges to the Bench of the Inn every year: and the Inn benefited considerably from their involvement.

My delight (and relief, as explained in chapter 13, 'Rehabilitation') to be introduced as a Bencher in July 1990 needs no elaboration. I have done all I can to play a full part in the life of the Inn ever since: not only as a member of Inn committees, but as a regular attendee at Council.

Participation in the Inn's memorable social events, such as Grand Day and the reopening of the Old Hall by Princess Margaret in October 1991, has also spawned memories. At about midnight when Princess Margaret, our Royal Bencher, attended for the Old Hall reopening, I was more than ready to go home. Peter Rawson and I vanished, en route to the loo – only to be hauled back by Malcolm Carver. 'You do not leave until she has done so,' he commanded. Thereafter, as the two junior benchers, we danced attendance on HRH. A languid hand stretched in one direction required a cigarette: another, a fresh glass of whisky. Unforgettable; and royalty finally departed about 2 a.m.

Similarly memorable was the first Grand Day I attended, in April 1991. Sir Michael Davies as Treasurer was keen to secure the attendance of Margaret Thatcher, no longer prime minister – she had resigned in November 1990 – but an Honorary Bencher; so he invited as his guest Sir Denis Thatcher, knowing that Denis would bring Margaret as his partner. Two memories stand out. First, entering the Drawing Room, she surveyed the replacement portrait of William Pitt the Younger – the previous one had been stolen. The replacement is an indifferent work by Hoppner, an artist of whom few have heard. Margaret Thatcher had been briefed about the replacement. As she stood in the doorway, she announced: 'Ah: Hoppner, I believe.' Second, and to my delight, I was seated opposite her at dessert after dinner in the library. The tables are narrow. For two hours I was the centre of her conversation and her attention. Returning home in the small hours, I inevitably roused Maxine – and tactlessly informed her that I thought I was in love with another woman!

George Hampel was a retired Australian judge with a passion for mentoring. In his youth he had been a ski instructor and a tennis coach. In retirement, he had applied those early skills to a scheme of advocacy training, which became transformational. An English Silk with links to the New South Wales Bar, and an advocacy trainer in Gray's Inn, encouraged George to come to London; and some Lincoln's Inn advocacy training enthusiasts attended his initial lecture. They were hooked. The simple key to the Hampel method, as it became known, was the assimilation of a single simple lesson under memorable headings:

HEADLINE: a succinct summary of the lesson being taught.
PLAYBACK: what the student had said, repeated verbatim.
REASON: why what had been said did not work.
REMEDY: a better way of achieving that objective.
DEMONSTRATION: a few lines only from the tutor, showing how the student might improve the performance.
REPLAY: after an interval, and some intervening 1:1 tuition that included playing a recording of the student's teaching lesson, the student presents a revised version of the exercise.

Stick-in-the-mud Samuels was initially adamantly opposed to the adoption of the Hampel method. 'I have been teaching advocacy for years and you can't equate a production line approach to the sophistication needed for contemporary advocacy.' More sneering: reminiscent of my confession in chapter 2 that I was an initially reluctant teacher.

Fortunately, my friend Roger Cooke was determined. 'We want you, John; but you will have to do it this way.'

After about a year of sulking, like Achilles in his tent, I succumbed. I learned to apply the Hampel technique; found it initially highly embarrassing to do so, particularly its public demonstration, but that it was hugely satisfying once I had mastered it. This laid the foundations of my subsequent experiences as an Inn mentor. Judicial monitoring remained well over the horizon.

As an Inn lead advocacy tutor, I routinely attended advocacy training residential weekends for pupils and new practitioners of the Inn. By the summer of 2008 I had progressed to the role of course director for the New Practitioners' Programme; and my relatively relaxed style seemed to be welcomed by both participants and my fellow tutors. I was sufficiently senior on the Bench of the Inn to be considered as a prospective Treasurer. Seniority within the Inn had previously dominated selection for election to the Bench and thereafter to the succession to the role of Treasurer.

Gavin Lightman had become Treasurer of the Inn in January 2008. We had been friends since we were both awarded a Mansfield scholarship in 1963. Despite his seniority as a Chancery judge – Gavin was appointed in 1994 – he seemed ill at ease when he presided at his first Council meeting after his installation as Treasurer, a characteristic that continued to dog him throughout his year in the role. At a residential weekend for students at West Dean in January, I had delivered the Friday evening talk; and the following morning noted in my diary that 'the Treasurer, sitting in rather lonely isolation at the front of the audience, pressed me hard – if not entreatingly – to sit next to him. His lack of confidence was as obvious as it was unexpected.'

The Inn limped along under Gavin's treasurership. In July, I asked him to consider nominating me as next year's entrant on the cursus: the pattern of office-holders in the Inn who, if all went to form, would end up as Treasurer four years later. I knew that, under the Standing Orders of the Inn, I needed to embark on the role of Treasurer before attaining the age of seventy-two, so that the latest year in which I could do so was 2012. Gavin's initial response was that I was 'ineligible' for the role, which he did not explain. Gavin told me to discuss the matter with David Hills, the Under Treasurer. I did so, and David characteristically and helpfully explained the position both to Gavin and me, and to others who needed to be informed.

The Treasurer subsequently telephoned me at home. He told me that he had now decided to nominate me for the fourth place on the Cursus. He added that this step had the full agreement of all those already on the Cursus. I wrote formally to him the following day to confirm what a privilege it would be to accept the nomination.

A formal notification of my nomination was sent out to all Benchers. I first saw this when we were returning from Cornwall on 7 September and had called in on Paul Heim. My pleasure was short-lived. There were other nominations, which polarised opinion. It emerged that the source of the bad feeling was that Gavin had failed to consult former treasurers before making his nomination.

Gavin asked me to meet him. He told me that a former treasurer planned to oppose my nomination at the forthcoming Council meeting. Throughout the meeting, Gavin displayed extreme agitation; and, probably increasing his agitation, I remained calm. While he walked up and down in his study, circumnavigating the central table several times, I remained seated. He said that this would by no means be the end of the election process: if I were to win an initial election, I could expect to be black-balled as Treasurer just before taking office. A single black ball would have been conclusive. I ended our conversation by saying that I would think about things, although the threat of being blackballed a few months before becoming Treasurer was particularly cogent. After reflection, I spoke to him the following day, and asked him to withdraw his nomination.

At the subsequent meeting of Council on 7 October, the Treasurer made a statement, recorded in the minutes, which includes:

'*During the year there was broad discussion and finally agreement that a fourth office be added to the cursus. A nomination to this office required to be made at the end of July. It was brought to my attention that by reason of age this was the last year in which HH John Samuels QC, if nominated, could be eligible to be elected Treasurer. Over 20 years he has made an unequalled contribution to the Inn and its core activity, education. In accordance with the rules I consulted all those whom I was required to consult, and they all unequivocally endorsed the proposed nomination. I accordingly made this nomination.*

A contested election for the office would be unprecedented and in the extreme unfortunate and potentially damaging to the Inn. In these circumstances, placing (as he always has) the interests of the Inn ahead of any interest of his own, John Samuels asked me to withdraw my nomination of him and I have done so.'

A group of former treasurers decided that only a new and clearly widely approved candidate could properly be put forward. Hence there emerged the name of Dame Janet Smith, then a leading member of the Court of Appeal. However, in terms of seniority she was then junior to at least four other Benchers.

A subsequent meeting of former treasurers decided that the Standing Orders of the Inn had to be modified to avoid a similar disaster. The black-ball procedure, particularly of a potential Treasurer shortly before assuming the role, was abolished; and the election of the Master of the Walks, the lowest rung on the Cursus, was henceforth to be achieved by a postal ballot of all Benchers (in contrast to those attending the meeting in question), subject only to the achievement of an appropriate majority of the votes cast, with a minimum number necessary to validate the election. These procedural changes precluded a resolution of the issue before Gavin ceased to be Treasurer. The subsequent nomination of Janet Smith was identified at the first meeting of Council by his successor.

Tempted though I initially was simply to walk away from involvement in the affairs of the Inn, I am unreservedly glad that I did not. For a further fifteen years I continued in my roles as a lead advocacy tutor and tutor trainer; the Pupillage Foundation Scheme went from strength to strength in supporting admirable candidates for pupillage to achieve their ambition, with heart-warming expressions of gratitude from those whom I had been able to assist; I have routinely presided as Acting Treasurer at a succession of dinners and other Inn events, when my non-speeches (it is an Inn tradition that we have no after-dinner speeches) have been well received; and I have steered the Euro Group to continued success and influence, despite the disaster of the Brexit catastrophe.

On 16 September 2010, Maxine and I held a party in the Old Hall. Ostensibly, this was to celebrate my fiftieth anniversary as a member of the Inn; but 15 August 2010 was also my seventieth birthday, so that was celebrated too. It demonstrated that despite what happened two years earlier, not only had I risen above it, but I had retained the affection and respect of so many friends and colleagues within the Inn, as well as outside it. The fact that four past treasurers, as well as the then current Treasurer, Lord Walker, attended the celebration – which took place on a gloriously sunny September evening – says much; and over a hundred guests, as well as David, Adam and Gabi, have been preserved in the photographs.

In conversation with a fellow Bencher before a Council meeting in July 2020, I mentioned that I was celebrating my thirtieth anniversary as a Bencher; and remarked on the number of meetings I believed I had attended. The minutes of the meeting recorded her disclosure: '*Judge Samuels had been made a Bencher 30 years ago. He had attended over 230 meetings. Council offered their congratulations to Judge Samuels.*' I believe this minute to be unique.

FIRST STEPS IN THE LAW

If a would-be barrister can be stopped from entering this profession,
it is in his own interest that he should be stopped. If he is the sort who is
stoppable, he is the sort who will fail. It is only those who cannot be dissuaded
who can safely be left to make the attempt.
Professor Glanville Williams (1911–1997), *Learning the Law*

'Do you think I might get a First, Geoffrey?'

It was one of those memorable mornings: early October 1962, the end of an Indian summer. I was in Queens' College Fellows' Garden, perhaps the most beautiful small garden in Cambridge, with my Director of Studies, Geoffrey Wilson. Geoffrey and I not only liked one another, but we had a joint and unusually expert interest in the etchings of Goya. To enter this garden, you had to be with a Fellow. The garden is sadly now destroyed and buried under the concrete structure of the ugly Fitzpatrick Building. 'Concrete is the material of the future,' proclaimed Sir Derek Bowett QC, later President of Queens', and my erstwhile tutor. Bowett was a great international lawyer, but a poor forecaster. Another forecast was: 'We shall have women in this College over my dead body.'

Geoffrey gave me a quizzical stare. 'Yes, I suppose you might, John, if you worked hard: but why would you want one? You are going to the Bar, aren't you? Why don't you just enjoy yourself?' I took his advice. In common with virtually all my Cambridge contemporaries who read law at Cambridge and went to the Bar, I graduated with a mediocre 2:2.

There were some more active spurs to the determination to become an advocate than this indolent approach. In spring 1961, Lord Birkett, who had been the foremost defence advocate of his day, introduced a series of radio talks on six outstanding early advocates; and concluded with his own summary of the qualities that make a great advocate. I listened, spellbound.

Birkett's exposition of the lives of his six great advocates are luminous. Birkett spoke specifically on the art of advocacy:

> '*I want to treat advocacy in rather a wider sense because I believe that advocacy is very much more than a mere legal accomplishment. Advocacy in the courts must always take pride of place because the opportunities for its most effective use are chiefly to be found there; but I like to think that every day the art of advocacy is being employed in much wider fields ... the most important element in all advocacy, whether in the courts of law or elsewhere, is the art of attractive and persuasive speech. It is not confined to the advocate in the courts of law; it is within the reach of all who aspire to influence their fellows in any walk of life, but the price to be paid is one of taking pains and exercising much patience.*'

Although I had joined Lincoln's Inn in July 1960, with vague ideas of wishing to become an advocate, it was these radio talks, delivered when I was not even reading law, that sharpened my determination to become, if I possibly could, a general advocate.

With the ebullience of youth, I said, 'That is what I want to do.' This was not only because of Birkett's mellifluous tones, or the simplicity of his exposition, but just because, as a great advocate himself, he pitched his message so perfectly that his audience was captivated by it.

My second memory is of one of the two outstanding figures in my legal life: both, to me, Tom (the other is Tom Bingham). The Right Honourable Lord Denning, OM – always Tom to his host of admirers – first entered my life in October 1961. He had been a member of the Appellate Committee of the House of Lords in July 1960, when the House reversed the decision of the Court of Appeal in DPP v. Smith, a capital murder case.

The issue was whether or not Smith, who by concession plainly never intended to kill his victim, a police officer, should nevertheless be guilty of murder if, judged by the standards of the reasonable man, he should have contemplated that grievous bodily harm was likely to result, and that the

My father, as Chairman of
the LCC, by Michael Noakes.
(Beginnings)

My mother by Ronald Ossory
Dunlop, RA (c. 1935).
(Beginnings)

Two early mentors: Peter Wainwright, and Lt-Col Owen Rowe (c 1957). (Then a Soldier?)

My parents greeting Lord Morrison of Lambeth at the LCC Chairman's Reception 1958.
(Beginnings)

JS: the new barrister and the aspiring politician (1964). (Politics and First Steps in the Law)

Dorking Platoon, A Company, 3 Queen's Surreys, TA (1964). (Then a Soldier?)

JOHN SAMUELS KNOWS THE HOUSEWIFE'S PROBLEMS

JOHN SAMUELS . . . at the age of 25 has already made a big impact on Reigate Constituency's political scene. In 1965 he slashed his opponent's majority by half when he contested the Reigate South-Central seat in the Surrey County Council election.

A barrister, he is a B.A. (Honours) of Queens' College, Cambridge. Before going to Cambridge University, where he was Chairman of the United Nations Association, he travelled extensively abroad.

John Samuels is the youngest member of the London Education Committee and holds special responsibilities for university and technical education. He is a governor of Brixton College for Further Education.

For seven years he has commanded a detachment of the local Territorial Army Battalion.

John Samuels is Secretary of the Surrey Federation of Labour Parties. He is also a member of the Fabian Society and serves on a law reform sub-committee of the Society of Labour Lawyers.

YOU CAN HELP . . .

JOHN **SAMUELS**

. . . FOR *LABOUR*

Contact:— *Central Committee Rooms, 164 Garlands Road, Redhill.*
Telephone: Redhill 64499—or any Labour Committee Room.

Published by D. Bettle, 164 Garlands Road, Redhill and Printed by Crawley Stationers, 9 High Street, Crawley.

SAMUELS

Parliamentary election campaign, 1966. (Politics)

Friends from Day One at Queens' – 50 years on! JS, Richard Rumary, Peter Abbott and John Groves. (Growing up)

Admiral Sir Peter Abbott GBE (King at Arms); KCB – an early mentee. (Growing up)

Maxine Samuels (MS) presiding at a school visit in Richmond Magistrates' Court, the proposed venue for a Greater London Community Court (c. 2005). (Judicial Monitoring)

The Community Court for Greater London almost happened (March 2006). Judge Robert Keating, founder of the prototype problem-solving court in New York, with JS, Lord Falconer, Lord Chancellor, Lord Phillips, Lord Chief Justice and Sir Mark Potter, President of the Family Division. (Judicial Monitoring)

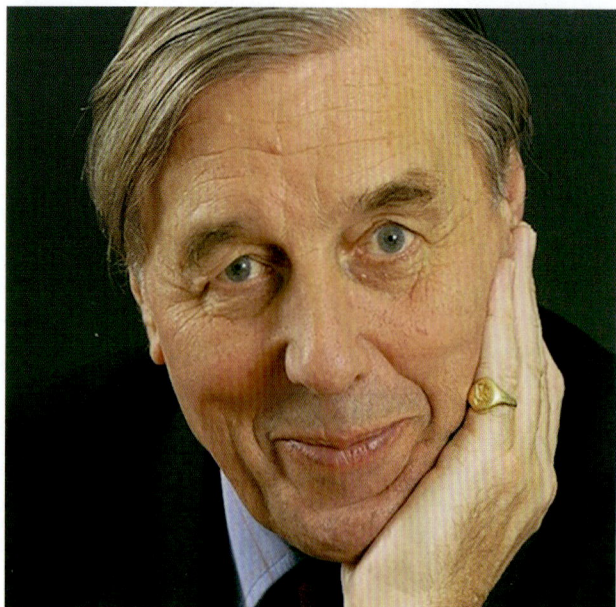

General the Lord Ramsbotham, GCB, CBE – mentor to so many in the cause of prison reform. (Preface and Envoi)

JS and MS at a Marryat shop party (c. 1995). (Never on Sunday)

officer died as a result. The decision aroused fierce controversy, and the judgment was roundly criticised, specifically by Dr Glanville Williams, later the Cambridge Professor of English Law, and the leading authority of his day in criminal law. His lecture on DPP v. Smith, one of the few I attended following Denning's lecture, was a step-by-step demolition of the logic of their Lordships' approach.

What stands out for me over sixty years after the lecture delivered by Denning to the Cambridge Law Society was his presentation of the facts. When Denning reproduced them in his lecture, the audience was wholly persuaded that only a conviction for murder would satisfy the enormity of Smith's callous recklessness in attempting to dislodge, when speeding in a built-up area, the police officer clinging on to its bonnet while banging on the windscreen with his right hand.

I had never heard such advocacy. I felt an overwhelming compulsion to write to the lecturer and tell him how inspired I had been by what he had said. I asked him for a copy of his lecture. His response deserves repetition:

'I am delighted to hear that you are coming to the Bar, and if my remarks were at all helpful to you in coming to a decision I am very pleased.

I much appreciate your kind reference to my speech. I am afraid I have not any typewritten record of it. A good deal of it was impromptu. It was kind of you to write.'

Denning had been stung by the chorus of academic criticism of the House of Lords' decision. In essence, the criticism was that the Lords had, by the use of the words 'reasonable man', introduced an objective test; whereas in the criminal law, the test of intent was invariably a subjective one. Denning sought to repair the damage in the Lionel Cohen lecture that he had delivered in the Hebrew University of Jerusalem in 1961. That lecture – 'Responsibility before the law' – was published by the Hebrew University when an honorary degree was conferred on Denning. I discovered the pamphlet in about 1984, when clearing out the bookcase of a deceased member of chambers. I only wish I had kept it: because that was, *verbatim*, the lecture delivered in Cambridge. Why did Denning wish to impress an already starstruck undergraduate that his lecture was impromptu, and that no text existed?

A few weeks later, there was a tap on my bedroom door.

'The President wants to see you, Mr Samuels.' It was my bedder, Derek.

'Go away, Derek: you only want to do my room.'

Half an hour later, Derek knocked again. 'The President really does want to see you: he has a judge with him, who wants to meet you.'

I reached the President's Lodge, panting. Arthur Armitage had taken a shine to me, as I was the President of the Queens' Bench, the college law society. I enjoyed that title long before it was later created (albeit with an important distinction in the apostrophe) to be conferred on my distinguished Cambridge contemporary Igor Judge, as the second-in-command to the Lord Chief Justice. I first met Armitage when he was senior tutor of the college in 1958, when he awarded me my place to begin, as we both then anticipated, after my National Service. As President of the college, he took a keen interest in everyone, but particularly the lawyers.

Armitage explained that his overnight guest, Mr Justice Lawton, had left; but wished to take me as his marshal. At that stage, I had no idea what a marshal was, or what the role entailed. It involved living with a High Court judge for six weeks or so as he tried cases at assizes. In hindsight, I realise that Armitage had engineered the whole thing. I did, of course, take up the opportunity; I subsequently met the judge in the Law Courts, and arrived in Carlisle on 2 October 1963.

This was not the only opportunity that Arthur Armitage took to promote my career. Midway during my final year, he asked what I had done about pupillage. Smugly, I said that I had organised everything. My first six months' pupillage had been arranged in Chancery Chambers, in which Sir Milner Holland QC was the leading member. The outstanding Silk of his generation, twice chairman of the Bar Council, Milner Holland had repeatedly rejected a judicial appointment. He was a friend of my father; and he insisted not only that I must join Lincoln's Inn (for which I remain eternally grateful to him), but that I should be a pupil in his chambers. He told me to make an appointment with the formidable senior clerk, Edward Jagot. I did so; and I knew that, once I had been called to the Bar, I should spend my first six months as a pupil with George Hesketh.

My forward planning was less productive than the haphazard approach adopted by my contemporary, David Latham. He was the secretary of the Queens' Bench. Asked the same question by Arthur Armitage, David said he had no idea where he might go as a pupil. Arthur suggested, with his diffident manner masking a razor-sharp mind, that David might like to meet a junior whom Armitage knew, Harry Woolf. David duly became Harry's pupil; he became a tenant in the chambers of which Harry was a member, and subsequently leaped to prominence as leading counsel to the inquiry undertaken by Lord Justice Woolf (as he then was) into the Strangeways Prison riot of 1990. After his retirement from a most distinguished career, including that of Lord Chief Justice, Harry became chairman of the Prison Reform Trust and has been a stalwart supporter of the cause of prison reform. Appointed to the High Court bench in 1994, David retired as Vice-President of the Court of Appeal (Criminal Division); and was then, for three years, chairman of the Parole Board, when we were both involved in identifying its future.

In September 1963, David had invited my flatmate, Peter Abbott, and me to his twenty-first birthday party. Peter wanted to cry off. I used all my persuasive powers to encourage him to accompany me. Peter protested that he could not come, as he had no black tie. I scoured South London to procure one for him. At the dance Peter met Sue, the love of his life, to whom he remained so happily married for fifty years. That wedding had critical implications for my own, as explained in chapter 3, 'Growing up'.

My journal of my formative experience as a marshal, first at Carlisle and subsequently at Lancaster Assizes, between October and November 1963, survives. I arrived at the Carlisle lodgings to be greeted by the housekeeper, Mrs Carruthers – 'I have been looking after the judges for over forty years, and they all call me Janet' – and the butler, Dearie (that was really his name!). Dearie was Irish, bald, with a fringe of grey hair, and his concession to modernity was to wear a nylon shirt. He was otherwise the perfect Jeeves, apart from the fact that he had a pronounced stammer. Inevitably, I had to address him as Dearie. Herbert, the clerk, greeted me with: 'Hello, Marshal, I have some papers for you to read.' An hour or so later, Judge and Lady Lawton arrived: again, it was 'Hello, Marshal', and I realised that, for the duration, I had lost my surname.

The following morning, I was woken by Dearie at seven o'clock with tea on a tray plus the *Daily Mail*. I felt modestly insulted until I found *The Times* in my place for breakfast. The High Sheriff and his retinue, including the Under Sheriff, then arrived to accompany the judge to court. Robed and bewigged, the judge moved off into the waiting Rolls. Cameras clicked as I tried to look appropriately solemn in my new morning coat. We made a stately passage down to the city with a police escort. Near the court the car slowed down and a heavier escort of police on foot, preceded by an enormous sergeant, led us to the court entrance. The liveried footman opened the door; out I stepped; the trumpets blew, and we processed into the building. In court, Herbert read the proclamation; and the clerk of assize proceeded to read the extraordinarily verbose commission.

The duties of a marshal are modest. Paid the generous sum of 2 guineas per day (£14.70 per week in modern currency), the marshal hovered somewhat uncertainly between the roles of the butler and the judge's clerk. When the judge's clerk was not sitting in court, the marshal swore in the witness ('Take the testament in your right hand and repeat after me...'); and would pour the preprandial drinks for the judge's guests. But his (there were never any female marshals in the 1960s) primary role was to observe and learn; to read the case papers; and to discuss any and every aspect of the case with the judge. It was a window into the role of the judge that is incomparable; and as a precursor to pupillage in chambers, invaluable. Pressure on the judiciary at High Court and Circuit level today means that a stint as a marshal rarely lasts more than a week. While any experience that provides the would-be barrister with a view from the bench is invaluable, the immersion in the thought process of an outstanding judge cannot be replicated in what is no more than a 'taster' experience.

The principal case at Carlisle was the murder of a child committed by her stepbrother. The case was notorious, since the child had been missing for many days until her corpse was discovered under the floorboards of the defendant's home. The defendant had, with many volunteers, participated in a search. Death was due to stabbing; and after death the child's private parts were mutilated. There was evidence of necrophilia. The defence case was that the stabbing was an accident, and the defendant thereafter wished the death to appear as if it had been the act of a sex maniac, as he was frightened of telling his mother – also the victim's mother – the truth. The prosecution was represented by Joseph Cantley QC (leader of the Northern Circuit) and David McNeill: both became High Court judges before whom I later appeared; and the defence was represented by Rose Heilbron QC and Ian Morris-Jones (again, judges before whom I subsequently appeared).

That evening, there was a 'special court' of the Northern Circuit. There was a ceremony, 'about which I am sworn to secrecy, but which involved a Herculean quaffing of port, followed by my being required to make a speech' is the contemporary diary entry. I can raise the veil to this extent. A claret glass filled to the brim with port was presented to me: I was obliged to down it in one go ('no heel taps'); and then to make my speech. While I retained my dignity for just long enough to return to the privacy of the loo in the judge's lodgings, I was very, very sick; and this coloured my subsequent approach to Mr Justice Cantley.

The following day, the leaders were invited to lunch. Rose Heilbron in her prime was strikingly beautiful. I was overwhelmed. It was my role to pour the drinks. I could not take my eyes off her as I mixed a gin and tonic for her: and the result was a massive helping of gin, which she lowered without batting an eyelid. My judge was less impressed; quoting Dr Johnson, on the dog that walked on its hind legs, he said of her: 'It is not done well, but the wonder is that it is done at all.'

Even when there were no guests for dinner, judge and marshal dressed formally in black tie. I remember a postprandial conversation, when in my eyes the judge was holding forth both pompously and rather antisemitically. I asked if I might say something.

'Anything you like, Marshal.'

After a deep breath, I replied: 'I'm afraid I find those remarks intolerable. As I hope to stay with you for the next six weeks, I don't think I can do so without speaking up.'

He pushed his chair back, and there was a long pause. Ultimately, he said: 'Well done, Marshal – you're quite right!'

We became good friends – and he actively supported me for Silk.

The Lawtons came to lunch with my parents in December 1963, and they returned that hospitality. I have a generous letter from Lady Lawton expressing regret that they were unable to come to our wedding. She added: 'I think your new wife is a very lucky girl.'

Following the conclusion of the criminal list, civil actions followed; and – what would be remarkable in modern practice – matrimonial causes as well. One evening, I wanted to go to the cinema, and suggested this. The judge said that this would never do: he might be recognised. I asked him to leave it to me; and, for anonymity, we would go in my ancient Armstrong, rather than the judicial Rover. The judge reluctantly agreed. I telephoned the local cinema and asked to speak to the manager. I told him, in confidence, that the assize judge wished to come to the cinema, but said that this was a completely private visit, and so no ceremony at all, please. When we arrived, the manager was waiting on the doorstep to greet us, wearing formal evening dress! Surprisingly, the judge was pleased with the attention.

Three weeks later, after quite a lot of local entertaining, we transferred to Lancaster. The assize court was historic, and I remember the branding irons, prominently hung facing the judge's bench: F for felon.

An usher told the judge that the deliberations of the jury were clearly audible outside the jury room. Without further ado, I received the following instruction: 'Marshal: go down to the jury room; stand outside the door; and report to me precisely everything that you can hear.' The secrecy of jury deliberations seem to have been overlooked.

Other memories: a plea of guilty to gross indecency resulted in what the judge described as the lenient sentence of twelve months' probation *plus* twelve months' inpatient treatment in hospital, designed to effect a cure for homosexuality. The gulf in social attitudes between then and now requires no elaboration.

I never forgot the way in which Lawton summed up: at the close of the defence speech, he routinely folded his arms over his notebook and simply addressed the jury. Despite the complexities of the evidence, he never needed to look at his notebook. His memory was prodigious, but he clearly worked hard on the summing up, early every morning. His opening observations to the jury were memorable, magical and never bettered: and I adopted them, to the best of my recollection without alteration, when I began to address juries in 1983. I did so with, so I believed, Fred Lawton sitting metaphorically on my left shoulder, for the next twenty-seven years.

––––––––––

On returning from my marshalling experience, I should have dedicated myself to my Bar exams. The old habit of doing just enough to get by had kicked in during the summer. A knowledge of Roman law, and the intricacies of how to free a slave, were regarded as essential to the knowledge base of the English barrister before he was let loose on the unsuspecting public in 1963; so over a weekend I assimilated the contents of *Teach yourself Roman law*, and duly passed the exam.

With that hurdle successfully overcome, I avoided whatever lectures might otherwise have been provided under the auspices of the Council of Legal Education, and focused on my role as volunteer election coordinator for the first GLC election. Any distraction was preferable to bookwork. I was flattered to be asked to speak at my prep school annual dinner in January 1964, following hard on the heels of Tom Bingham, who had left the school immediately before my arrival in 1947.

The Bar finals finished on 1 May 1964. The Bar final results were duly published in *The Times* on 5 June; and my name was there. I owed my success to the dream question I was asked in the Criminal Procedure paper: *Describe the course of a criminal trial from arraignment to verdict*. As a former marshal, I could answer that in my sleep. There were no awards in Class I, but the later Lord Hoffmann occupied the penultimate place in those awarded a 2:1. It is notable that 693 candidates then took the Bar final, of whom 237 passed, including 78 who received conditional passes. The pass rate in the current Bar course compares rather favourably with that failure rate of 66 per cent.

Before the introduction of the parking meter, I had driven to London to eat a compulsory dinner in Lincoln's Inn. Of parking restrictions in St James's, I knew nothing. I picked up a fixed penalty notice, requiring me to pay £2. This seemed unfair. Derek Bowett told me I had no defence, and to pay up. Determination kicked in. My case was listed at Bow Street, and by coincidence before the then Chief Metropolitan Magistrate. I was correctly dressed, as I was going to another Lincoln's Inn compulsory dinner. I summarised my few points of mitigation. He smiled at me. 'Are you by chance going to the Bar? If so, may I wish you all success; and give the usher £1 as you leave.' A result!

On 15 June I started as the pupil of George Hesketh; and on 23 June I was called to the Bar by Lord Denning, Treasurer of Lincoln's Inn. When the Bench retired to the library with the newly called barristers, as was then the modest custom, I was lucky to be seated next to the great man; and, as was his wont, he spoke engagingly to me – as he did to so many generations of students. My souvenir of the occasion is not only his signature on my dinner menu, but also his apparent interest in me, despite my insignificance.

The following day I received my first instructions, from the solicitor who had arranged my Call to the Bar at camp (see chapter 4, 'Then a Soldier'). This involved the redemption of a rent charge. I could make neither head nor tail of it. I asked George Hesketh for help. He generously did so; but added: 'This is really very difficult indeed.'

George Hesketh was a mountain of a man. He must have weighed between 30 and 35 stones. He had an enormous double-sided partners' desk in his room, and the pupil perched, diffidently, on the far side. He had an amazing intellect; but, with his size, sleep was never far away. His habit after lunch was to waddle back from the Bench in Lincoln's Inn, reach for *The Times* cryptic crossword, complete it within ten minutes, settle his many chins on his chest, and fall sweetly to sleep until the knock on the door announced tea, for him, and a plate of biscuits for Lucky, the mongrel who slept on his feet. There were, of course, neither biscuits nor a cup of tea for the pupil. Tea completed, George was wide awake, and ready for the afternoon conference.

It was the chambers tradition to go for coffee in the Bar restaurant in the crypt in the Law Courts, and the corner table was reserved for them. Pupils were only invited when they had presented a particularly distinguished piece of work, so my invitations were rare. George Hesketh was still alive to welcome me to the Bench in July 1990.

The 1964 intake to the Bar was the last for which the barrister was not required to have the *cordon sanitaire* of non-practising pupillage. The profession was tiny, compared to its current size: 1,956 members, to be contrasted to the some 17,500 in 2024.

In September 1964 I received instructions to appear in Wandsworth County Court, to recover money paid in mistake of fact. I prepared a careful opening, contrasting the recoverability of money paid in mistake of fact to money paid in mistake of law. The hearing was before the registrar. He was *very* deaf.

As I rose, he barked, 'Prove your case.'

I had no idea what that meant. I ploughed on.

He repeated the instruction, *fortissimo*.

I looked blank.

'Call your witness.'

The penny dropped. I did indeed do as directed (swearing a witness had been my speciality as a marshal).

My first 'criminal' case – a plea in mitigation – was in November 1964. I was instructed by Douglas and Co, a firm in which my father was also a partner; and the brief was to represent manufacturers of shoe trees who had infringed the requirements of the Petroleum Regulations. As this was all local to Battersea, it was no surprise that the case was listed in the Battersea Magistrates' Court; but it was a surprise, to both of us, when I walked into court to find Dad, as a lay magistrate, in the chair. While today this would no doubt break many of the provisions in the Code of Conduct, the potential for conflict of interest occurred to no one. The clients generously supplied me with some shoe trees, which I continue to use almost sixty years later.

Remarkably, as these were Chancery Chambers, not only did I have a fellow pupil, but she was female. Lilac had no intention of practising: but we did enjoy one another's company in the rather squalid accommodation then reserved for students in Lincoln's Inn where coffee was available. On one occasion, we lingered rather longer than was objectively appropriate. On my return, George looked distinctly and unusually grave.

'While you have been away – no doubt enjoying yourself, John – our beloved Head of Chambers has collapsed and died.'

Apart from a spluttered 'I am so sorry', it was difficult to know the correct etiquette for that unexpected development.

The Head of Chambers, Joe Wolfe, was a junior, despite his distinction. In his will, he bequeathed his Law Reports to the senior clerk, Jagot. That was no empty gesture. Jagot read every opinion before it left chambers. He not infrequently returned an opinion to a junior member of chambers, expressing the view that it was incorrect and instructing the author to revise it. One of my predecessor pupils, who left the Bar never to return (but subsequently developed a highly successful career in commerce, plus a knighthood), had a significant clash with Jagot. 'Mr X,' Jagot announced one day, 'I have noticed that you are in the habit of using the lavatory at 12 noon every day. That is the time when *I* use the lavatory.'

Fortunately, my exchange with Jagot was milder. Dad had arranged for me to receive instructions to wind up a company. Some three months later I was at home for the weekend, and he wanted me to be paid. The fee was £9.60 in current coinage. He asked me to request a fee note.

The following day, I tapped on Jagot's door. 'Excuse me, Mr Jagot. You may remember that my father's firm sent me a winding up petition. My father has asked me to request a fee note.'

Jagot's response was typical. 'Mr Samuels, your job is to learn the law. My job is to deal with fee notes. Good morning.'

Jagot had been a wing commander in the war. He remained a commanding presence. He and Milner Holland were inseparable. Every afternoon when Milner was not in court, they would go into The Seven

Stars, the seventeenth-century pub in Carey Street, immediately behind chambers. Jagot kept chickens, and routinely presented Milner Holland with fresh eggs to take home. One summer day, both were walking back to chambers, past the Victorian offices that then existed on the west side of Serle Street. A typist with an expansive cleavage was bending over her typewriter. Milner Holland – leader of the Chancery Bar and a pillar of rectitude – reached for an egg, took careful aim, and lobbed the egg, as in grenade practice, through the open window. It hit its target; and the ever-faithful Jagot ensured that nothing, but the story itself, ever harmed his hero.

Two George Hesketh memories. First, in the summer of 1964, George was due to go on holiday. He needed some bathing trunks, and telephoned Lillywhites. There was a gasp at the end of the telephone as he described his measurements. The second memory was more educational. George was undertaking a case for a water authority near Oxford; and he had a holiday home on an island in the Thames near where we had to appear the next day. He invited me to stay. After supper, we reviewed the papers – quite a slim brief – together. I believed I had read everything I needed to know about the case and, at about 10.30 p.m., excused myself and went to bed. At about 2 a.m., I heard George tramping upstairs. It was only when he opened the case the following day that I realised how many hidden depths in the case he had plumbed, and how meticulous preparation is the key to effective advocacy.

My second pupillage, in a common-law set, had similarly been organised well in advance. This was with Marcus Anwyl-Davies ('Mark'), a friend of John Talbot, my father's solicitor partner. I started with Mark on 4 January 1965. His support during the next fourteen months was all that I could have hoped for. For most of the next six months I was usually with him in court, although I was often used by the clerks on my own account: a regular diet of attendance at inquests, representing insurers (the golden rule was to ask no questions at all, and to keep a full note); and on Saturday afternoons representing, in the Lambeth Magistrates' Court, ladies involved in neighbour disputes who had cross-summonsed one another for assault. I devilled for Simon Brown, the junior tenant in 2

Garden Court – later to become Treasury Counsel, and ultimately a Lord of Appeal and a Supreme Court Justice – and I was welcomed to Simon's home for dinner.

There was a memorable trial in the High Court. A marine surveyor was severely injured on a vessel in dock, and his personal injury action failed. Mark was led by Owen Stable QC, a relatively new Silk; but as the son of a High Court judge, he was very grand. The defendants were duly awarded their costs.

Stable QC was tying up his papers and about to walk out of court when the lay client, in tears, pleaded: 'Mr Stable, what am I to do? Should I just go away and shoot myself?'

Stable completed tying up his papers, said, 'I shouldn't do that, old boy', and stalked away. I decided that was not how I wished to treat my lay clients.

———

From July 1965 I was flying free, albeit a 'squatter'. I was told by the Head of Chambers, Granville Wingate QC, that as soon as the chambers acquired extra accommodation, I should be a tenant. The senior clerk, Peter Plager, encouraged me to frequent those public houses and other establishments in the vicinity of the Temple in which barristers' clerks were regularly found in the 1960s.

I had settled in generally in the chambers and was frequently boxing and coxing in the County Court with Simon Brown. In 1980, when I was considering an application for Silk, I asked Harry Woolf (by then already a High Court judge) whether I might potentially succeed Simon as Treasury Counsel, or should instead forget that aspiration and apply for Silk. Harry encouraged the latter. What he knew, and I then did not, was that these appointments were closely linked to membership of chambers. Had I stayed at 2 Garden Court, my history would have looked very different.

Although I routinely undertook all Mark's paperwork – he had an extensive County Court practice representing defendants in accidents at work on the instructions of insurers – I was never paid devilling fees by him, and this was the *quid pro quo* for the fact that I occupied the tiny pupil table in his room. On the credit side, it certainly taught me how to become an accomplished pleader: pleading being rather like learning to ride a bicycle. On the debit side, he had a good bargain, as my pleadings were usually adopted without correction.

I was not the only pupil in 2 Garden Court. From about October 1965, when I was already a squatter, Jonathan Mance, another Carthusian, arrived as the pupil of Bill Macpherson. Jonathan was younger than me, and I saw little of him: Bill's room was at the other end of the chambers, and I was usually at court. It was recognised that Jonathan was in any event destined for the more elevated pastures of insurance work in 7 King's Bench Walk after cutting his teeth in the rough-and-tumble of common law. Appointed to the High Court in 1993, he has been a Lord of Appeal, and later a Supreme Court Justice, since 2005. He wrote to acknowledge my congratulations:

> *'I too look back to those distant days in Garden Court – indeed even further to my first meeting with Granville there before I had even decided on the bar as a career. We were lucky in our pupillage home. In one sense the Lords will be a home from home, since just round the corner from my small room will be Simon Brown in another cramped slot!'*

Mark was not a natural pupil master. There was no 'instruction' as such. I read Mark's papers, tried my hand at pleading, and observed how he then undertook the task. The essence of good pleading is to tell the story, as well as identifying why you are entitled to the relief that your client claims. Whether by osmosis or luck, I became a skilful pleader: and my earliest attempt at legal writing was to edit the chapter on Pleading in *Halsbury's Laws of England*.

Unless I had my own brief, I invariably accompanied Mark to court; and he often invited me to his home for supper, where his wife and family were very welcoming. On an occasion when we were in the Marylebone County Court, we went to have coffee with his father, an eminent specialist in venereal diseases, whose consulting rooms were in the London Clinic in Harley Street. Dr Anwyl-Davies asked me, with great solemnity, whether I ate apricots. I was unclear whether this was to ward off venereal disease, or to enhance virility: but for years I adopted his advice, with positive results.

I returned to Chambers on 1 April 1966 after the Parliamentary election (see chapter 5, 'Politics'): a date properly described as 'All Fools' Day'. Mark was sitting behind his desk. He neither looked up nor spoke. I sat down at the little table, which was the pupil's perch. There were some briefs, instructions and cheques already there. I pretended to be absorbed by them. After twenty minutes or so of silence, Mark looked up. He had the most piercing blue eyes, even behind his heavy horn-rimmed spectacles.

'The time has come, I think' – long pause – 'John' – longer pause – 'for you to find other chambers.'

I was sorely tempted to react and, with considerable pleasure in hindsight, withstood the temptation. I quietly left the room. Mark's room adjoined the clerks' room; and Peter Plager saw me emerge. He knew that something had happened, and asked me what it was. I repeated what Mark had just said.

'Don't worry about that, sir,' – Peter always called me 'sir', even when he took me out to inappropriate drinking clubs – 'it's just the election. It will all pass.'

I was on my high horse. 'No one talks to me like that, Peter.'

I stalked out of chambers, found a convenient red telephone box, telephoned Neville Sandelson (whom I had known since 1952: see chapter 5, 'Politics'), arranged to meet him for lunch; and by 3 p.m. the same day had a tenancy in the chambers of which he was a tenant, which objectively was probably the least appropriate set of chambers in the Temple.

Shortly before I left 2 Garden Court, I was asked to advise a tenant whether the unreasonable refusal of his landlord to agree to the assignment of his lease entitled the tenant to damages. I advised that it did. During my absence in March 1966, the instructions to draft a statement of claim were diverted to Bill Macpherson. His enduring claim to fame is as chair of the inquiry into the death of Stephen Lawrence, following his retirement from the High Court bench. Had Bill been less busy, he might have remembered that he had previously been counsel for a similar plaintiff in

Rendall v. Roberts and Stacey in 1960, in which the judge, applying a long line of authority going back to 1874, had struck out the statement of claim as disclosing no cause of action. The case returned to me after a defence had been served; and in June 1966 I settled further pleadings. Thereafter, I received a characteristically courteous letter from my opponent, Tom Bingham, which informed me that unless I abandoned the claim, he would apply to strike it out. We met to discuss the claim. I stood my ground. The case was struck out. I appealed. Mr Justice Waller affirmed the decision of the Master. I advised an appeal to the Court of Appeal; and the appeal in Rose and Rose v. Gossman came before Lord Denning and Lord Justice Danckwerts on 12 December 1966.

In a typical Denning judgment, the Master of the Rolls said: 'If I were free to construe this document without the aid of previous authority, I would be inclined to say that the landlord promised not to withhold his consent unreasonably', but the authorities precluded him from so finding. Denning added:

'Mr Samuels wishes to challenge that long line of authority in their Lordships' House. I do not know that he will have much chance of success, for it has stood for so long. However, Mr Samuels strikes me as a persuasive young barrister; and I for one will not deprive him of the opportunity of attempting to do so. If the tenants wish to keep the point open for argument in the House of Lords, they should not be prevented from doing so when the application to strike out has come so late.'

The fatal error of the defendant had been to request further and better particulars of the statement of claim, and to permit the plaintiff to serve further pleadings, before launching the application to strike out. Even Homer can nod: and I never knew Tom to err again.

A Court of Appeal success, before the Master of the Rolls, within a year from achieving a tenancy, was not a bad start. To achieve this against Tom Bingham made it even sweeter. When Tom was appointed Master of the Rolls, I wrote to him:

'*You will not remember our first forensic encounter – but as my earliest experience before Tom Denning in 1966 it remains ever-memorable to me! The overwhelming impression was not so much the exhilaration of being successful in the C.A. – sweet as that was; but the almost tangible calm which you displayed as an advocate.*'

Tom replied:

'*Of course I vividly recall your triumph on the question of unreasonably withholding consent – which is, as a result, one of the very few bits of law that I shall never, ever, forget. Some of one's forensic Waterloos are blanketed by merciful oblivion, but not that one.*'

After my departure, 2 Garden Court (now 39 Essex Chambers) went from strength to strength. It was not long before they recruited John Laws, who succeeded Simon Brown as Treasury Counsel in 1984, and John retired as a Lord Justice of Appeal in July 2016. They were later joined by John Dyson. He too retired in July 2016, having previously been a Supreme Court Justice and Master of the Rolls.

————

My tenancy chambers had been established by a New Zealander, John Cope. Cope's success was in inverse proportion to his ability. He had a charisma that encouraged the friendship of successive Lord Chancellors: both Gerald Gardiner and Elwyn Jones were visitors to his home in Halkin Street, Belgravia, and through such connections he acquired good work. I became his regular 'devil', which provided a healthy source of income.

Who were the other tenants? In addition to Neville Sandelson, who became a Labour MP in 1971, there was Jeffrey Thomas, another Labour candidate, who was first elected to Parliament in 1970. Jeffrey became a leading criminal Silk, but died, out of Parliament and addicted to alcohol, aged only fifty-five. Virtually my contemporary was Lawrence Giovene, an idiosyncratic Italian who had been president of the Cambridge Union.

Lawrence is the sole survivor. Our young clerk, Walter Sandham, was enthusiastic but painfully inexperienced: he was aged twenty in 1966.

I had little experience of crime. I had no experience of defending a criminal trial at quarter sessions. One of my TA soldiers, Cpl Kane, had been charged with racing on the highway, and he wanted my help. I introduced him to some Reigate solicitors. When his case was committed for trial, I told him firmly that he needed a more experienced barrister.

'I want you, sir.'

My attempts to dissuade him fell on deaf ears. I arrived in Winchester for the trial. There was only one witness for the prosecution, a police officer. I had no idea how to conduct a cross-examination. I cleared my throat, raised my voice, and said, 'I put it to you, officer, that you are lying.'

The officer collapsed in the witness box. After an interval, he climbed to his feet. The kindly deputy chairman asked the witness whether he was all right.

'Yes, I think so, sir.'

'Can you continue with your evidence?'

'Yes, sir.'

'As a matter of interest, do you know why you fainted?'

'I was lying, sir.'

The prosecution immediately offered no further evidence; my astonished client was duly acquitted; and I never subsequently achieved such immediate forensic success.

John Cope had active links with solicitors in Kent: and within days of my arrival in his chambers, I was encouraged to join the local Bar mess. Shortly afterwards I was in Maidstone, taking sherry at lunchtime. 'So whose chambers are you in?' rather grandly enquired John Gower, the chairman of the Bar mess. I told him. 'I say, chaps: this is Samuels, and he is in that shit Cope's chambers' was his unforgettable comment.

I was asked to deputise, at short notice, for Cope in addressing a social gathering of Kent solicitors. This resulted in my introduction to several firms who became loyal clients: none more loyal than Basset and Boucher, and their assiduous managing clerk, Tony Crowhurst. Shortly afterwards, I received instructions to represent a driver in the Dartford Magistrates

Court, charged with causing death by dangerous driving. These were committal proceedings: and I was delighted subsequently to receive the defence brief at Maidstone Assizes in November 1966.

The trial was listed before Mr Justice Melford Stevenson, whose reputation preceded him, and by whom I was duly terrified. I used all my persuasive powers to ensure that the case was listed before the other judge, Mr Justice Howard, of whom I knew nothing. They arranged to go out on circuit together.

My tactics could not have been worse. During my final speech for the defence, a juror interrupted, saying, 'I don't agree with that.'

'Nor do I,' echoed the judge.

I paused, dramatically. 'Ladies and gentlemen, may I ask for five minutes more of your patience, and I shall seek to persuade not only all twelve of you, but His Lordship as well.'

My client was duly convicted, but he managed to avoid a custodial sentence. To my surprise, the insurers continued to instruct me to represent them in the subsequent Fatal Accidents Act proceedings in the High Court. By the time the Fatal Accidents Act claim came to trial in 1968, my client was also dead (for reasons unrelated to the road accident). Oliver Popplewell represented the widow. He should have wiped the floor with this novice. He was in fact charm personified: a delightful Old Carthusian and Old Queensman. We shared the same birthday, until his recent death, aged ninety-six.

———

Another case was equally memorable. It started in a conference. The client was an elderly English spinster. She had formed a close attachment to a Thai student, and she asked me whether she could formally adopt him in order to ensure that he remained within the jurisdiction. She was accompanied by the prospective adoptee. I asked his age.

'Twenty, I'm not twenty-one until next month.' (The age of majority was only lowered to eighteen in 1971.)

I asked him whether he had parents who were still alive.

'Yes, my father is a general in the Thai army, and my mother lives with him.'

'Would they agree to your adoption by this lady?'

'Certainly not; my father wants me to return, to do my military service. I want to stay here.'

That was the shortest conference I can remember: within five minutes, the spinster, the student and my solicitor were walking out of my room, with a firm rejection of their adoption plans.

Three months later, I attended North London Magistrates' Court. The Thai student had overstayed. I envisaged a formal hearing and a perfunctory mitigation. On my arrival, I discovered a very senior official within the office of the Director of Public Prosecutions, accompanied by a detective chief superintendent. Both were particularly pleasant to the novice barrister.

'We just have to ask your client one or two questions.'

'What about?' I asked.

'Only a formality.'

'Can you give me a bit more information?'

'No.'

I spoke to a far more subdued client than the one I had met three months earlier.

'There are two gentlemen here who want to ask you a few questions. They won't tell me what they want to ask you. My advice is not to answer any question until they tell me what this is all about.'

The client nodded. The senior police officer came into the cell.

'We have found a woman's arm, neatly dissected at the elbow, on a track near your home. Each of the fingernails has been painted in a different colour of nail varnish. We know that you are a medical student; and that you have recently worked as a mortuary attendant. We have examined your car; and traces of blood have been found in the boot which match the blood from the severed arm. Where is the rest of the body?'

The student remained silent.

Police inquiries continued. There was a similar experience at the next hearing. The stipendiary magistrate was becoming impatient.

'Unless you can proceed,' he said, 'I intend to deal with this case by accepting the guilty plea and imposing a conditional discharge.'

This is exactly what happened: the client walked out of court, into the anonymity of North London.

Time passed. Some two years later, the same solicitor telephoned me.

'Do you remember Miss... [the would-be adoptive parent]?'

Of course I did.

'She has been arrested in Bangkok. She has been charged as an accessory after the fact to some murders of prostitutes, whose dismembered remains have been found in the home which she shared with the former medical student.'

The British consul provided effective consular service, and she returned to London. The young man confessed all, and he was executed. He was my first client to be convicted of murder. But of whom?

———

There were some memorable cases at Inner London Quarter Sessions. The first was a defence case, missed in the list by my clerk. I rushed to court by taxi. There was little time to discuss the case. The defendant was charged with street robbery, and with making off into the streets of Brixton. The complainant had described him to police as 'a young black male'. My speech to the jury was succinct. 'How many young black males do you think there are in Brixton?' That resulted in a swift acquittal.

By the end of 1966, there was active dissension in chambers. This was primarily fomented by Neville Sandelson and Jeffrey Thomas; and we were just caught up in it. Neville Sandelson left for other chambers; and Jeffrey Thomas, Lawrence Giovene and I, together with our clerk, Walter, left to join chambers of which the head was Dick Bingham QC. This was a set comprising Northern Circuit Silks, primarily practising in Liverpool and Manchester, but using the London chambers as a base.

The merger was an initial success. In time, however, the South-Eastern Circuit members of the new chambers were focused exclusively on crime; and my civil practice was growing. I began to look elsewhere. To his credit, Walter recognised where my future lay, and was actively helpful in ensuring that I moved successfully.

DEVELOPING ROOTS

You'd scarce expect one of my age
To speak in public on the stage;
And if I chance to fall below
Demosthenes or Cicero,
Don't view me with a critic's eye
But pass my imperfections by.
Large streams from little fountains flow,
Tall oaks from little acorns grow...
David Everett (1769–1813)

No, I hadn't heard of Everett either. I stumbled across these lines in the *Dictionary of Quotations* (3rd edn, 1979), when looking for something completely different. The final couplet seems to describe, with wooden idiom, the plodding tenacity, coupled with stilted phraseology, of the young barrister I was between 1968 and 1980: obsessed very largely by the requirements of my junior practice, to the exclusion of the other interests and activities that had rounded my earlier life. Serendipity, listed as my primary 'recreation' from my first appearance in *Who's Who* in 1982, triumphs again.

Judicial characters were far more pronounced than in the post-millennial era of the Office for Judicial Complaints. A judge notorious for both rudeness and unfairness was Ewen Montagu QC, chairman of Middlesex Quarter Sessions. While I had no particularly memorable spats with him, his bias against defendants was obvious. I was present when he was trying to control the far more idiosyncratic Harold Cassel.

'What is Your Lordship going to do about it then?' Cassel had a nasal twang, which took on a sing-song tone when he was becoming angry. 'Bury me in hot sand up to my neck? The Japanese did that, and it didn't work.'

Montagu was clearly bettered by that remark. Also a legend in his time, Cassel's way of dominating proceedings before Montagu was to address the jury, standing with one foot raised on the seat beside him, and gazing in a lordly way at the ceiling of the court. He knew that this irritated the judge.

'Mr Cassel,' Montagu once said testily, 'would you pay the jury the compliment of looking at them when you are speaking to them?'

'Certainly, My Lord: is there any particular member of the jury Your Lordship would like me to look at?'

While less overtly biased, Reggie Seaton, chairman of London Quarter Sessions, seemed to have no spark of human empathy. He looked as animated as a cod on a fishmonger's slab. To hear him sentencing a repetitive stream of young men on a sentencing day with just the two words 'Borstal training' was unforgettable. His obvious lack of interest in their future encouraged my later enthusiasm for judicial monitoring and supervision.

Rudeness was not confined to the full-time judges. I experienced a combination of rudeness coupled with drunkenness on the part of the chairman of the Ealing Bench in October 1968. My attempts to mitigate were constantly interrupted, and he concluded: 'You can be sure that however bad you are, we shall not hold that against your client.' I sat down, and then left the court. I was followed by the clerk, who encouraged me to complain. He said that this had been going on for years. I did complain; and my complaint was forwarded to the Lord Chancellor. The upshot was that 'the Lord Chancellor caused enquiries to be made and in the result the Chairman of the Bench has expressed his apologies for his conduct and has asked that these be conveyed' to me. I was told that the chairman had given an undertaking that he would no longer take the chair, and on that basis he was not required formally to resign from the Bench. I was asked if I agreed. My reply – rather magisterial, in retrospect, for a barrister of four years' Call – was to say that this was a matter for the Lord Chancellor.

A similar judicial 'character' was Judge Claude Duveen QC. Duveen had two pet hates: applications for adjournments, and women at the Bar. A female pupil was instructed to apply for an adjournment. A solicitor, knowing what was likely to happen, passed a note to the judge: 'Go easy on her – I think it's her first case.' The note only reached the judge's clerk, who was asleep. The application was brusquely dismissed, and the pupil had almost reached the shelter of the court door when the clerk woke and passed the note upwards. Duveen read it swiftly.

'Ms X,' he roared. Counsel came back into the front row. 'I have just received a communication which informs me that this is your first case. I sincerely hope it will be your last.'

I represented the plaintiff alleging fraud. The defendant was a local solicitor. In cross-examination, I extracted a damaging admission. Looking straight at the press bench, Duveen asked whether there was a representative of the press in court, and was told that there was.

'I cannot order you not to report that question and that answer; but I would regard it as a personal favour if you did not do so.'

I protested, predictably.

'Oh, do get on, Mr Samuels.'

I knew the likely outcome. However, as often happened, Mrs Duveen came into court, and sat on the bench. I decided to address her in my closing speech. Duveen knew what I was doing.

'Mr Samuels, you are addressing my wife. You think that when I get home I shall get it in the neck from her for failing to agree with you. You are probably right: but while I am the judge of this court you will please address me.'

I had many similar spats with Duveen; but the one that turned out to be my last appearance before him gave me the greatest pleasure. I was instructed by a supermarket whose refrigeration plant allegedly represented a noise nuisance. The plaintiff's house was located on the other side of a large car park, and noise was said to be audible only after 11.30 p.m. My expert evidence was that no noise was audible. As I was instructed shortly before the trial, I amended the defence to plead that since the claim was primarily for an injunction and not for damages, the court had no jurisdiction to hear it. This involved the citation of much authority; and my opponent and I argued the point over the first half day of the trial. Duveen summarily dismissed my objection and added: 'You can take me to the Court of Appeal if you like.'

Over a year later, appealing the inevitable adverse decision, I did so. By this time, the successful plaintiffs had dispensed with counsel. Lord Justice Megaw interrupted my opening.

'The court has received a communication from the trial judge: no doubt you have seen it.'

This was news to me.

'The judge says that he has read the notice of appeal. He thinks there is nothing in it; and the issue of jurisdiction to which it refers was never argued.'

This roused my fighting spirit. 'If Mr Williams [my erstwhile opponent] were here, he would confirm that it was.'

'Let him be sent for,' replied Megaw.

At 2.15 p.m., with no opportunity for warning, Jon Williams entered Court 1, fresh from some other court hearing. He was effectively cross-examined by Megaw.

'Yes, I remember this case well. I took a car full of books to Slough. We argued the point for half a day, and I remember the judge saying, "You can take it to the Court of Appeal if you like, Mr Samuels".'

It was satisfying when the Court of Appeal ruled that, save in exceptional circumstances, a trial judge should not comment on a notice of appeal; if in exceptional circumstances he did so, he must send those comments additionally to the parties; and in that rare situation 'it behoves the learned judge to get his facts right'.[2]

––––––––

In October 1968, when I was still routinely undertaking criminal work, I had a difficult case. Representing three shopbreakers at Surrey Quarter Sessions, I was asked at the end of Day 1 how their case was going. I told them it was unlikely that their story would be accepted. They asked what

––––––––

2   *Vockins and Others v. Hallmark Stores*: 15 May 1975

sentence they were likely to receive; and I advised them that if they were to plead guilty, they might expect some leniency. With their agreement, I negotiated a guilty plea. Their response was: 'We knew we were guilty, but we thought we would have a run for it.' I asked them to come to court the following day with any witness who might help with mitigation.

The next morning, there was a change of mind. The clients told me they wanted to continue with their not guilty pleas. This was embarrassing, as they had each admitted that their jointly concocted defence was untrue. I told them I could no longer professionally present that case: either they would need to ask for other representation, or they should act in person. After an adjournment, the deputy chairman agreed that both I and my solicitor should withdraw. Unfortunately, the court transcript gave the impression that I had abandoned them.

Following their conviction, the clients appealed. The Court of Appeal noted the exchange between the defendants, the deputy chairman and me, and referred my conduct to the Bar Council. The Court of Appeal stated: 'These three defendants refused ... to accept certain advice which Mr Samuels gave them. In consequence Mr Samuels was eventually released from taking any further part in the proceedings.' The court requested 'an inquiry into the circumstances in which counsel abandoned the defence of these three accused'.

I explained the background in a detailed note, which owed much to the careful editorial improvements made by Dick Bingham QC, who provided a model of the care and support that a junior tenant should expect.

The Bar Council responded: 'Your letter and enclosed comments were considered by the Professional Conduct Committee on Wednesday. They are satisfied that you have not been guilty of any professional misconduct. They would like your consent for me to send a copy of your letter and comments to the Court of Appeal.'

The Court of Appeal replied: 'I am directed by Lord Justice Phillimore to inform you that, having read Mr Samuels' comments and explanation, he and the other members of the court concerned entirely agree with the view of your Council's Professional Conduct Committee that Samuels had not been guilty of any professional misconduct.'

If only my subsequent experience of the disciplinary process of the Bar Council (see chapter 13, 'Rehabiltation') had been as exemplary and expeditious as this!

———

From apparently routine cases, opportunities appeared for the novice barrister out of a clear blue sky. Such was the case of Hanning v. Maitland. Mr Maitland, a bachelor of limited means, was on a walking holiday. He was a few feet from the verge, walking down a country lane, in the dark. A group of cyclists, travelling at speed, came up behind him. The lead cyclist passed him safely; and the third cyclist shouted a warning. However, the middle cyclist, Mr Hanning, collided with Mr Maitland and sustained a fractured skull. Assisted by legal aid, he pursued Mr Maitland for damages. The claim was dismissed. The trial judge, having been told that the cyclist could not satisfy the claim for costs of Mr Maitland, adjourned his claim, as the regulations required, for the Law Society to consider his application for costs against the legal aid fund. He added that it would, in his judgment, 'be a wicked thing if Mr Maitland had to make any contribution towards the costs of an action which was a complete waste of time'. So far, so good. Mr Maitland's costs amounted to £325.

Relying on recent authority, the taxing Master, and later the judge in chambers, declined to award Mr Maitland anything. I had to persuade the Court of Appeal to conclude that their earlier decision in Nowotnik v. Nowotnik,[3] in which the leading judgment had been delivered by Lord Denning, was wrong. Denning took the bull by the horns:

'*Those figures show one of two things: either that the Act itself was badly worded so that it did not give effect to the intention of the makers of it; or the courts have interpreted it wrongly so as to defeat the intention of Parliament. I am afraid that it is the second. We can and should learn by experience. In the light of it I must confess that this court in* Nowotnik v. Nowotnik *interpreted the Act wrongly. This present case affords us the*

———

3   [1967] P 83

opportunity of putting the matter right for the future; and I think we should do so.'

Not only was the earlier, relatively recent decision that of a court over which Denning had also presided, but it was a court of five judges: and normally the Court of Appeal was bound by its own decisions. Hanning v. Maitland was a milestone case.[4]

––––––

Despite my Chancery pupillage, motions in the Chancery Division remained areas of hidden reefs. In early January 1969, I was instructed to oppose a motion. Its bland terms meant nothing to me. The relief sought could have been based on any kind of foundation. I so advised. 'Don't worry, John,' my solicitor reassured me. 'If you find yourself in difficulty, I am sure the judge will give you an adjournment.'

On 14 January 1969, I appeared outside the court of Mr Justice Buckley. My opponent arrived with a trolley filled with law reports. A glance enabled me at least in outline to understand the point of law on which his motion was to be based. With ill-placed confidence, I rose to seek the necessary adjournment. I explained that it was only moments before the court sat that I could glean, from my learned friend's authorities – this was well before the convention that you identified in advance to your opponent a list of those cases on which you would rely – what was the ambit of his application; and that I needed a little time to review them. The response was crushing.

The judge, perhaps still recovering from the fact that he had been installed as Treasurer of Lincoln's Inn the previous evening, with the refreshment that this is likely to have included, provided a historic put-down. 'Counsel, no doubt practising in the common law courts, applies to a judge of the Chancery Division for an adjournment so that he can research the law. In this Division, counsel know the law. This application is refused.' It was an uncharacteristic remark. Denys Buckley had first met me in Cambridge in

––––––

4   It appeared twice in the Law Reports: [1969] 1 WLR 1885; and [1970] 1 QB 580

1963, when he offered to move my Call to the Bar. In the Court of Appeal, he was invariably courteous; and I joined the Bench of the Inn while he was still able to attend social events.

I had tried to address the application and failed. It was a trade union case, turning on the rules of the union. Judgment was given for the plaintiff. Three days later I was in consultation with Peter Pain QC, a leading expert in trade union law. He was delightful.

'If only you had seen me before,' he said. 'It is clear that the judge has gone wrong. We shall put it right on appeal.'

At the end of the consultation, I asked for a further word. 'I have now researched these authorities, and I do think the judge was right.'

Pain was reassuring. 'When you have been doing this work as long as I have...'

I remained doubtful.

The appeal came on swiftly before Lord Denning on 13 March.[5] Despite all of Peter Pain's careful argument, not only was the appeal dismissed, but the respondent was not called on to reply. I was vindicated!

In November 1968 I had advised a husband, whose wife had left him for another man, whether he should agree to have a blood test that was likely to determine if he was the biological father of his young son. I advised him not to do so. The child was four, and had at all times lived with my client. If he agreed to a blood test, it seemed likely that the test would show he was not the natural father; and this would undermine his claim to custody. To my concern, Mr Justice Baker directed that the child should be blood-tested. For the first time, I advised taking in a Silk for an appeal. James Comyn QC was instructed.

I attended for a pre-hearing consultation. My client and his solicitor were present. The leader was not. After fifteen minutes or so, James arrived. He was unshaven, and looked dreadful. I went into his room on my own. He upended his briefcase: papers flew in all directions. 'So which is this

---

5   Braithwaite v. E.E.T.U-P.T.U. [1969] 2 All ER 859

case?' I briefly summarised the issue; and once I felt he had pulled himself together, introduced him to the client.

We walked over to the Law Courts. By the time we had reached Lord Denning's court, Comyn was transformed. His opening sentence simply grabbed the attention of all members of the court. 'My Lords, this could have been an appeal from Dr Ormrod.' Mr Justice Ormrod, who had been in chambers with Comyn, was – as everyone knew – also qualified as a medical practitioner. He was wont to apply his own specialist knowledge in substitution for the evidence. That, in essence, was what Mr Justice Baker J had done. The appeal was triumphantly successful. But what an initial cliff-hanger![6]

––––––

A case with curious undertones in October 1969 was that of R v. Anthony Haydon. He was charged with burglary at the home of Lionel Bart, well known at the time as the author and composer of the musical *Oliver!*. There was no doubt that the burglar had a comprehensive knowledge of Bart's alarm system: and as Haydon was normally resident in Bart's home, this was unsurprising. What could not publicly emerge, however, was the nature of the relationship between Bart and Haydon. No one would turn a hair today to learn that Bart was gay, and that Haydon was his partner. In 1969, it would have ruined him.

The trial judge, Murray Buttrose, belonged to the class described by the Bar as a 'jungle judge': he had returned to sit in England after a lengthy spell in the Colonial Service. When Bart gave evidence, he protested his firm belief in Haydon's innocence. This assertion provoked an outburst from the bench, directed at me, that startled the hearing into silence:

'I do not care 2 hoots what Mr Bart thinks. What he says is absolutely irrelevant. Are you asking that Mr Bart should supersede the jury? Mr Bart is not the judge nor the jury in this case. The jury will decide in this matter, not Mr Bart. The fact that Lionel Bart thinks the accused did not

––––––

6   B v. B and E [1969] 3 All ER 1106

commit the robbery is completely irrelevant. He was in America when this happened. He employed this man for a short time, and this was a long time before the offence occurred. He does not know the facts except that it is a friend and erstwhile employee who is accused. I shall tell the jury firmly and categorically that whether they think the defendant had committed the offence has nothing to do with Mr Bart.'

The grounds of appeal identified repeated cross-examination of Haydon during his evidence; constant interruptions of my closing speech; a failure to put the defence in the summing up; personal cross-examination of the defendant on his notice of alibi; disclosing privileged communications between the defendant and his solicitors; and finally directing the jury that Haydon must have lied to his solicitors. I retain a letter from the client: 'I am lost for words to explain my gratitude for all that you have done for me...' All in all, an egregiously biased judge.

———

By early 1970, I was almost five years out of pupillage. While I was still instructed to appear in criminal cases, the bulk of my work was civil: and I routinely appeared in the County Court and the High Court in a variety of matters, including a regular diet of cases in and from Kent and in Devon.

Advocacy is not only about persuasion: it requires judgment. I believe that, even as a novice, I displayed rather more judgment on one of my rare forays into the law of defamation than my leader, a libel specialist. The lay client was notorious. Former Detective Sergeant Challenor had been well known at West End Central police station in the early 1960s for his aggressive style of policing. This included, as emerged during the subsequent high-profile prosecution of Challenor and subordinate officers for conspiracy, that evidence, specifically fragments of broken brick, had been planted in the pockets of those who were arrested during a disturbance. While the other officers were sentenced to terms of imprisonment, Challenor was found unfit to plead, and was committed to a mental hospital.

Following his discharge, the *News of the World* published an article about Challenor, claiming that he was a paid police informer. Such persons were the 'lowest of the low'. Challenor denied ever so acting and maintained that the article was defamatory. So far, so good. I should have been prepared on his behalf to accept the proffered apology and modest damages and call it a day. Not so my leader, Michael Kempster QC. He wished to deny that Challenor had ever been involved in the initial conspiracy; and he was technically able to do so because a finding of unfitness to plead did not amount to a conviction. With considerable hesitation, I prepared a pleading on this basis. That was an open goal to the rest of the press. They relished the opportunity to retry the facts of the notorious case. Legal aid was unavailable for libel actions; I was on my own, as Kempster QC accepted a judicial appointment in Hong Kong, and I had to use such negotiating skills as I had to extricate myself and my client from a looming financial catastrophe.

In June 1971, I had my first forensic experience of the House of Lords. Derek Hodgson QC, who occupied the next-door room to mine, had undertaken a major appeal: Todd v. Davison.[7] Judgment had been reserved, but I was asked to represent the respondent when costs were being dealt with. Derek assured me that there was nothing to do: full argument had been presented on costs by both his opponent, John Cobb QC, and him. At the Lords Chamber, the formidable Viscount Dilhorne presided. He had forgotten that costs had been ventilated by both Silks, and required me to deal with the costs argument there and then. Some forty minutes later, in some exasperation, he required the costs argument to be adjourned for the attendance of both Silks. Despite my subsequent appearances in the Appellate Committee of the House of Lords as a Silk on some fifteen occasions, none was as terrifying as that one.

With the benefit of what we now know about historic sex abuse, the behaviour of my fashionable art dealer client in the summer of 1971 would

7   [1972] 2 AC 392

seem more suspect than I made it appear in the Marlborough Street Magistrates' Court. He was the proprietor of a particularly smart gallery in the heart of the West End, and he had advertised for a personal assistant. A young woman attended, and claimed that the job interview included an indecent assault. My starting point, as with many similar cases, was to ask for a view; and this informed my subsequent cross-examination of the complainant. Returning to chambers just before Christmas, following my client's triumphant acquittal by the stipendiary magistrate, I was delighted to find a note of profound gratitude attached to an excellent vintage bottle of Perrier-Jouët champagne. I was far less delighted to discover that, in the spirit of Christmas, my clerks had drained the bottle.

———

It was the variety of my practice that led to some of the most memorable conclusions. A routine conference in June 1971 with some residential tenants in dispute with their new landlord did not initially look as if it was to become the principal item of news in the London evening papers, as it later did. Ten residential tenants had occupied their bedsits in Paddington for many years without a problem. Their landlord assigned the lease. The new owner immediately served notice to quit on all the tenants, and purported to double their rent. I advised an immediate application to the Rent Tribunal, and to defer the operation of the notice to quit.

The landlady, in a threatening letter, told the tenants that their rooms were required for immediate renovation. I advised the issue of proceedings, alleging breach of the covenant for quiet enjoyment of their premises, and obtained an injunction the same day. The landlady continued her campaign of harassment. Despite being granted security of tenure, within days all the tenants had been driven out. Proceedings for contempt of court, for breach of the injunction, followed. The landlady was warned by the judge to seek representation, but she refused. She declined to give evidence. The judge said: 'Counsel for the tenants, whose conduct of the case has been marked by great restraint, argues that this is a case in which I should award exemplary damages.' The judge did so. He also committed the landlady to prison for contempt.

The County Court decision was the front-page news item in the *London Evening News*, and was prominently reported in every national newspaper. She appealed to the Court of Appeal and, pending the appeal, was released on bail. The appeal was pursued on the technicality that the County Court lacked the power to impose imprisonment for breach of the injunction. The argument, brilliantly presented by Simon Goldblatt (who occupied the next door room in 2 Garden Court when I was a pupil there), accepted that his client was responsible for each of the acts and omissions found by the judge, but submitted that only the High Court had jurisdiction to commit for contempt for breach of an injunction when the injunction ceased to have effect, since the tenants had already left when committal proceedings were launched. Simon referred to over forty authorities, and he had only one sheet of paper in his hand. On it was listed the authorities, in the order in which he intended to cite them; there was no other note. I have never observed such a bravura performance. The hearing lasted three days, and the court reserved judgment. I had all the merits: but was the law on my side?

The court returned to give its judgment. Before they did so, I was embarrassed. At about 10.45, I was phoned in chambers by the clerk to Lord Justice Salmon.

'Good morning, Mr Samuels. How are you?'

'Very well, thank you, Peter. How can I help?'

'If it is not too much trouble, would you please come over to the Court of Appeal: their Lordships have been waiting for fifteen minutes or so to come into court.'

My clerk had missed the case in the cause list. I ran, and of course I grovelled once I arrived. Counsel are responsible for the acts, and usually the omissions, of their clerks.

After judgment was delivered dismissing the appeal, Simon advanced an eloquent mitigation, saying that Mrs Baker had suffered enough, and had learned her lesson. The court rejected the plea. The way in which they dealt with it, in the *ex tempore* judgment of Salmon LJ, deserves citation in a collection of contemporary literature.[8] It included a gracious nod in my direction:

> *'A woman as intelligent and highly educated and resourceful as the defendant showed herself to be must have realised that if she went into the witness box and told this story she would be subject to cross-examination and that her story was unlikely to stand up. She heard the witnesses whom she did call cross-examined with devastating effect.'*

Simon received a letter of congratulation on his stellar performance. It included the phrase: 'I find it personally somewhat offensive to receive such a sophisticated argument from counsel wearing a stuff gown.' Simon took the hint, and took Silk the following spring.

———

Most judges in 1972 were well aware of the statutory purpose of the Rent Acts, namely to provide security of tenure for those tenants to whom the acts applied, and to protect them from capricious eviction by profit-seeking landlords. Those judges did not include Bernard Lewis, the County Court judge at Uxbridge County Court. My client occupied an eighteenth-century cottage in the grounds of Cowley House, a manor house in what had been the village of Uxbridge. He and his wife occupied it as their home for many years, at a modest rent. Cowley House, including the cottage, had been acquired by a property company. They served notice to quit the cottage, on the ground that suitable alternative accommodation was available for the tenants' occupation, and that it would be reasonable to make the order. The alternative accommodation was in a terraced property, built just before the First World War. The issue at trial was whether it would be reasonable to make a possession order.

At the end of the first day, following a view of both sets of premises, and when only limited evidence had been called, the judge required both counsel to see him in his private room. He said it was obvious that a

---

8   See Jennison v. Baker [1972] 1 All ER 997; [1972] 1 All ER 997 at 1010 – 1011

possession order would have to be made. He added that he expected the landlords to provide some financial inducement to the tenant in a sum that he indicated should be about £500. I pointed out that compensation was irrelevant.

On the next day, the director of the landlord company unsurprisingly offered the tenant £500, as well as to accommodate him in the proposed alternative accommodation. However, after my cross-examination, when I deliberately avoided any reference to the financial offer, both counsel were again summoned to the judge's room. He told them that £500 was not enough. My opponent asked him what he thought might be appropriate. £1,000, said the judge. Despite my disagreement with this Dutch auction, the judge remained obdurate. When the hearing resumed, the director was re-examined and asked if he had reconsidered his offer to the tenant. I predictably objected, but the judge allowed the witness to tell the court that he now proposed £1,000.

The trial became a travesty. When the tenant gave evidence, the judge constantly interrupted him, stating that the topics I wished to lead in evidence were irrelevant, despite clear authority to the contrary: anything a tenant wishes to say in relation to his occupation of premises of which possession is sought on these grounds is relevant in relation to the issue of reasonableness.[9]

The judge continued to badger me, saying that if my client did not accept what was being offered, he might receive less compensation, and might well have to pay the costs of the action. Unsurprisingly, the judge made a possession order; and left the compensation undisturbed.

I pursued an appeal with confidence. It was listed thirteen months later. The normal outcome of such an appeal, if successful, would have been a direction that the case should return to the County Court, to be reheard by another judge. However, the Court of Appeal concluded that there were simply no grounds on which the landlords could, on the established facts, recover possession. My notice of appeal pulled no punches. It included the fact that the judge expressed a conclusion on the reasonableness of making

---

9   See Cresswell v. Hodgson [1951] 2 KB 92

a possession order before hearing any material evidence, and then refused to consider the subsequent evidence. It referred to the financial offers being made, and increased following the judge's intervention, by the landlords, despite objection. For good measure, it mentioned that the finding of the judge that the property would be demolished and redeveloped ignored the fact that no application for planning permission had yet been made. That was the end of the case – but not the end of my dealings with Bernard Lewis.

Some years later, I was sitting as a deputy County Court judge in the Brentford County Court. Bernard Lewis came into my room, all smiles. 'Samuels, I have such a busy list today. Would you be kind enough to take this case, which I just won't have time to hear?'

What could I say, but agree? The case involved a dispute between neighbours, neither of whom spoke English, with inadequate interpreters on both sides. Both parties appeared in person. I was trying to make some sense of the pleadings when I looked out of the window. It was about 11.15 a.m. There was Bernard Lewis, driving away in his Rolls-Royce, having finished in court for the day. I imagine he believed that he had evened the score.

———

On the face of my initial instructions in Chelmsford Auctions Ltd v. Poole,[10] there appeared to be no more than the determination of an idiosyncratic local judge to make life difficult for my auctioneer clients to justify the prosecution of an appeal. The judge had struck out a claim brought by the auctioneers to recover the unpaid purchase price of a vehicle from the buyer, claiming that the auctioneers were fully reimbursed in respect of their own commission from the sum they took from the buyer as a deposit. The auctioneers had, in the meantime, paid their principal the balance of the purchase price: and the issue was whether the auctioneers could sue in their own name for that balance. The compelling reason for the appeal was the direction of the local judge that any further action brought by the auctioneers in his court, based on their standard conditions of sale, would be stayed.

———

10   [1973] QB 542

This case provided an unexpected opportunity once again to observe Denning at his best. The appeal was closely argued; and the leading case had been decided in 1788. At the conclusion of the respondent's argument, I thought that I had lost; but this turned out to be one of those rare cases in which I succeeded in turning the tide in my reply.

There were two consequences. First, Denning stopped me in New Square, a few days later: 'We all thought you did this case really well, Samuels. When are you going to take Silk?' Second, and unknown to me at the time, Dad, who had hoped I would join him as a member of the Athenaeum, had written to Denning, asking for his support. Denning replied:

'I shall be delighted to support John's name for the Athenaeum – I do not often go there but I will hope to do so soon and sign the book. He is doing splendidly – we all thought he argued the auctioneers' case very well – the next step will be to take Silk – but that will be a little time yet.'

I was duly elected, just over a year later. Denning had proposed me, and Dad seconded the nomination. I only went to the club infrequently, usually to join Dad. Maxine hated it, because of the then discriminatory rule that ladies entered via a separate staircase and used the basement annexe. With some misgivings, I discontinued my membership some years after Dad died in 1982; and have subsequently visited periodically as a guest, including as a guest of lady members. Fortunately, I was subsequently persuaded to join the Garrick, and have been a happy member there: its practices have also changed.

———

Throughout 1973, I was counsel representing a fellow member of the Bar in heavily defended divorce proceedings. His wife was a spirited American: this had been the initial attraction in a whirlwind romance, which quickly turned sour. My abiding memory of the case is that, standing outside court waiting my turn to come in, in one of those interminable moments of kicking one's heels – and recognising that, in accordance with the traditions of the Bar, I was acting for no fee – I asked my client why he had selected me. His candour was memorable: 'The solicitors gave me four names to choose, and you were the only one I had never heard of.' In fairness to him, at the conclusion of the case he presented me with two magnificent antique silver coffee pots. In the only substantial burglary we ever had, they were stolen before they were insured.

———

A number of civil cases were coming to the boil throughout 1973; none of them came to trial until I had moved chambers, as described in the next chapter. My growing civil practice was accompanied by increasing difficulty in arranging cover: the juniors preferred to sit behind a leader earning what were then the very high fees achieved by the criminal Bar, rather than to rush around the County Court as my temporary cover.

Walter Sandham recognised the problem. Initially, he tried to persuade me to stay, but once he saw that my mind was made up, he supported my move elsewhere. That was not until after he had landed me with what was perhaps my most memorable criminal appeal. Through a listing error, an appeal came on that had been missed. The trial at the Central Criminal Court had lasted over six weeks; the summing up had lasted over a week; and I was the first appellant. I received the brief at 4.30 p.m., worked on it all night, and opened the appeal at 10.30 the next morning. Lord Justice Scarman expressed gratitude to me for ensuring that the case could be dealt with. I remember that Walter achieved a *very* large brief fee!

———

A quasi-criminal case with a difference was that of Chiltonian Ltd. They were biscuit manufacturers, and it was alleged that they had manufactured a biscuit from which a pin projected point first at an exact right angle: and that this had been spotted by a mother just as her toddler was popping the biscuit into its mouth. I was initially instructed to admit responsibility: but I was suspicious. After a conference and a view at the factory, I persuaded the clients to undertake an experiment. I asked them to drop a box of 400 pins in some biscuit mixture and see what happened. They were terrified of losing some of the pins, with further claims down the line. Each pin was accounted for. The results were illuminating. In no case was a pin fully buried in the biscuit; and to the extent that pins were covered by biscuit at all, they projected at odd angles, but not at right angles. This hardened my determination. With the photographic evidence of the subsequent experiment, the mother agreed in the Peterborough Magistrates' Court that she had indeed inserted the pin herself, to obtain compensation from Sainsbury's. The prosecution collapsed.

TRANSPLANTING THE SAPLING

'How vainly men themselves amaze
To win the palm, the oak, or bays,
And their uncessant labours see
Crown'd from some single herb or tree,
Whose short and narrow-verged shade
Does prudently their toils upbraid'
Andrew Marvell (1621–1678)

Sydney Aylett was a legend among barristers' clerks in 1973, but not for the usual reasons. Sydney's principal claim to fame was his longevity. In his really dreadful book of memoirs, *Under the Wigs: The Memoirs of a Legal King-Maker*, he describes his fifty-eight years as a clerk in the Temple. Much of it is inaccurate; and while he was indeed the senior clerk to both Lord Diplock and Lord Hailsham, perhaps his primary reputation should be that of the promoter of the magnificently endowed film personality Sabrina (who occupies a disproportionate quantity of those memoirs).

Sydney's obsession with Sabrina and her physicality was far more prominent than his interest in the barristers whom he left at 4 Paper Buildings on his retirement. Maurice Drake QC, Head of Chambers on my arrival, told me that he had had some difficulty in persuading Sydney to modify the draft manuscript, which he had been asked to review before publication. The draft suggested that, once Hailsham had left to become Lord Chancellor, there was no talent left in the chambers; Maurice was only taken on as a tenant four years after his pupillage ended; and the dismissive way in which, even after editorial revision by Maurice, Sydney referred to the rest of his barristers emphatically explained why he was not the clerk for me.

My first contact with the chambers was some eight years earlier, and left an indelible impression of a shambolic administration. I had been saddled with William Wells QC as a leader in a Boundary Commission inquiry; as a Labour MP, he was of course available *pro bono*, and as a then aspiring politician I was keen to get in on the act. I first met Sydney in what was no more than a cubbyhole for the clerk; and was then escorted into the Silks' room – which was as filthy as any I have ever known, with a large hole prominently in the middle of the stained Turkey carpet. I vowed never willingly to go there again.

My conscience was modestly salved, because I subsequently met and formed an excellent impression of John Woodcock, the junior clerk who took over after Sydney's retirement. John was indeed an admirable clerk, and when I arrived in January 1974 his feet were well under the clerks' room table.

———

Stephen Yeoman was the first heavy damages case that I conducted. Stephen had been riding a motorbike when he was in collision with a car and was flung against a brick wall. Aged twenty-four at the time of the settlement of his claim, a brilliant academic career had been forecast for him. His father was a practising vet. Quadriplegic, Stephen was initially not expected to survive. His mother, a nurse, was convinced that he could, and her dedicated full-time care so improved his condition that, following twelve months' inpatient care in hospital, he was discharged to her. By the time the case came to court in March 1974, he was able to sit up in a chair and communicate normally. I was led by Stephen Brown QC; and the agreed settlement was £30,000. This sum in later years would look microscopically mean, even during my practising career, when such claims routinely attracted seven-figure awards.

I first met Stephen Brown under the auspices of Queens' reunions, at which as a former pupil of Arthur Armitage he was a diligent attender. He became my leader of choice in personal injury cases, as Tom Bingham was my favourite leader in commercial matters. It was a modest disappointment when, as President of the Family Division, Stephen declined to permit me to train (and therefore to continue to sit) as a deputy High Court judge in that division. He explained that, in his view, those who now sat in the Family Division had to be exclusive specialists. I pointed out that he had been my favourite leader in personal injury, and that following his judicial appointment (initially to the Family Division) he had transferred to the Queen's Bench Division, before returning via the Court of Appeal to the presidency. Disarmingly, he said, 'I see you, John, as a natural for the QBD' – in which I had also then sat as a deputy for some time.

———

The following month, I represented the son and heir of Littlewoods Pools in negotiating and agreeing a divorce settlement. The discussions were protracted. The doyen of the divorce bar, Joe Jackson QC, represented the wife. Once agreement over financial provision was reached, it should all have been plain sailing; but negotiations almost foundered over the matrimonial chattels. The sticking point was a particular oil painting. The wife insisted that my client should have it; and he adamantly maintained that his wife should remove it. It was of no value, but each spouse hated it. I cut the Gordian knot by telling my client: 'You keep it and put it on your bonfire.'

———

Another memorable case from 1974 was that of Re Ager. The scene was set on the eighteenth floor of an office block under construction overlooking the road works at the commencement of the M3 motorway at Sunbury. Mr Ager had gone to the eighteenth floor, leaned out of the window aperture, and was found dead on the canopy above the entrance. At the subsequent inquest, the coroner rapidly concluded that this was death by suicide. Mrs Ager first saw me after the inquest. She had not long been married. Of particular significance, although it would be churlish to say of paramount importance, was the fact that her husband had life insurance, which excluded death by suicide. I advised a challenge in the

Divisional Court: suicide must be proved to the criminal standard. The challenge was successful. The initial inquest verdict was quashed, and a new inquest took place. Very unusually, the new coroner permitted me to question every witness, and even to address the jury before he summed up the case. Everyone left court to enable the coroner to complete the formal inquisition with the jury. I had forgotten my raincoat. I knocked on the door and entered. As I did so, I heard the foreman say to the coroner: 'We all knew it was suicide, but we felt sorry for her.' I said nothing. Mrs Ager generously presented me with a set of whisky glasses, which remain in use.

———

It was difficult not to feel some sympathy for Herbert Kelly. A remand prisoner in HMP Wandsworth, he consistently complained of a progressively inflamed sore throat, over a period of five months. His complaints went unheeded. Eventually, it was discovered that he had throat cancer; and to save his life his larynx was surgically removed – the same operation as was undergone by the well-known actor Jack Hawkins. Maurice Drake, my new Head of Chambers, led me. We drove to Wandsworth prison in his low-slung Volvo sports car for a consultation; HMP Wandsworth was the first prison I entered. It was easy to see why Maurice had been awarded the DFC: he drove fast, aggressively and impervious to the growing anxiety of his passenger. We survived; and in February 1975 the case came on for trial. All went reasonably well as the plaintiff croaked through his evidence in chief, with his Dalek-like voice box (the sophistication of Stephen Hawking's apparatus lay far in the future). The principal witness for the Home Office was the prison senior medical officer. Before starting cross-examination, Maurice turned round languidly. 'You take this witness, John.' I refused. Not only had I not prepared the cross-examination, but I knew that if I were to attempt it, and it went wrong, the client would crucify me. 'Only joking,' said Maurice, as he rose to cross-examine. Sadly, we lost.

———

Jeffrey Archer and Jonathan Aitken were both destroyed by their pursuit of libel cases, and lies they told in the witness box. Interestingly, I have known both. Jeffrey Archer was a Tory member of the GLC when I was on the Education Committee of the ILEA; and while I knew him as someone who lunched in the members' restaurant, we were only on nodding terms. Jonathan Aitken, by contrast, has become a recent friend. Following Jonathan's experience of custody, he has become an active prison reformer. It is in that capacity that we have become collaborators as well as friends. He has taken up the cause of problem-solving courts and sentencer supervision, and we jointly undertook the creation of a paper promoting these twin concepts, published by the Centre for Social Justice in September 2017: 'What happened to the Rehabilitation Revolution?' This is amplified in chapter 19, 'Judicial Monitoring'.

This is a Beethoven-like introduction to the far lower profile case of Mr Reginald Sheppard, the Conservative opposition leader on the London Borough of Brent, whose election to that council I formally challenged in March 1975. Election petitions are rare; and the election petition that I was required to promote for Mr Brian Ereira, defeated Labour candidate in the Sudbury ward, failed to achieve more than ephemeral notoriety in the *Wembley Observer*. What was all this about?

Councillor Sheppard had certified, in his nomination paper for the forthcoming local election, that he was normally resident within the ward for which he sought election. There are interesting parallels in 2024, with the far more newsworthy case of Angela Rayner, deputy leader of the Labour Party. Our case was that this was a sham: Mr Sheppard had, at best, parked a suitcase in the home of a resident within the ward, and his normal residence was in Harrow Park, outside the boundary of the London Borough of Brent. There was a formal hearing by an election court. Having called my witnesses for the petitioner, I embarked on the questioning of the respondent councillor. He was obviously finding cross-examination uncomfortable. He muttered a reply to one of my questions. I did not hear what he said. I asked him to repeat his answer. Truculently, he said that he had said nothing. I asked him again to repeat it. He declined.

Turning to the commissioner, I said: 'Sir, the witness said something. I did not hear it. I believe it to be relevant. Will you please direct him to repeat *precisely* what he previously said?'

The commissioner obliged. Blushing bright red, the councillor did so: 'I said, why don't you fuck off.' That was the end of his credibility.

———

Train-wrecking is not the kind of criminal offence you automatically associate with a highly respected senior member of the staff of an established firm of stockbrokers. That, however, was the charge my client faced in July 1975. Section 35 of the Malicious Damage Act 1861 was the first count in the indictment to which Francis Dodgson pleaded not guilty at Chelmsford Crown Court, before a High Court judge: and he pleaded guilty to count 2, the lesser offence of placing himself on a railway and thereby obstructing an engine using the railway.

Mr Dodgson was one of several commuters from Manningtree station who, in March 1975, had become increasingly frustrated by the cancellations of their regular trains to Liverpool Street. On 5 March, his train had broken down and was cancelled. There was a large group of passengers on the station. It was known that the Hook–Harwich express regularly passed slowly through Manningtree on its way to Liverpool Street; and that that train, usually empty, would stop in exceptional circumstances. Other passengers asked if the express could be stopped and were brusquely told 'No'. Mr Dodgson, carrying a briefcase and a rolled umbrella, stood on the line; the driver of the express saw him and brought the train to a gentle stop. The waiting commuters gratefully piled on to the train. The unscheduled stop delayed the train by four minutes. Mr Dodgson immediately identified himself to railway police by saying: 'It seems to be me who has caused all the trouble.'

In advising Mr Dodgson to plead guilty to the offence, to which there was no defence, I hoped that the judge might treat the case as one deserving no punishment. I had not then appreciated the lack of humour to be displayed by a High Court judge who was fortunate to have been promoted from the Circuit Bench. I had encouraged the prosecution formally to admit all the facts that supported my mitigation; and they did so. My mitigation included:

'*Given the cumulative effect of delays and frustration which commuters from the station had to endure over the previous three or four months, there comes a time when the most social of men does something which he might in the quiet light of dawn realise only too well was wrong. That is the relevance of the agreed schedules; that is the relevance of the delays; the cumulative effect of a man who is faced with a wall of silence and no explanation ... I wonder if I may deal with the appropriate sentence in this case?*'

Mr JUSTICE TALBOT: 'It might help you to know I do not intend to send him to prison.'

Mr SAMUELS: 'I am very much obliged for that indication. If I may say so with the utmost respect, I was anticipating that would be Your Lordship's view.'

I concluded by inviting the judge to discharge my client.

In the result, Mr Dodgson was fined £100 and ordered to pay £100 costs. What the judge did not know, when I told him that I would arrange to pay by cheque, was that Mr Dodgson's friends and supporters had gathered more than enough to pay the fine, the costs *and* his legal expenses.

There was a sequel. A few days later, I was before a Queen's Bench Master on a routine summons. The case had been widely reported in the press. He asked me to stay behind. 'I was on that train, Samuels. To whom should I make a contribution?' So much for the majesty of the law, and its uniform application by *all* its officers.

————

Although I knew Harry Woolf, then Treasury Counsel, socially well before October 1975 when we met in the court corridor, I believe that this was the only occasion on which our interchange was less than cordial. We routinely walked across Waterloo Bridge together. My client, having slipped on a patch of custard in the canteen of her factory, had been injured. The issue was whether or not her injury had occurred during the course of her employment. I challenged the decision of the National Insurance Commissioner, who had concluded that her employment had not begun, and therefore that she was not entitled to industrial injury benefit.[11] Harry arrived to find that I was relying on some relevant authorities. Not only had I provided these to the court, but I had sent a list over to his chambers. Harry denied all knowledge of the list. I showed him a written receipt. In all my subsequent dealings with him, his courtesy and friendship towards me was unfailing. Maxine and I have been guests at his home, as have Marguerite and Harry to ours (Marguerite was Maxine's predecessor as chair of the Richmond Magistrates' Family Panel). The moral is: first impressions should not count, even if they are memorable.

Dr Chaterjee[12] was a highly unusual matrimonial client. At the material time, he was aged seventy and in poor health. He had married his wife in 1952 and they divorced in 1955. From 1961 onwards they cohabited for thirteen years, for five of these as husband and wife, during which the wife gave birth to an illegitimate child, whom my client accepted as its father. For eight years between 1966 and 1974 they remained under the same roof. At first instance, Mr Justice Arnold had ridden roughshod over the relevant statutory provisions; and I advised an appeal. The issue in the Court of Appeal was whether or not the relevant statutory provisions introduced by the Matrimonial Proceedings and Property Act 1970 were retroactive. If they were not, the wife's claim for a lump sum and/or a transfer of property order was bound to fail.

I argued that, on the particular facts, the wife should not receive the relief that she claimed, and not to contend that the statutory provisions lacked retroactive effect. Lord Justice Ormrod, having articulated the jurisdiction issue, continued:

'*Mr Samuels gallantly shouldered the burden of arguing the point which he had not intended to argue and, as he later explained, he personally did not think a good one. This court is extremely grateful to him for his able and lucid guidance through the undergrowth which surrounds this question. It might have been resolved very simply by including in the Act*

---

11   R v. National Insurance Commissioner, ex parte East [1976] I.C.R 206

12   Chaterjee v. Chaterjee [1976] 1 All ER 719

an express provision whether or to what extent each of its provisions was intended to have retroactive effect. In the result, the question can only be answered by detailed examination of the Act and some of its predecessors.'

At the conclusion of the appeal, I was asked whether I had any objection to the matter being remitted to Mr Justice Arnold for final determination. Since I believed that his approach to the case would be guided by what the Court of Appeal had stated, I readily agreed. In the ensuing application, the judge had no problem in adopting what he had said and done before: and this taught me a memorable lesson. There must have been no hard feelings on his part, because in 1981, when I took Silk, he was then President of the Family Division. He congratulated me and added: 'You are the only family Silk of 1981.' I protested that family law was only a small part of my practice. 'It will not be now,' he replied. Within a few months, and at his nomination, I was invited to sit as a deputy High Court judge in the Family Division.

WIDER STILL AND WIDER

Wider still and wider
Shall thy bounds be set
from 'Land of Hope and Glory' by A. C. Benson (1862–1925)

My first visit to Niagara Falls was in 1967: a honeymoon expedition, to soak up the atmosphere of Ontario's finest tourist destination. Whether or not I appreciated at the time the importance of the falls to the generating capacity of Ontario Hydro or that they provided the bulk of the electricity supply for the whole of New York State, these aspects have faded, unlike so many other memories of the honeymoon generally. They came into prominence some years later when, acting for Hopkinsons, valve manufacturers of Huddersfield, I was asked to resist a claim that an allegedly defective valve had been responsible for closing the Ontario Hydro and the electrical supply to much of New York State.

The clients were clearly happy with the advice, because not only did they successfully avoid liability for the massive consequential loss claims formulated against them, but they returned for further advice in relation to what started as a trade dispute, and developed into a saga, embracing domestic and international politics, and chicanery on the part of current and retired politicians. It culminated in a high-profile trial.

Draughtsmen employed by Hopkinsons, who included the national chair of the trade union in dispute with the management, were dismissed. The response of the sacked men was to lock themselves into the offices of the company, intimidating female staff and jamming the locks with superglue. During their occupation, the strikers found documentation – which they passed to the *Guardian* newspaper – revealing that Hopkinsons had supplied spare parts for a power station in what was then Rhodesia, in breach of the then sanctions regime.

My instructions were to regain possession of the company's offices. An injunction was readily obtained. Following its grant, ACAS intervened. Both the company and the trade union were each invited to appoint two representatives to a committee to be chaired by the former Labour cabinet minister Frank Cousins. I was appointed as the second representative of the company. I naively assumed that Frank Cousins would act as an independent chair. Time showed just how experienced a negotiator he was, and how partisan. After two long days of negotiation, Hopkinsons rolled over, reinstated the dismissed strikers and resolved the pay dispute.

The *Guardian* subsequently published an article that prompted the DPP into action. I suggested that any potential prosecution of the company for breaching the sanctions regime would not be in the public interest, given the circumstances in which the breach, if it existed, had been brought to the attention of the authorities via the newspaper. I arranged a meeting with the Solicitor General, Peter Archer, in which I sought to persuade him not to continue to prosecute Hopkinsons based on documents clandestinely obtained by the strikers. Peter Archer courteously explained that he fully intended to continue the prosecution. With my clients' agreement, I put the facts before Ian Percival QC, then a shadow law officer. Percival told me that he considered the prosecution misconceived. Shortly after these abortive discussions the Labour government fell, and Ian Percival was appointed as Solicitor General. I wrote to him formally and invited him to enter a *nolle prosequi* – a direction, with which the DPP was bound to comply, that no prosecution should continue.

He replied that the law officers would not enter a *nolle prosequi*, nor would he be prepared to see me. There was no explanation. I discovered that the word of a politician is not the same as the word of a barrister.

That left the prosecution on track for a state trial. There had been some committal proceedings, when Dai Tudor Price QC, leading Treasury Counsel at the Central Criminal Court, represented the prosecution and told me that I had no defence. A directions hearing followed at Leeds Crown Court, when the judge told me much the same.

'How long is this case going to take, Mr Samuels? I can't see it going more than a day! I have read the papers.'

'With the greatest respect, I have also read the papers; I have advised my clients that they have a defence; and I maintain my time estimate.'

The judge snorted. Arthur Hutchinson QC, representing the co-defendant, was so terrified by the judge's reaction that he advised his client to plead guilty.

The case came to trial in York in September 1979. I had a different judge. I had secretly agonised about the prospects of addressing a Yorkshire jury as 'PLC' ('posh London counsel'); and had arranged for Maxine and the boys to come up to York to stay for the first weekend. My fears and my plans melted like summer snow. On Day 2 of the trial, the judge accepted the last of my submissions. These were based on the well-known proposition that a company can only be criminally liable when it is shown that the act in question arose from what was done by those directors or managers who represent its 'directing mind and will'.[13]

It was unnecessary then to show one's hand in a defence case statement. The jury were directed to acquit. The following day, an embarrassed Arthur Hutchinson mitigated on behalf of his client, who received a modest fine.

Before the events leading to the Hopkinsons prosecution had unfolded, another saga was under way. In the spring of 1976, a US-based entrepreneur, Leonard Weisman, who carried on business via a Delaware corporation, had obtained a default judgment in the state courts of California against his erstwhile partners in a joint enterprise. Those partners were a Serbian conglomerate, Interexport, and Emo, a Slovenian factory based in Ljubljana. Weisman had persuaded Emo to turn the whole of their production line over to the manufacture of 16- and 32-foot steel containers, to his own design; and the issue was whether or not that design was capable of being manufactured, either in bulk or at all, to suit its role as a lightweight

---

13   Tesco Supermarkets Ltd v. Nattrass [1972] A.C. 153

but robust steel shell, suitable for the transportation of freight by road, rail and sea.

Following the default judgment in California, enforcement was being sought against the then Yugoslav state airline, in part owned by Interexport. Enforcement of the judgment grounded the airline worldwide. Marshal Tito, then the president of Yugoslavia, demanded action. The default judgment was set aside on terms that the dispute between the parties would be submitted to a London-based arbitration. Each party appointed its own arbitrator; and a London barrister was appointed as the umpire. I attended the Commercial Court so that directions could be given for the conduct of the arbitration. My opponent was the experienced Kenneth Rokison QC. As was becoming a bit of a habit, the judge leaped to the conclusion that I had no leg to stand on. I took the cowardly line, and recommended a Silk.

Norman Tapp QC was reassuring and methodical. He identified the parameters of the subsequent arbitration; and, before I understood the general outlines of our case, sadly dropped dead. I assumed that he would be replaced with another leader. Stuart Benson, my solicitor, whom I first knew as an articled clerk, had other ideas. He was confident that I could take over. We embarked on an odyssey that lasted for five and a half years, embracing multiple visits to Belgrade, Ljubljana and New York, and proved an invaluable introduction to the politics of pre-war Yugoslavia. When the lawyers representing the two clients came to London, Stuart arranged to wine and dine them well. The advocate representing the Serbian entity, Advocate Ilic, had little English, but looked exactly like Leonid Brezhnev, then General Secretary of the Russian Federation; his sidekick, a very able Croatian lawyer with perfect English, could not be left in the same room as the Slovenian lawyer representing Emo, Rudi Selic. Rudi was a former president of the Yugoslav Bar but had been a partisan during the Second World War. His opposite number had been a Chetnik. The political passions that ran deep in the former Yugoslavia boiled over later.

At an early visit to the Emo factory, the managerial representatives of the clients refused to speak to Stuart and me. Gradually, we discovered why. As representatives of the enterprise, they were responsible for entering into this contract; and if it went sour, as seemed likely in the communist world in which they operated, they would pay for their errors with their lives. It took both patience and multiple visits to win their trust. Having done so, they opened an Aladdin's cave of critical and relevant documents, carefully housed in cupboards surrounding an extensive boardroom. I took much pleasure in informing my New York opposite number, Mr Liner, that he was welcome to inspect them: 'The good news is that only some of the documents are in Slovenian. The bad news is that the rest are in Serbo-Croat.'

A piece of the jigsaw involved identifying precisely which piece of Delaware corporate law governed the activity of the plaintiffs. Our New York attorneys proved to be hospitality personified on our frequent visits between 1977 and 1980 – usually flying on Concorde. Long hours of 'chewing the fat' in the attorneys' offices were leavened by trips to the theatre. *The Best Little Whorehouse in Texas* stands out.

The strategy we adopted, to avoid getting bogged down in lengthy arbitration proceedings, was to seek security for costs against the plaintiffs, who were technically insolvent. Despite wriggling hard, they failed to provide the necessary security, and the claim was permanently stayed.

Some memories persist. First, in ancillary proceedings taking place in New York that had potential consequences for our London-based arbitration, the clients arranged representation by an elderly former New York judge of appeals, now practising as counsel, to impress the state judge. On our arrival, the retired judge promptly handed over the case to a young associate. I stayed up for much of the night, giving him all the necessary background.

Mr Liner opened proceedings: 'Your Honour, there are two gentlemen from London, England whose very presence in your Honour's Court is inimical to the interests of justice.'

The wise judge replied: 'I am sure the gentlemen from London will behave: if not, they're out.'

The hearing began. Within moments, Liner invited his novice opponent to enter a stipulation, a formal agreement for the purposes of the litigation, that would, if agreed, have a prejudicial impact on our case in London. I leaped from the back of the court to the front. 'Don't do that!'

Without drawing breath, Liner said: 'There you are, Your Honour: I said he wouldn't behave.'

Fortunately, the judge found in favour of the Yugoslavs.

The overseas visits included six days in Slovenia in September 1976, including some wonderful trips to the countryside around Ljubljana; six days in New York in November 1977; three days in Belgrade in June 1978; four days in New York in November 1978; and four further days in New York in March 1980. All were the equivalent of truly memorable holidays; and I should have paid handsomely for the privilege.

———

In March 1978, Maurice Drake was appointed to the High Court bench. There were no other Silks in chambers and, objectively, we needed one. Although there were other juniors who were senior to me, I took responsibility for finding a suitable replacement. In the event, I found two. Richard Rougier QC was exceptionally able, and equally idle. His practice in Silk had become 'quiet', and he relished the opportunity for an injection of new work. When I took Silk, three years later, Richard's advice was to ensure that I always took a two-week break after every case, even if it had been no more than a short appointment before a Master. Richard became a High Court judge in September 1986.

Harvey McGregor QC was a polymath: a brilliant lawyer, he was practising in 1978 as a specialist tax Silk, although he was the leading authority on the law of damages. He was also a pianist – a latter-day Noël Coward – and his soirees for students in New College, Oxford, were legendary. He was also perhaps the world's worst advocate, failing to see the wood for the trees as he bolted down every interesting-looking rabbit hole. He relished the opportunity to come to 4 Paper Buildings; and my task was to persuade both to come in partnership.

Richard Rougier was also attracted by the large room overlooking the Temple gardens, in which he installed his mother's extensive library – the historical novelist Georgette Heyer undertook more detailed research than her son. Harvey McGregor, a bachelor of eclectic taste, divided his time between New College (of which in due course he became Warden) and the Bar; and the prize he offered me, in gratitude for the introduction to 4 Paper Buildings, was the junior brief in resisting a major claim against those responsible for the design and construction of Ronan Point, a famous tower block in East London. As a result of a gas explosion, a corner of this block had collapsed in May 1968.

A careful public inquiry into the collapse had been chaired by Hugh Griffiths QC, and was the foundation of his subsequent pre-eminent reputation as a judge. Press comment at the time was that 'Ronan Point collapsed like a pack of cards'; a complaint that had repeated echoes in the subsequent protracted litigation. The block was one of five tower blocks designed and built by Taylor-Woodrow Anglian Ltd, a consortium of architects and contractors formed for the purpose. The building owner was the London Borough of Newham. The case, shorn of its technicalities, was developed in contract, the relevant contractual duties being specified in the building contract, and in tort: a failure to take such care in the design and construction that would have avoided the collapse.

Harvey focused on the contractual duties and spent almost six months researching the intricacies of the massive documentation. The case came to trial before Mr Justice O'Connor. The trial began on 25 April 1979. On 4 May, Harvey phoned me. He was in agony.

I reassured him: 'Don't worry, I am sure I can get the case adjourned.'

He had only just started his cross-examination of the plaintiffs' first witness. I rang our opponent: Gerald Moriarty QC was sympathetic and accommodating. I rang O'Connor's clerk: he too was reassuring. I went into court to apply for the adjournment.

'How lucky you are, Mr Samuels, that Monday is a bank holiday. If Mr McGregor is not better on Tuesday, I expect you to continue.'

My heart sank. I knew how much time and effort had been devoted to the preparation of this highly technical cross-examination. Fortunately, Harvey was in his place on 8 May; and he continued his cross-examination for a further nine days.

The plaintiffs' second witness dealt with the tortious aspect of the claim. He was to be cross-examined by me. He was a leading light in the Institute of Structural Engineers. At the end of his evidence in chief, the judge was getting tired. 'Yes, Mr McGregor,' he sighed, without looking up. Answer came there none. I was on my feet, as planned.

My initial questions annoyed the witness. I read from some technical articles that I had unearthed and asked him if he would comment on the propositions that the articles identified. They were all inconsistent with the evidence the witness had given. He roundly rejected each proposition. I asked him whether he might be interested in who had written the articles of which he was so dismissive. He shrugged; and I teased him a little bit, before putting to him that the authorship of the view that was so diametrically opposite to that which he had advanced in his expert evidence was surely worth identifying, since such an author might be well regarded in the profession. Reluctantly, he agreed to be told who it was. 'It was you,' I said, as I sprang the trap.

The trial lasted forty-one days. It was one of the lengthiest pieces of civil litigation then known, albeit there have been more recent claims arising out of banking litigation that have lasted for years.

The judge found that the defendants were not liable in negligence; and many of the contractual claims against them also failed. However, he concluded that in respect of the limited failure to design and build a structure in which gas could be safely used, they were in breach of contract; and were thus liable to reimburse the building owner in relation to the cost of strengthening the five blocks that Newham had incurred.

Harvey ascertained from our clerk, John, that I had no red bag, and generously presented me with one. He inscribed it '*In memoriam* Ronan Point: for omnidirectional [a reference to a feature of the expert evidence] aid'. An unusual aspect of that assistance was tying Harvey's white bands in the robing room: despite his intellectual brilliance, tying any bow defeated him. I had always understood that a red bag should be reserved for a junior who gave outstanding assistance in the House of Lords, and that only three such red bags could be presented during a Silk's career. I certainly limited my gift of red bags to these criteria. I note, with some regret, that the wish of more recent leaders to obtain work from their juniors has diminished the currency significantly; and red bags have become as cheap as chips.

This long trial was only concerned with the issue of liability. It was followed by an appeal to the Court of Appeal, limited to that issue. The appeal began in June 1981, by which time I was in Silk. Harvey had been leading me for just over three days when our solicitor, recognising the growing disaster that was developing as a result of Harvey's failure accurately to read the reaction of the court, demanded that Harvey should sit down and let me take over as leading counsel. While I was fully prepared, in the sense that by then I knew the case well, I had no warning of how I should present this volte-face either to Harvey, to our opponents, or to the court. Somehow a *modus operandi* was achieved; and I was on my feet in the front row for much of the next five days. Unsurprisingly, we were unsuccessful in the Court of Appeal; and the subsequent petition for leave to appeal to the House of Lords was rejected.

That left the issue of quantum. After protracted delay, the case was eventually listed before a judge reluctantly transferred to the Official Referees' corridor. Following four hearing days (a drop in the ocean, contrasted to the liability hearing), a reserved judgment awarded the plaintiffs a substantial sum.

That was by no means the end of the case. Apart from a token application for leave to appeal to the Court of Appeal, I still had a card to play. I was authorised to settle the case for the amount left in the insurers' pot. The plaintiffs had not realised that their claim was being met by insurers alone (and not the well-known contractors who had formed the relevant consortium to design and build the five blocks); or that the insurance cover provided was itself limited to £1 million. That is what I was instructed to disclose; and in late July 1985 I concluded the claim of the London Borough of Newham in this saga, which for them had begun in May 1968, for the token sum of £1. The rest of the insurance pot had been spent on the litigation.

————

While I cannot now remember the name of our client, I have the clearest recollection of her claim for ancillary relief, in the aftermath of divorce proceedings. Her husband had asserted that her entitlement should be reduced, on the grounds that she had not only hit him over the head with a silver candelabrum, but that in so doing the candelabrum was damaged, and it was a family heirloom. The husband was represented by John Mortimer QC (the creator of Rumpole); and I was led by Joe Jackson QC. Very much to the surprise of her representatives, not only was the wife's conduct ignored by Mrs Justice Lane, but she was awarded what, for that era, was a generous lump sum. There were two consequences. First, the judge had second thoughts about her generosity, and so informed Joe over lunch in the Inner Temple. Before she had a chance to do anything about it (I doubt whether she could have done, in any event), the wife requested a consultation, in order to discuss increasing the award. Joe Jackson listened to her complaints in silence. The wife was a Scottish lady, with a particularly irritating whine to her voice: she was, perhaps, fortunate not to have been on the receiving end of the candelabrum. She maintained, in the teeth of the evidence, that she was left destitute: 'Mr Jackson, do you know what I had for my Christmas dinner? A boiled egg!'

Joe tied up his papers quickly, threw them down on his desk, and said, 'Madam! I have nothing else to say to you. Get out!'

I wondered whether I could do the same to a difficult client; but I never did. As it is, I cherish some of Joe's miniature teapots, which I bought at auction after his death, and which I cannot look at on their display shelf without thinking of that whining Scottish client.

The case of De Winter in April 1977 was a straightforward claim arising out of a road accident, maintained by a husband against his wife (the driver) and another motorist. What was unusual was the fact that I had been provided with a leader, with a concomitant uplift in what would normally have been my brief fee: the fee was far higher than my 'tariff' fee for such a case in 1977. On the morning of Day 3, my leader announced that he had to leave the case the following day, as he had a commitment in the Industrial Tribunal. This seemed strange: first, the High Court invariably took precedence over a case in an industrial tribunal, and in any event the case had been listed for four days. I told my leader that if he insisted on leaving the case (about which I was less than happy), he must so inform the lay client. The lay client was even less happy.

'I am sure we can get your case settled now,' airily announced the leader. He sought out our opponent, and returned with a settlement offer. He put that offer to the client, whose response was:

'I am not interested in your views: I want to know what Mr Samuels thinks.'

In the result, we did settle the case; but I was never led by that Silk again. I did, however, have two more recent experiences. In 1986, I represented American clients in a case relating to trading in gold futures, which Mr Justice Bingham had transferred from the Commercial Court to the Chancery Division, as the Commercial Court was clogged with work. The same very grand Silk represented the plaintiff; and the trial judge was Mr Justice Harman. The case had been listed for a week. For the first two days, the opening was interspersed with anecdotes between Bench and Bar, relating to the previous year's summer holidays when the judge had been a guest on leading counsel's yacht in the Mediterranean. When not a word of evidence had been called on behalf of the plaintiffs, I had a long-distance call to New York. I told the clients they were on a hiding to nothing, and that I wanted their authority to secure the best settlement I could. Those clients never appreciated the nuances of a close relationship between Bench and Bar. Fast-forward to November 2016. I bumped into leading counsel at an event held by a think tank in London. He hailed me as a long-lost friend. We chatted generally, and he asserted that he felt sure he had once led me. I agreed; but felt it unnecessary to add any of the detail.

––––––––––

The Matrimonial Causes Act 1973 revolutionised divorce law. Instead of the old grounds for divorce on which I had cut my teeth, the sole ground permitted by the reforming statute was that the marriage had irretrievably broken down. Proof of that breakdown was to be provided in one of five ways, the most significant of which, for present purposes, was that the parties had lived apart for a continuous period of at least five years. My client had married and separated from a Greek lady in 1969. The wife petitioned for divorce in 1974 on the grounds of her husband's unreasonable behaviour. The husband denied the behaviour alleged, and cross-petitioned for divorce on the grounds of more than five years' separation. The wife admitted the five years' separation but opposed the husband's cross-petition on the grounds that, as a practising Christian, her conscience would be affronted if the marriage were to be dissolved otherwise than for grounds of substance. I advised that the wife's reply should be struck out, on the grounds that there was no continuing issue to be litigated. That application succeeded at first instance, and before the judge on appeal. The wife appealed to the Court of Appeal, which on 4 May 1977 rejected her further appeal.[14]

In January 2017, the principal topic of news was the unprecedented and very public resignation of the UK ambassador to the EU, Sir Ivan Rogers. He told his staff that he did so because his role as the UK's representative in the forthcoming negotiations over Brexit, and the departure of the UK from the EU, was simply impossible to discharge in that he was not being provided by the politicians with the tools with which to discharge his role. His behaviour as a civil servant was said to be unprecedented because it is the responsibility of officials loyally to implement the decisions made by politicians. Was there ever an occasion when I simply refused to comply with instructions given by my client, with which it was lawful for me to comply, and when I was not professionally embarrassed by doing so?

The short answer is Yes: and this introduces a custody dispute between a Bulgarian father and his American wife. The parties had been living in Paris with their two children when the mother clandestinely removed the children to England and started divorce proceedings, before returning to the USA. The mother left in the father's home a diary spanning over two years in which she explicitly described a succession of adulterous liaisons. I had to cross-examine the mother in relation to what she had recorded in her diary, with the result that in November 1978, after a three-day hearing

---

14   Grenfell v. Grenfell: [1978] 1 All ER 561; [1978] Fam. 128

when emotions were running very high, the judge awarded custody, care and control of the two children to the father. The father's proposal, accepted by the judge, was that the children would return to the former matrimonial home in Paris, to be looked after by their paternal grandmother, and would continue to attend their former school.

The following Monday, my solicitors relayed their client's instructions that I should return to court to vary the order obtained the previous Friday, by requiring the court to return the children to the care and control of the mother. I asked the reason. I was told that the client had wanted to prove his point. I refused to comply. My cross-examination had for practical purposes destroyed the mother as a fully functioning adult; and prior to the separation she had been undergoing treatment, including psychoanalysis, for her disturbed mental health. Quite apart from the inappropriateness of returning the children to the care of a potentially unsuitable carer, the father's motives were disturbing. He said he had no further interest in the children. My response was: 'He can do his own dirty work.' I doubt whether I was professionally justified in doing so.

———

There was another occasion when I turned a Nelsonian eye towards my instructions. In August 1985 an aircraft caught fire on the runway at Manchester Airport. I was instructed on behalf of the pilots, by their trade union. Even though the aircraft never took off, and remained on the runway, fifty-five passengers died. Prior to the inquest, I learned that the incident had been fully recorded on the black box flight recorder. That recording exonerated the pilots from all responsibility: their reaction to the incident was a textbook one. However, I was specifically instructed that this material must not be deployed. The concern expressed by the trade union leader who attended the consultation was that if the contents of these recordings were admissible in air accident investigations, they would probably identify pilot error; and so on balance the voluntary arrangement whereby pilots agreed to their use should not be disturbed by creating a means of prejudicing pilots in future litigation.

The captain gave impressive factual evidence relating to the sequence of events. However, during the cross-examination of the co-pilot, it was suggested that the captain had been at fault in not allowing the aircraft to be brought more quickly to a halt. Such an allegation should have been put to the captain. It potentially undermined the evidence of both pilots. I had to make a snap decision. I knew that if I introduced the evidence of the flight recorder, it would exonerate both pilots. I also knew that my instructions precluded me from doing so. I took the view that my primary professional duty was owed to the pilots, whose reputation was literally in my hands.

Perhaps the most difficult decision an advocate must take is whether to re-examine a witness. The normal rule of re-examination is 'Don't'. There are, of course, exceptions; and, if that exception applies, the advocate needs to know precisely how far, and in what way, it is permissible to do so.

I decided to introduce the flight recorder evidence in re-examination. The second-by-second transcript could not have been more dramatic. I read each entry, slowly, to the witness: and it was accurately transcribed by the large press presence. Each word subsequently appeared in the comprehensive press reports in the national press.

There were two immediate consequences. First, both my ankles were black and blue, from being savagely kicked by my junior as he tried in vain to stop me. Second, by the end of the short re-examination, everyone regarded both pilots as heroes.

––––––––

Berni Inns were, in the 1970s, the location of choice for middle-class England seeking a good-quality evening out in a reasonably priced restaurant. It was thus significant when, in May 1980, Southampton City Council laid a total of twenty-one summonses against the local branch of the chain, alleging not only that the food-handling arrangements within the kitchens were unsatisfactory, but that the steaks supplied were unfit for human consumption. I was delighted to be instructed for Berni Inns.

At the close of the prosecution case, the magistrates dismissed four of the twenty-one summonses. Witnesses were called on behalf of the

JS and MS: appointment as a Circuit Judge (March 1997). (The Bench)

JS as a Crown Court trial judge, but **not** when acting informally as a judicial monitor. (Judicial Monitoring)

JS with Yvonne Gayle, his longstanding court clerk and early enthusiast for judicial monitoring and supervision (c. 2003). (Judicial Monitoring)

MS at the celebratory party in Lincoln's Inn (2010). (Lincoln's Inn)

Parenting is mentoring:
David, the editor-in-chief and publisher.
(The Unexpected Mentor)

Parenting is mentoring:
Adam completing the Pennine Way.
(The Unexpected Mentor)

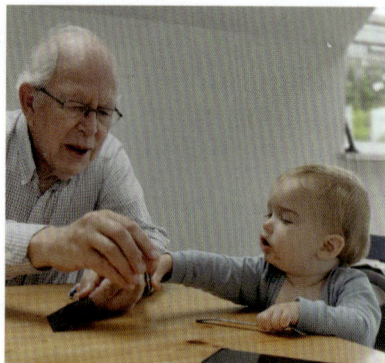

The next generation of mentees: JS with Rafael (August 2022). (The Unexpected Mentor)

Grandpa as mentor: JS with Maximilian and Hardy (August 2020). (The Unexpected Mentor)

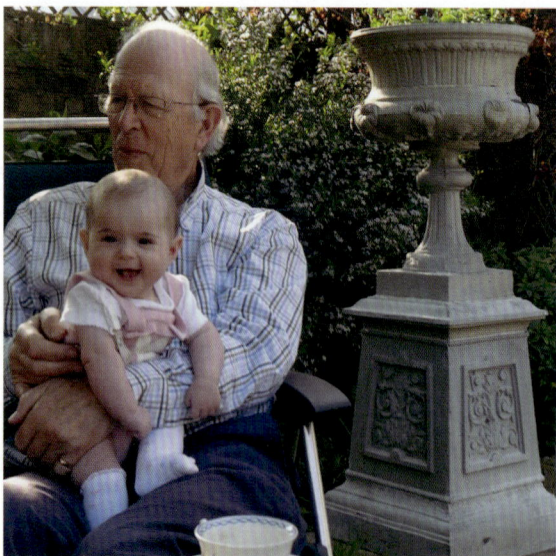

The next generation of mentees: JS with Heidi (April 2019). (The Unexpected Mentor)

JS, Steve Gallant and Ryan Walker of 'Learning Together'. (Judicial Monitoring)

Advocacy training: three outstanding mentees from Lincoln's Inn – Ellie Brown, Antonia Benfield and Dilpreet Dhanoa (2019). (Lincoln's Inn)

JS reaching out to prison reformers: with Jan Cunliffe, co-chair of Joint Enterprise Not Guilty by Association (November 2023). (Judicial Monitoring)

JS with Ingunn Seim of the Norwegian Correctional Service, whose friendship inspired the theme of this book (January 2024). (Judicial Monitoring)

Dear John,

Thank you for giving us your time, advice and guidance throughout the years. You went where others dared to. You are truly appreciated. Never doubt the difference you made. It's huge - and so is the gratitude in this little note.

You will not be forgotten.

Beyond grateful,

Thank you for your continued support and for the amount of genuine concern and care you have shown for us as people and as prisoners. Your efforts will not be forgotten. Hopefully your work ethic and mentality will affect many people for the rest and benefit of the CJS.

Thanks for everything and all your advice

Best wishes & thanks for your support.

Thankyou for time, support and encouragement to always doing the right. Best Wishes

Hope to see you outside!

Dear John,

Thank you for many a thought-provoking and inspiring conversation since we first welcomed you to Coldingley in August 2018! It has been a real honour and pleasure to be able to meet regularly with you, stimulate the grey-matter, and piece together meaningful reform proposals to help contribute to change within our justice system. I shall miss our group, but I wish you and the family well, and hope our paths may cross again in the future! Good luck and God bless

---

Dear John

Thank you for everything that you have done with us, enjoy the future

God bless

Dear Judge Samuels,

Thank you so much for all the time, dedication, care and friendship that you gave to forgotten people like us. Seeing you on a monthly basis for the past 5-6 years has been one of the most rewarding parts of my sentence. God bless ya and I pray that you receive your reward of excellence and stewardship from the one who sees and knows all.

It had been very nice meeting you, thank you for your time.

Thank you for all you have done in support of us.

I just wanted to have a moment to express my sincere gratitude for all the time and effort yours put into supporting the group and myself your dedication and support have made a significant impact in my life and I truly appreciate everything you've done thanks you so much.

John,

Thank you for giving us your time, advice and guidance throughout the years whilst visiting us in Coldingley. You attended every month without fail. You are truly appreciated. Never doubt the difference you made. It's huge - and so is the gratitude in this little note.

Beyond grateful,

Thank you for your time and sharing your knowledge with us

Thank you Judge John for all your help and Support!!

Hope you are safe and well in the future mon you years

Dear Judge John

Thank you for all your support, knowledge & being brave, to get us access to decision makers. You have helped me to find a voice. Best wishes for the future.

Two retirement cards from HMP Coldingley (April 2024). (Judicial Monitoring)

defence. These explained that the discolouration of the steaks observed by the local authority inspector was attributable to the way in which they had been vacuum packed; a healthier colour infused the steaks when they were removed from their packaging, and they were objectively fit for human consumption. Other summonses, relating to the condition of the walls and work surfaces of the premises, were dismissed on the facts. However, the Bench included a law lecturer at Southampton University, coincidentally sharing my surname. Alec Samuels, no relation so far as we both believed, was a fellow member of JUSTICE. He was keen to demonstrate his legal acuity.

Having disposed of all save six of the outstanding summonses, the magistrates were faced with a submission from the defence that, as drawn, they disclosed no offence. The Council alleged a failure to provide soap, a supply of nail brushes and clean towels for each wash-hand basin in the kitchen, but identified each failure as a discrete offence. My submission was that the breach consisted of one offence only, namely a failure to provide each hand basin with the stipulated items. Because I was sure that this was the correct construction, I had called no evidence; and submitted that there was no offence of which the defendants could be convicted.

The Bench dealt with that submission in an unorthodox way. They announced, without any application for leave to amend being made by the prosecution, that the summonses would each be amended, so that each identified a failure to provide a supply of nail brushes, soap and towels; and thereupon convicted the defendants. They refused my application for an adjournment, so that I could call evidence to address the amended summonses. I advised an appeal.

In their case stated, the magistrates agreed with the defence submission, namely that it was an offence to fail to provide an adequate supply of each of the named items for use with a wash-hand basin, and not an offence to fail to provide the individual items. They went on to say, however, that 'it was appropriate to amend the informations; and that as Berni Inns had in no way been misled by the informations as originally laid ... an adjournment of the case was inappropriate'. The eventual appeal focused on the propriety of the conviction of Berni Inns on the three amended summonses. The upshot was that the Divisional Court agreed with my argument; and Berni Inns were acquitted of everything.

There was a happy sequel. My solicitors were so pleased with the outcome of this case that I became their standing counsel. In 1982, I embarked on the representation of their clients B&Q Ltd, in what became the Sunday trading saga. This lasted for some twelve years. and gets its own chapter, entitled 'Never on Sunday' (chapter 14).

———

One of my former colleagues in chambers used to say how disarming it was when he arrived as junior counsel for a consultation with a fashionable family Silk. He knew that his parents had been involved in acrimonious divorce proceedings. That memory did not objectively need to be stirred by being hailed, in front of his lay client, as 'You must be the child of that custody dispute!'

While I hope I never displayed such a crass reaction in relation to the offspring of my former matrimonial clients, I cannot mentally avoid being reminded of one of them when I watch TV. A well-known presenter is clearly the son of my erstwhile client since he looks just like him. Those heavily defended divorce proceedings lasted for almost three years, concluding – just after I took Silk – in April 1981.

There were a couple of memorable interludes. First, there was an appeal by the wife petitioner against the refusal of the registrar to require the co-respondent to file details of her own financial resources. (It seems bizarre today to think that the means of the husband's then girlfriend could possibly have been of relevance to the parties' squabble over ancillary relief.) The wife was represented by an erratic and explosive barrister: J.J. Davis. The co-respondent girlfriend, whose role both before the registrar and the judge in chambers was largely that of a bystander, was represented by my old school friend Christopher Sumner, subsequently a well-regarded judge of the Family Division.

During the hearing, Davis had helped himself to one of my law reports. At its conclusion, as he was tying up his papers and placing a strap round his law reports, I quietly asked for its return. 'It's not yours,' he snapped.

I invited him to look inside the front cover, where he would see my book-plate. He did so, thrust the volume forcibly towards me, and, in taking it from him, I inadvertently knocked off his glasses. He blazed up, believing that I had done so deliberately. He started to attack me with his fists, and was dragged away from me, in a bear hug, by the quick-thinking Sumner. Davis, whose temper was only equalled by his lack of judgment, appealed to the Court of Appeal. The further appeal[15] was dismissed.

There was a sequel. Some ten years later, I was sitting as a deputy judge in the Family Division. Fam 128 Davis represented a party in my list, and he passed a message via the court usher that I should recuse myself from hearing his application. I asked him to come into court to make whatever application he wished. He did so; but in a veiled way. I asked him if he had any authority on which he wished to rely. His answer was succinct: 'Wynne v. Wynne and Jeffers, My Lord.'

'Mr Davis,' I replied, 'that case has nothing to do with this one. While I vaguely remember it, I assure you that it will not affect my conclusion in this case.'

The hearing proceeded; I found against Davis; and to my surprise I received an uncharacteristically charming letter from him, congratulating me on how fairly I had dealt with his case.

---

15   Wynne v. Wynne and Jeffers [1980] 3 All ER 659

SILK

We are all Adam's children; but Silk makes the difference
Thomas Fuller (1654–1734)

Despite my busy junior practice, I had not thought about making an application for Silk before I was sent for by Melford Stevenson in 1978, when he expressed his appreciation for giving his son a 'normal' pupillage, rather than the hothouse one he had experienced in the commercial chambers of which Melford was a founder member (chapter 2, 'The Unexpected Mentor'). He encouraged me to do so. I had previously been asked to think about becoming a Recorder, since I had some experience of sitting in a public-facing capacity. I asked Melford if he would support an application from me. He replied: 'Yes, you must of course apply for a recordership and by all means name me as a referee. I would have thought the important question is whether and when you want to apply for Silk.' I explained that I simply was not ready: I was, after all, of only fourteen years' Call. Melford said: 'Well then, I shall make you a Recorder.' While he could not achieve this – appointment as a Recorder was in the gift of the sovereign – within a week or so I was sitting as a deputy County Court judge in Barnet County Court.

In 1980, I began to think that I need not be a junior for ever. The grindstone of pleadings and paperwork was inescapable; and it became a constant juggling act, not only to satisfy the proper demands of home and family life, but to identify which case would settle and which would stand up and fight.

There were two events that concentrated my mind on a prospective application. First, I had appendicitis, and I had been overdoing things.

Second, several of my contemporaries had been successful in their Silk applications in 1980; and I decided to seek advice, initially from Fred Lawton. His reply was not only positive, but he offered to be a referee.

I had made no reference in my letter of congratulation to Tom Bingham, appointed to the High Court bench in 1980, to our early encounter in the Court of Appeal: but with his good memory and personal charm, he emphasised it in his reply:

> '*Thank you very much for writing. And thank you for your good wishes. I well remember our encounter in the Court of Appeal, not least because (as I recall) you had the extreme bad taste to win.*
>
> *I shall very much hope to see your name in some shortly forthcoming list of new silks. Do not leave it too long. It does not ease the pressure very much, but it is much more fun and you will do very well.*'

Later that year, I sounded Tom out. He replied:

> '*It would of course be a great pleasure to support your application. I am delighted you are making it & I trust you will be successful. It would help me in due course if you could drop me a line giving some detail of where & how you spend your professional time. I shall then do all I can to help.*'

I went to see him. He was forthright: Yes, I should do so. 'Would you be one of my referees?' I asked, with some diffidence. 'Definitely not,' he replied. My disappointment must have shown on my face. 'That is because I so much want you to get it. You need support from those who are far more senior than I am.'

I did not wish to approach a second referee based on social acquaintance. Because I had appeared regularly before Lord Justice Ormrod, both at first instance and in the Court of Appeal, but we had had no social contact, I concluded that if he was prepared to support me, I was being supported for the right reasons. The fact that we had had some vigorous exchanges in court, when I had maintained my client's position in the face of some equally tenacious opposition from him, only underlined this. He generously agreed to support me.

I was sure that my mixed practice would need at least three applications before any success, so in April 1981 we set off for a family skiing holiday; and while still there, I received a telephone call from John Woodcock. 'There is an envelope here – it is the right size, and can I please open it?' I agreed; and the news, couched in arcane language, provided the confirmation.

I returned from Switzerland on Maundy Thursday, when the announcement was published; duly paid my £100 to the Paymaster General; and Jim Wadsworth (also successful as a Silk – 4 Paper Buildings was the only set in 1981 to boast two Silks) left me with a note that authorised me to make arrangements for a joint celebration in chambers, provided it cost no more than £100. As the then modest tradition was to limit any party to colleagues in chambers and immediate family members, that sum was more than sufficient. Today, it is routine to find Silks' celebrations costing well in excess of £10,000; and they are designed as marketing opportunities for chambers.

———

I remember little else about the ceremony, save for the gloomy comment made by the Lord Chancellor, Lord Hailsham: 'Some of you may succeed; most of you will fail; but do not blame me. By this time next year, I shall be dead.' Hailsham survived for a further twenty years. However, there was one fortunate meeting. Immediately ahead of me in the queue of new silks was Stephen Williamson, a bluff Yorkshireman with an exceptionally keen brain. We exchanged notes in relation to our respective practices: Steve was a criminal practitioner, exclusively in the North-East; and I had no criminal practice. As we parted after all the bowings as we processed round the courts, we agreed that it would 'be good to meet in court one of these days'. Little did we then know that we should be engaged, antlers locked, in one of the most remarkable solicitors' negligence actions of the era: Blueglade Ltd v. David Coates & Co.

A Leeds firm of solicitors was jealous of the fact that my clients had established a practice on their 'territory', and attempted, via a bogus negligence claim, to ruin them. The case had initially been adjourned after three days, when there was a mysterious delivery at court of highly relevant documents in a brown paper parcel. It started again before Mr Justice Michael Davies, and ran for a further two weeks. By the end of the nine-day trial, in March 1982, there were two sets of counsel on the plaintiffs' side of the court: those representing Blueglade, and another representing the plaintiffs' solicitors, who feared that the trial judge was going to refer them to the DPP. Because I was sure the judge could not find against my clients, and their insurers did not want to throw good money after bad, I called no evidence. This upset the judge immensely. He believed that a solicitor was duty-bound to give evidence when criticised; and to hide behind the commercial decision that to extend the trial would throw good money after bad was professionally improper.

It would have been relatively easy for Steve and me to fall out over this case: in fact, despite the need to resort to the use of every weapon in the forensic armoury while in the courtroom, a firm and sustained friendship between Steve and me persisted. When Steve was Treasurer of the Inner Temple, he generously invited Maxine and me to his Grand Day; and we met routinely to celebrate the anniversary of taking Silk, with our spouses, until shortly before his death.

Unfortunately, the judge's disapproval of my insurer clients spilled over into the next two cases that I conducted before him, long before he finally gave judgment for the defendants in Blueglade.

Claire Warren was aged seven when she accompanied her mother to work in her uncle's small butcher's shop. There was a mincing machine in the preparation room in which Claire's mother was working, only a few feet away from her daughter. Her uncle was not in the shop. Claire thrust her hand into the machine and sustained a traumatic amputation of her hand and forearm. I advised that the responsibility for Claire's care and safety was her mother's. However, the judge concluded that her uncle was responsible for the consequences of the accident, in that he had failed to ensure that she did not enter the preparation room during working hours, or that she was instructed not to play with or touch the mincing machine.

I confidently advised an appeal. When the appeal came on in October 1983, I was optimistic. My opponent, Paul Kennedy QC, seemed entirely relaxed. All his submissions to the Court of Appeal were treated with deferential respect. At the end of the argument, I asked for an explanation. 'I'm not supposed to tell you. They know, but it's still confidential, of my appointment as a QB judge.'

The outcome in Claire Warren's case can be explained by the sympathy due to a pretty little girl, maimed for life, when her uncle was represented by insurers. However, the next case in the list, while receiving equal sympathy, did not deserve it.

Mrs Liggins had slipped at work as a cleaner in 1973. She was not eligible for legal aid. Having consulted local solicitors, her claim was repudiated. The solicitors failed to bring proceedings within the limitation period. Unusually, and confident of defeating the claim on its merits, the insurers agreed not to claim that it was barred by limitation. I submitted that Mrs Liggins was only entitled to nominal damages.

The judge took a shine to Mrs Liggins. Before I cross-examined her, it was objectively obvious that he intended to award her substantial damages. On Day 2, I was instructed to offer her a reasonable sum, plus costs. The judge wanted to know why I had not offered indemnity costs. The short answer was that my offer of settlement included costs on the usual basis. The judge's subsequent criticism of both leading counsel, as well as of the defendant solicitors and their insurers, was the subject of extensive publicity in the national press.

The Blueglade judgment was reserved for over four months, with the judge trying to find some way in which to pin liability on the defendant solicitors. When Treasurer of Lincoln's Inn in 1991, some nine years later, Michael introduced himself to Maxine, saying: 'You must remember the great case of Blueglade.' Maxine replied, truthfully, that she did not know what he was talking about.

———

After the festivities around the Silk ceremony, I carried on much as before: a good deal of paperwork, winding down my old junior practice, and a succession of short conferences. The rule then was that a Silk could continue to settle pleadings for a year; but the iron curtain then fell. Webb v. BRB in May 1981 was a more than memorable personal injury case. Not only was it one of my first cases in the front row, but it had a sequel both in the Court of Appeal and the House of Lords that remains evergreen. Mr Webb was a trainee railway guard. His goods train started off; he fell under the wheels of the train and sustained brain damage as well as the loss of a leg. He could remember nothing of the accident. It seemed clear both to me and to my opponent, Swinton Thomas QC, that if the train started up when the guard was on board, he won; but if, as the defendants maintained, he was trying to jump on board a moving train, lost his footing and fell, his claim failed. There was no direct evidence. Mr Justice Staughton, a commercial practitioner with a speciality in shipping, had just been appointed to the Bench. He found that Mr Webb was not on the train when it pulled away, and that he was attempting to board the moving goods van. However, he concluded that the defendants were half to blame for the accident, in failing to give their employee adequate training.

The case was inevitably appealed. At the door of the Court of Appeal, Swinton Thomas offered a compromise: my client could keep one half of his award, plus the costs. To the lawyer, this seemed a reasonable offer; but Mr Webb would have none of it. He had lost not only his leg, but his working capacity; and that modest offer of one quarter of his total claim would be of little use to him. My persuasive powers, despite the new silk gown, were useless. In the Court of Appeal, the new member was Christopher Slade, hitherto a distinguished Chancery judge. Characteristically, he said nothing until Day 2, when he asked a devastating question: 'Mr Samuels, Mr Thomas, can you tell me where the lavatory was on this train?' As a goods train, it had no facility for its staff. How this information enabled Slade LJ to concur in the result, which sadly allowed the appeal of the British Railways Board, I have no idea.

By this time, my sympathies were fully engaged on behalf of the disappointed Mr Webb. A petition for leave to appeal to the House of Lords was presented. The appeal came on before a committee headed by Lord Diplock, who by then was breathless with emphysema, and not far from his eventual death. With long pauses, he made it plain that he was against me.

'Mr Samuels, this is a pure question of fact. Their Lordships are not – in the slightest – interested in a pure question of fact.'

I had arranged for Mr Webb to attend the House of Lords, and he was sitting awkwardly and uncomfortably on one of the Pugin chairs. No wells of human sympathy flowed in Court 1 that day. I was sorely tempted to reply: 'My Lords, my client, present in court, has lost his leg; and because of his brain damage will never work again. Those are, of course, pure questions of fact; and he hears what your Lordships have said about your lack of interest in questions of fact.'

But I chickened out.

———

On 8 January 1981, Mr Madhvani, a Ugandan Asian who, with his wife, had lost a final appeal against their deportation to India, killed his wife. Because his parents were British subjects, and their children had been born in the UK, the deportation order did not extend to the children, and it was envisaged that they would remain here. Mr Madhvani and his wife were liable to deportation to a country in which they knew no one. It was his case that the killing was a suicide pact; and that due to his depressive illness he was liable to be convicted not of murder, but of manslaughter by reason of diminished responsibility.

As a brand-new Silk, I was nominated by the Attorney General to conduct the prosecution shortly after acquiring my new status. The thinking was that the new Silks would be 'tried out', to see whether they had the right qualities ultimately to become High Court judges. This was before the creation in 1986 of the Crown Prosecution Service, and its insistence that only those who are experienced criminal lawyers would be responsible for the prosecution of the gravest offences.

I made what the professional officer at the DPP thought was a highly unusual request: 'May I have a consultation?'

'Why?'

'I want to discuss the case, both with you and my junior.'

'Will it take long?'

I explained that it would take only as long as was necessary; and I reassured him that it would not interfere unduly with his adult college class in Italian (which was his major concern). The consultation turned out to be of critical importance. My instructions were to accept a plea on the grounds of diminished responsibility, since three psychiatrists instructed on behalf of the defence supported that course. No one had examined the defendant on behalf of the Crown. In the consultation, I gleaned not only that the case had previously been listed before another High Court judge, who had refused to agree to the plea tendered by the defence, but that the new judge was Mr Justice Boreham, fresh from trying the case of the Yorkshire Ripper, Peter Sutcliffe. In that notorious case, the Attorney General had agreed, on a preliminary basis, to accept a plea on the basis of diminished responsibility; the judge had refused; and Sutcliffe went on to be convicted of all the murders with which he had been charged. Had I offered to accept the plea, and before that judge, my reputation as a prosecutor would have been extinguished before it began.

Those facts had been omitted from my instructions. I advised that arrangements should be made for the defendant to be seen by a psychiatrist instructed by the DPP. In the result, Dr Paul Bowden concluded that the defendant was not suffering from a disease causing an abnormality of mind before the killing. Upset, depressed and unhappy he most certainly was; but, inconveniently for the defendant, he had written a detailed letter that explained his then state of mind. In the light of what Dr Bowden stated, the case was bound to proceed.

The defendant was represented by Barry Hudson QC, a criminal Silk of the 'old school'. In the robing room, Hudson demanded to know why I was not prepared to accept his client's plea on the basis of diminished responsibility, supported as it was by the evidence of three consultant forensic psychiatrists. I stood my ground.

'I have been doing this work since before you were born,' he thundered.

'May I correct you? You were called in 1943, and I was born in 1940.'

Hudson glowered at me. 'Do you want to see the judge?' He continued to mutter – and his false teeth clacked. However, on we went with the trial.

Despite the conflict in the medical evidence, it was difficult not to feel sympathy for this defendant. There was the clearest evidence that he had tried to kill himself after killing his wife.

The trial lasted three days. Quite apart from the conflict over the medical evidence, three unrelated features stand out. At breakfast on Day 2, David Cocks (by then a senior junior representing the defendant) asked me if I had heard the commotion in the night. I had not. Barry Hudson had been taken to hospital by ambulance with a bleeding ulcer. I asked solicitously whether I was responsible. David carried on with the trial.

Asked to lunch by the judge, and making small talk with Lady Boreham, I congratulated her on her diligence on sitting in court throughout. Her response amazed me: 'I have been to court with Leslie every day since he was first called to the Bar.' My subsequent experiences with Lady Boreham, always in civil cases, wholly confirmed that; and the wise advocate tailored his submissions to be as attractive to her, sitting alongside her husband on the bench, as they were to him.

Finally, and as I was more recently reminded by my then young junior (now herself a senior Silk), just before I made my speech to the jury, I walked around the cloisters of Norwich Cathedral, reciting *The Ballad of Reading Gaol*:

> *Yet each man kills the thing he loves*
> *By each let this be heard;*
> *The coward does it with a kiss,*
> *The brave man with a sword!*

Mr Madhvani was convicted; and in May 1994, there was a news item about him. He had remained mute in prison. He refused all visits, and never saw his children or family members again. Tiring of this regime, he decided to starve himself to death; and following the refusal of all food and water, he died.

I trailed earlier the comment made by Sir John Arnold, by then President of the Family Division, when I took Silk (chapter 9, 'Transplanting the Sapling'; but I had no reason to anticipate the arrival of the letter, just over two months later, from the private secretary to the Lord Chancellor, which informed me that 'following consultation with the President, the Lord Chancellor has it in mind to add your name to the list of Silks who may be invited to sit in the Family Division as Deputy High Court judges'. I accepted the invitation, and started to sit in the Family Division shortly afterwards.

In time, I progressed to sit as a deputy High Court judge in the Queen's Bench Division as well as the Family Division, and I found this work equally rewarding. It came as something of a disappointment when in 1989 the President, Sir Stephen Brown, told me that I was no longer eligible to sit as a deputy in the Family Division.

Shortly after that, and following the personal intervention of Lord Justice Tasker Watkins behind the scenes, in early 1990 I was told, to the embarrassment of Mr Justice Michael Davies, judge in charge of the Queen's Bench list, that he had been directed by Tasker to pause my sittings as a deputy High Court judge. This was a direct consequence of what Tasker had learned during the hearing, in December 1989, of the Bar Council case described in chapter 13, 'Rehabilitation'.[16] Until this issue was resolved, I could not sit as a deputy in the High Court; but my sittings in the Crown Court as a Recorder were uninterrupted. Thereafter, I resumed sitting as a deputy in the QBD for the next seven years.

––––––––

The early part of my first Long Vacation in Silk could not have been more different. With considerable courage, Maxine entrusted David and Adam to me for a week; and we spent it on a canal boat, navigating (if that is the right word) the Wey navigation to its blunt end at Godalming. A phone call to Maxine passed on a message to ring chambers. This told me that I

––––––––

16   R v. General Council of the Bar ex parte Percival [1991] QB 212

was to receive my first brief in the House of Lords[17] – I emerged from the phone box, metaphorically feeling 10 feet tall.

————

With hindsight, Cornwall, and particularly the village of Polzeath on the north coast, has played an immense role in our family life. I first went there in 1947 with my parents, and took my earliest steps as a surfer on a wooden bellyboard. Serendipity brought us back, when David was two weeks old, and we wrecked the shiny wheels of his new pram on the broad sands of Polzeath beach. With our family, including four grandchildren, we have spent annual and more frequently regular holidays there. While probably out of sequence, the next part of this chapter may show a corner of my personality of relevance to my later role as a monitor.

As an Assistant Boundary Commissioner, holding a lengthy public inquiry in Plymouth, it made sense to use our Polzeath home as a base. En route to Plymouth, I popped into the village newsagent to buy a news-paper. The proprietor, whom I then merely greeted anonymously in my holiday clothing, amazed me when she replied, 'Mr Samuels, you do look smart wearing a tie'! The hearing in Plymouth Town Hall was memorable too. There was an unfenced gap of about four feet from the Lord Mayor's dais; and at the conclusion of my opening remarks, I duly fell off.

Once on the Circuit Bench, I asked – like many other London-based judges – to sit for a few weeks a year on the Western Circuit. I was lucky to do so in Truro, a magnificent building, with welcoming staff and a highly supportive local Bar. I realised that there was a vacancy for a resident judge. I broached it with Maxine. She knew that Truro was a small pond, and I would never settle to bridge parties and local gossip. Very wisely, she said I could come home each weekend. That was clearly impracticable.

To the dismay of many London-based judges, sittings on the Western Circuit were terminated by Igor Judge, as Senior Presiding Judge, because a particular London-based judge was so unpleasant to the local Bar. It was

———

17   R v. Hillingdon LBC ex parte Islam [1983] 1 AC 688

more politically correct to stop the practice for everyone than to grapple directly with the presenting problem.

I produced a lot of verse in Polzeath, and include one piece as an example.

Polzeath Beach – August Bank Holiday

The rock, primeval guardian of pre-history's secret store
Lay smooth and glistening in the dew as dawn bewitched the shore.
Below the beach stretched level as the ebbing water spanned
From headland crag to headland bluff – a Hall and Co of sand.

That scene at 7: but the sun, now sullen, now a tease,
At 10 will bring the Emmets out, broad busts and hairy knees.
The bay, once wide enough to lose the fleets of Allied powers,
Will fill to Frith capacity in a brace of sweaty hours.

The sports parental hollow-based, the sports connubial dry,
The dogs, the ice cream van, the kites, the leaden, threatening sky,
The surf wind-tossed, the outraged gull, the screams of queried glee,
The plunge, the board, the questioning, the false identity.

Among these thoughts, an incident to gel the squamous brain,
To check the random shrimp-like thoughts bound straightways down the drain:
A family, no different, descend to find their place
As Grandpa slips upon the rock and falls flat on his face.

The blood (and there's a lot of it) the shale incarnadines.
While poet – helpless – stands and stares, and ponders plodding lines.
But as he stares, and others aid – he finds a chord so rare:
A note of human sympathy, to human frailty there.

The sorrow of a child's mute grief as down she turns to shed
A glut of shocked and generous tears about that well-loved head.

The patient will recuperate, the happening at an end;
His wounds well stitched, his bruise resolved, the trauma soon will
mend.
The chord of human sympathy it was that quickly died,
And washed away, with all the blood, the very next high tide.

A few necessary explanations:
- Hall & Co, sand and gravel merchants throughout south-east England, were my initial employers when I was a management trainee in 1959 (see chapter 3, 'Growing Up').
- 'Emmet' is the conventional term in Cornwall for a non-local tourist.
- W.P. Frith was a Victorian artist. *The Derby Day* is his most famous crowd scene.

I simply cannot now remember why the London Borough of Hillingdon latched on to me as a brand-new Silk. Not only were they instructing me to represent them in the House of Lords, but, potentially even more significantly, I was asked to advise on a forensic challenge to the new fair pricing policy for London Transport presented by the GLC in the aftermath of the election in May 1981. This had been the linchpin of Ken Livingstone's election campaign. I could immediately see the potential value of such a challenge for a new Silk in terms of the Silk's career; what continued to puzzle me was any basis upon which it could legitimately be argued, in the context of a judicial review, that the policy was liable to successful challenge in the Divisional Court. After considerable heart-searching, outlined in a lengthy opinion, I concluded that it could not, and that were the GLC to raise a supplementary precept to pay for their proposed policy, this would not be challengeable on the grounds that it was beyond the Council's statutory powers; and the margin of appreciation would be left to a council as to how to exercise those powers.

My reluctant opinion was not shared by the London Borough of Bromley, who, advised by other counsel, embarked on a challenge. I discussed the basis for the challenge informally with David Widdicombe

QC, the vastly more experienced local government Silk instructed by Bromley. His response was relaxed: 'I have no clear idea, but I feel sure that something will crop up once we get to the Court of Appeal.' How right he was.

While his challenge was initially unsuccessful in the Divisional Court, it succeeded in the Court of Appeal before Lord Denning, Oliver LJ and Watkins LJ. Should any student of twentieth-century judgments be tempted to think that the courts were blind to political considerations, the language in which Lord Denning and, more particularly, Watkins LJ expressed themselves[18] shows pellucid hostility to the decision-makers, as well as to the decision.

It seems strange that I now remember so little about my first leading brief in the House of Lords. The hearing lasted four days; but this was because it was listed with another case raising similar issues under the Housing (Homeless Persons) Act 1977.[19] For pragmatic reasons, that appeal preceded the Hillingdon appeal. The Lords more clearly identified the merits in that appellant's case than Lord Denning had done. His conclusion that Mr Islam 'occupied' a home in Bangladesh at the same time as he was resident in Uxbridge, on the grounds that his wife and family resided in that home in Bangladesh, and that when they arrived in England to share his accommodation, which was only suitable for one person, he had made himself, and them, intentionally homeless, is objectively out of kilter with so many Denning merits-based judgments.

———

In November 1981, the appeal of Langdale v. Danby began before Lord Denning, Dunn and Fox LJJ. In 1964, Mr Langdale and his wife had purchased an estate near Hull that included a cottage. They thought the cottage might in the future be a suitable home for one of their three daughters. They offered the cottage for sale at a price of £2,650, on terms that they would reserve an option to repurchase at the same price within

18   See [1982] 1 All ER 129 at pp 136 and 149 respectively

19   Din and Another v. London Borough of Wandsworth [1983] 1 AC 657

twenty-one years. Mr Danby, who had done some work on the cottage, urgently needed accommodation. His employer introduced him to Mr Langdale. Mr Danby agreed to purchase the cottage on the terms proposed but could not afford the purchase price. On Mr Danby's behalf, Mr Langdale procured a mortgage advance for the bulk of the purchase price, with a second mortgage in favour of his wife and himself for the balance. He undertook all the conveyancing for no fee. In 1979, the Langdales exercised their option, offering to pay Mr Danby £3,500 above the original purchase price.

Mr Danby refused to sell. Proceedings for specific performance of the option agreement were combined with the County Court proceedings initiated by Mr Danby. In December 1979, specific performance was granted in favour of the Langdales. It was only when the Langdales sought to enforce their judgment, after a lengthy series of delays orchestrated by Mr Danby's solicitor, that Mr Danby sought, almost two years later, to appeal.

Before I was instructed, leave to appeal out of time had already been granted. Gerald Godfrey QC, a formidable Chancery practitioner, acted for Mr Danby. The substantive appeal came on for hearing two weeks later. The appeal succeeded; and the subsequent history is rehearsed in the judgment of Lord Bridge in the House of Lords.[20] That appeal was unanimously allowed.

My clients had been pilloried in the press over the case; and their daughter, for whom the cottage had been intended, attempted suicide. This pitiable story was rehearsed in detail in the judgment of Lord Bridge; and the Langdales were awarded all their costs. Mr Langdale came to see me in consultation, to discuss whether he had any remedy against the media, which had so vilified him. At the conclusion of the consultation, and to my amazement, Mr Langdale produced a personal letter written to him by Lord Denning. The notable facts are (i) the timing of the decision of the House of Lords, which was published on 29 July 1982; (ii) the fact that Denning retired as Master of the Rolls in a memorable ceremony on

---

20 Langdale v. Danby [1982] 3 All ER 129 (HL) at pp 132–140

30 July 1982 (I was present); and (iii) that Denning chose to write to Mr Langdale on 1 August 1982 in his own hand: note the date.

> *'Dear Mr Langdale*
>
> *I am glad to see that the House of Lords have allowed your appeal and I do hope you get all your costs from the Legal Aid Fund.*
>
> *I see that they thought it 'surprising' that the Court of Appeal gave Mr Danby leave to appeal on 6 October 1981: and I think we owe you an explanation. We (were) very much influenced by the 'blaze of publicity' that the case had received; and felt that, if leave to appeal were refused, it would look to the public as if the administration of justice itself was at fault in allowing a wrong decision to be made, and then refusing leave to appeal. Looking back on it, I can see that we ourselves were mistaken, and should not have been influenced by the 'blaze of publicity'.*
>
> *I realise that this must have involved you in much anxiety and distress and I am very sorry that this has been so. But I am glad to see that you have been vindicated by the House of Lords.'*

Professional success and the interests of my clients were not the only thing on my mind in the autumn of 1981. About that time, Dad had been diagnosed with lung cancer, and my predominant concern was to do what I could to promote his welfare, and to enable Mum to cope with the inevitable. Dad had much enjoyed the fact that I had taken Silk and was there with Mum at the celebrations. I clearly remember a one-day appeal in the Court of Appeal when I managed to turn the argument on my reply. As the three Lords Justices rose to retire, I knew we had won. I turned round to my junior and said: 'That was OK, wasn't it', and to my amazement saw Dad in the public seats. That remains a magical moment, I think for both of us.

My diary from 1982 only hints at what was growing emotional pressure. I had boasted of having broad shoulders. In addition to the requirements of practice, Dad's deteriorating health and the need to be in chambers and in Reigate virtually simultaneously, there was a chambers meeting on 13 May (about which I comment below).

On 13 June I took off for Norwich, where I was due to prosecute a further murder. By this time, I was actively worried about whether Dad would survive. Torn as I was between professional and personal responsibilities, I shall never forget that drive. I stopped every half hour or so, whenever I found a public telephone box. On arrival in Norwich, I was delighted to learn that the Crown psychiatrist was asking for the trial to be postponed; and I thought I had a cast-iron reason for an adjournment. I asked to see the judge. I explained the request of the psychiatrist. Mr Justice McCowan was unimpressed. Disappointed, and with diffidence, I mentioned my father's condition. His response was: 'John, of course you must have an adjournment.' I have never been so grateful. I went straight back to Reigate; and Dad died a few days later. Meanwhile, in addition to making all the necessary administrative arrangements following his death, I conducted the House of Lords appeal in Langdale v. Danby on 23 and 24 June; and on 25 June I represented B&Q Ltd in the first substantive hearing of the Sunday trading campaign.

———

Prior to the chambers meeting on 13 May, there had been a particular irritation. As a self-employed group of idiosyncratic individuals, the Bar does not promote cooperation among its members. I had arranged to move my room, from a rather dismal annexe to a really pleasant room with a garden view. The new room was refurbished, and I bought a new carpet. This was duly fitted, while I was out in court. The old carpet was piled up, in the rain, in the basement area. I returned from court, for a consultation in my newly refurbished room. As a 'joke', the filthy, rain-soaked carpet had been piled up in the middle of the floor, on top of the brand-new carpet. I knew the culprit; and I was not amused, as I struggled to ensure that my room was ready for the consultation.

The purpose of the chambers meeting, which I could not attend, was to discuss a novel system of contributions to chambers. Hitherto, our contributions were based on an agreed percentage of our receipts for the preceding quarter; but it was now proposed that contributions would be based on receipts for the preceding twelve months. Since I had taken Silk twelve months earlier, the bulk of my junior earnings had flooded in, so that by the end of May 1982 my annual receipts were over £107,000: small beer today, but a very substantial sum at the time. I had two reasons to be worried. First, I was concerned that my earnings in Silk would not keep step with those I had enjoyed as a junior, and might significantly fall; and second, I knew I was going to be financially responsible for twenty-four-hour nursing care for my father, as soon as I could arrange for his return from hospital; and had no idea how long this would be needed.

My dismay was perceived by John Woodcock. John was reluctant to remain at 4 Paper Buildings; and as is the habit of experienced clerks, he let it be known within the gossipy world in which the Bar operates that I was also dissatisfied. Initially, he sought to persuade me to leave chambers and start afresh with him; but I refused.

Knowing that John wanted to move, I arranged an introduction to Tony Hoolahan QC, the head of specialist defamation chambers, and our friend and neighbour in Richmond. The meeting was productive, and John left 4 Paper Buildings in the summer of 1982. He left behind his first junior, Stephen Smith, who was promoted to become the senior clerk. He remains at 4 Paper Buildings (now Hailsham Chambers) and has become one of the doyens of barristers' clerks. When we now meet, he tells me that he can never understand why I ever left!

I was invited to meet Ian Percival QC, then Solicitor General, which led to a meeting with Paul Batterbury, the administrator of the chambers of which Percival was the head, on 1 June; and ultimately a meeting with the members of Percival's chambers at 3 Hare Court a fortnight later. The timing of these events could not have been worse.

TEMPTATION

I couldn't help it. I can resist everything except temptation.
Oscar Wilde (1854–1900), *Lady Windermere's Fan*

If only...

How often has that two-word thought bubbled up? Standing at the crossroads, you have gone rushing down the cul-de-sac instead of taking the highway. If only I had accepted the advice of Arthur Armitage, President of Queens', to pursue a pupillage with Harry Woolf. If only I had not flounced out of chambers on 1 April 1966. And if only I had not, infuriated by a trivial incident over a new carpet, exacerbated by the proposal to modify the basis on which my contribution to chambers expenditure would be collected, let it be known that I was even contemplating a move to other chambers, there would have been no meeting with Ian Percival, and no decision to leave in June 1982. Hindsight provides a wonderful viewing platform; but I echo the more recent comments made by Stephen Smith, Michael Pooles and Martin Spencer (both the latter having become in their turn head of what is now the successful Hailsham Chambers) that my move was inexplicable at the time, and ultimately disastrous.

I have explained how gossip about my dissatisfaction reached the ears of Ian Percival, and he sent for me. He told me that Paul Batterbury, who was running his chambers at 3 Hare Court while he was a law officer, would shortly receive a judicial appointment, and that he would not return to the Bar. In due course, he expected either promotion within government or a senior judicial appointment. Were I to move to 3 Hare Court, I could expect to be its Head of Chambers shortly. The temptation was obvious. A subsequent meeting with Paul Batterbury confirmed what I had been told by Percival; and when I met some of the members of 3 Hare Court informally, all seemed to go very well.

Paul was a long-serving major in the TA – his communications owed much to the military style – and as an administrator he was sound and conscientious. The chambers at 3 Hare Court had for some time planned to encourage the arrival of a 'mythical silk', which turned out to be me; and I was offered the largest and most attractive room I could have imagined: airy, bright and with a good outlook over Middle Temple Lane.

The minutes of a chambers meeting held on 19 July 1982 (which I did not attend) recorded that my 'acceptance of Sir IP's invitation to join Chambers was unanimously approved, and the meeting was told that he would arrive in Chambers sometime in September 1982'.

I only learned of the basis upon which Ian Percival had delegated responsibility to Paul Batterbury for the running of chambers while he was acting as Solicitor General once I succeeded to that role, because the document outlining this, prepared by Percival, was in the chambers minute book. It read:

1. *In the traditional manner IP remains head of Chambers, not merely in name but continuing as the tenant and retaining ultimate control as under.*
2. *PB will continue to deal with the day-to-day running of Chambers much as before, only more so in that broadly speaking he will only consult IP:*
   a. *On the granting of new tenancies, and then hopefully with specific proposals agreed by all as to who should be given seats; and*
   b. *On any matter which appears to him to present problems of which IP should be aware and/or which IP must himself resolve.*

Even now, this is all as clear as mud to me: but its ambiguity became more relevant.

———

I moved into 3 Hare Court on 16 September 1982. Following Dad's death and his funeral, Mum had initially stayed with us in Richmond; but she then stayed with a supportive friend for the rest of the summer, before returning to Reigate. I encouraged her to sell the family home, and to purchase a flat locally. Progress was slow.

However, despite concerns about my mother, I flourished in the new arrangements at 3 Hare Court. Paul Batterbury continued with his role as chambers administrator: there was a delay in his appointment to the Circuit Bench, and this suited me well, as he continued the administrative role while I concentrated on my practice. Alan Brewer, my new clerk, had only recently been appointed, and he was as anxious as John Woodcock had been to promote the professional interests of the newly arrived Silk.

By the end of December 1982, in addition to the provision of routine opinions and consultations, I had, in my first term in the new chambers, undertaken nine briefs in the Queen's Bench Division; two in the Family Division; and one each in the Court of Appeal and the House of Lords. The expectations of the chambers in relation to their 'mythical silk' were being met.

On 13 June 1983, Mrs Thatcher reshuffled her team, and sacked Percival as her Solicitor General. Contrary to his expectations, she did not provide him with a judicial appointment.

There were two immediate consequences. First, I was asked to see Percival in his flat in the Temple. I told him that, following a chambers meeting, it was the unanimous decision of members of chambers that he was unwelcome to return. To my surprise and horror, Percival began to cry. It was a long time since I had seen an adult male in tears, and I had not expected this, more particularly from an MP and recent minister. He assured me that he would not interfere in any way with the running of chambers. I knew, from a letter sent by Percival to the chambers' bank when Paul Batterbury was appointed to the Circuit Bench (and copied to me), that Percival told the bank I 'had stepped into Paul's shoes'; and I also knew from the circular prepared by Paul, dispatched to all his solicitors on the day his appointment was announced, that he had told them: 'As you may know, I have been acting as head of these Chambers at the request of the Solicitor General ... and that responsibility will now fall to Mr John Samuels QC.'

The second development is reinforced by my contemporary note of a subsequent meeting in chambers. Despite an overwhelming reluctance from those members of chambers who had experienced Percival's conduct as Head of Chambers prior to his appointment as Solicitor General to agree to his return to practise in chambers, I persuaded the meeting that the personal assurances I had received from him, coupled with the problems we might face if his return was rejected, should carry the day.

For at least a year, there were no problems. Maxine and I held a party for all members of chambers at our home in July: not only did Percival and his wife attend, but he swam vigorously in our pool at its conclusion. We repeated the summer party in 1984, and it was an equal success. In 1985, Percival told me that it was no longer 'appropriate' to hold such an event at our home, and that he would do so instead. He never did.

On 23 July I took off for a week-long visit to Houston and Dallas, to pursue what developed into memorable litigation on behalf of Robert Ogden, a millionaire client from Yorkshire, against Arthur Andersen LLP. The claim was based on the fraudulent misrepresentation of the Texas partner in this once highly respectable firm of accountants, who enjoyed a worldwide practice and a stellar reputation. After the Enron case, however, the Arthur Andersen worldwide practice disintegrated. Meanwhile, and to the surprise of all, our client's claim was successful. I believed that, despite the constant hard work, all was going well.

The beginning of August 1983 marked the start of what turned out to be another saga: the Queen's Hotel fire. Instructed on behalf of insurers, I confidently advised them to repudiate liability in relation to a fire that had destroyed the Queen's Hotel in Ramsey, Isle of Man, earlier that year. The facts were striking. A wedding party had taken over the hotel at the end of March. After the wedding, the proprietor insisted that everyone should leave the hotel for an afternoon promenade. Despite the blustery weather, everyone did so. The proprietor led the walk, taking his pet cat on a lead. Within less than ten minutes of the party's departure, a major fire broke out; and a subsequent investigation found not only the use of accelerants, but multiple seats of fire. There was evidence that at least one unidentified person was spotted running from the scene. In consultation, my solicitors asked whether it was right to repudiate liability in a fire fraud without direct evidence to support it. I replied: 'It's a small island: we'll get the evidence.' Some twelve years later, with masses of additional evidence in relation to the impecuniosity of the proprietor, and the insolvency of the corporate entity responsible for the hotel, we never did. However, the litigation was resolved in favour of insurers, despite protracted and often ill-tempered interlocutory hearings and appeals, because the plaintiff company was unable to satisfy our requirement for security for the defendant's costs.

What are the highlights of a twelve-year saga? First, my finally successful attempt to be specially admitted to the Manx Bar, to represent insurers. This was opposed by those representing the plaintiff company, on the basis that it was 'such a straightforward case' that anyone could handle it. My response to the Lieutenant Governor, who had rejected the application, was to ask him to supply reasons, which would be challenged before the Privy Council. He backed down; and the certificate of my admission remains as a framed souvenir.

As a visiting Silk, I had the luxury not only of an English solicitor, but also two juniors from the Manx Bar to support me in the succession of interlocutory hearings. The senior junior, Geoffrey Karran, went on to become the President of the Manx Bar; and his articled clerk, David Doyle, became the senior Deemster on the island. We last met in Guernsey in February 2016, when I was taking part in an advocacy training event and he was sitting as an ad hoc judge of the Court of Appeal. We had a couple of meals together. He said, flatteringly, that he had learned more from me than from any other advocate!

Second, while staying with my solicitor, Trevor Chamberlain, on one of our innumerable visits to the Isle of Man, our evening meal was interrupted by someone who had much direct evidence to convey about the causation of the fire. Knowing how critical it might be to avoid any contact with a potential witness, I left Trevor to interview him alone. At breakfast the next morning, Trevor told me the good news and the bad news. The good news was that the informant had made a comprehensive statement, identifying in detail all we had suspected about 'bonfire Billy', the former mayor of the town of Ramsey and the proprietor of the Queen's Hotel. The bad news was that he had adamantly refused to sign the statement.

———

There were no grounds for thinking that any problems existed in relation to my running of chambers, as their *de facto* head, until well into 1985. Percival then began to press me for details of what members of chambers were earning, so that he could assess how successful he was in comparison with others' – and specifically my own – earnings. I refused this information. It had always been the practice from the time when my predecessor was administering the chambers to keep such information confidential; and only the person responsible for assessing the contribution to chambers expenses and the senior clerk needed to know this. However, to my pleasure, not only did all members of chambers thrive, but their income had risen considerably. This had positive consequences. With the benefit of hindsight, I should have disclosed the existence of what was becoming a healthy surplus. However, Alan Brewer persuaded me that it was not in the interests of chambers that I should do so. This was because some of the more senior members of chambers had been historically parsimonious about making any but the most modest contribution to the rent and levy; and if, as we hoped, chambers were to move to more prestigious and more expensive accommodation, a healthy balance in the account would be a condition precedent to doing so successfully.

In July 1985 there was a surplus of £15,000 in the account (in the sense of not being required for immediate expenditure), and that sum was transferred to a deposit account with Barclays, the chambers' bankers. I had a personal account with a building society, and I knew that the interest achievable on that account significantly exceeded the interest being paid on the Barclays deposit account. Alan Brewer and I made arrangements, as the sole signatories on the chambers account, to transfer that sum to a new account with the building society. Because I had no wish to alter the current description of the account, we identified this as an account in the name of 'the Trustees of Sir Ian Percival QC Chambers account' (which, as the sole signatories, we were).

Shortly after Christmas 1985, Percival, without notice to Alan Brewer or me, transferred £20,000 from the chambers bank account to a deposit account. Alan only discovered this when he received the bank statement early in January. Alan had drawn a quantity of year-end cheques on the current account, which I had signed, in the belief that funds would be available in the current account. Alan arranged with the manager of Barclays to return the £20,000 to the current account. This episode undoubtedly exacerbated what was becoming an unhappy relationship between Percival and me; and the fact that Alan also disliked the way in which he had been treated by Percival over his own employment contract only added fuel to the fire. Recognising as we both did that there remained £5,000 more than immediate requirements, Alan and I transferred that sum to the building society account; and made a further similar payment in March 1986.

Percival continued to press for information. He applied to Barclays for duplicate bank statements; and when these disclosed the existence of the two cheque payments of £5,000, he acquired the paid cheques from the bank. He flourished them at me. I should have brought his conduct to a chambers meeting immediately: but, in a vain attempt to keep a lid on things, I repaid these two amounts on the same date to the chambers current account, and said nothing.

When I next reported on financial matters in detail, at a meeting that took place in November 1986, I provided chambers with a comprehensive account of what the surplus had been, and where it had been located. This was designed to draw a line under the financial disagreements between Percival and me. Sadly, that was not the case. On 4 February 1987, without notice to me, Percival purported to dismiss me from my role as administrator of chambers. There was an immediate response from chambers as a whole, demanding an urgent meeting; and following that meeting, I was unanimously reinstated as the chambers administrator, on the nomination of Percival. He recognised the strength of feeling against him; but he was biding his time.

On 5 June 1987, at a time when I was sitting as a Recorder, my court clerk said that Percival wished to speak to me urgently. I interrupted a summing up; and he told me that he was requiring me to leave chambers forthwith. He said that I would discover the reasons when I returned to chambers. On my return, I discovered that he had written to every member of chambers, and had attached to his letter a bound dossier extending to more than 160 pages. This came out of a clear blue sky. It was well known that I was just about to undertake some heavy litigation, on which I would be engaged for the next few weeks. Meanwhile, Percival told the members of chambers that from his contacts with other Inns, he could confirm that no accommodation in any Inn would be available for me or any member of chambers who wished to accompany me.

Fortunately, Lincoln's Inn came to our rescue. The bulk of our chambers had been offered excellent accommodation, to which we and all the clerks successfully moved in September 1987; and we were joined there by other barristers with good practices. Many members of the judiciary, including Tom Bingham and the Treasurer of Lincoln's Inn, attended our happy opening party. However, on 30 December 1987, over six months after his formal dissolution of the previous chambers, Percival presented a formal complaint to the Bar Council, asserting that I had been in breach of professional conduct.

REHABILITATION

The only person you are destined to become is the person you decide to be.
Ralph Waldo Emerson (1803–1882)

In January 1988, the Bar Council faced an unprecedented dilemma. Ian Percival had accused me of professional misconduct: an accusation that, if established, would have ended my career. I was not only a well-regarded head of a successful and expanding chambers but had played a leading role in the Bar Council and its predecessor for six years; was a member of its Professional Standards Committee; and chaired an important regulatory committee of the Bar Council and the Inns of Court. The Bar Council knew that Percival was not only a former Solicitor General but was soon to be the Treasurer of the Inner Temple.

The Bar Council instructed Lionel Read, a leading Silk, to advise what, if any, disciplinary issues the copious documentation disclosed. He advised:

'*The highest one could reasonably put the last sentence of Samuels's note of 5 February 1987 is that it was less than frank. In my opinion, therefore, a charge could not properly be preferred alleging dishonest conduct or accordingly professional misconduct on that basis. There can, in my view, be no halfway house on this point. It is all or nothing, and in my view it is nothing. The third alternative ground of complaint ... is that Samuels failed to observe the ethics and etiquette of the profession and the terms of paragraph 6 (c) of the Code. This is hazy territory. No breach of any of the other many paragraphs of the Code is or can be alleged ... I have to say that any charge based on breach of ethics and etiquette, if prima facie sustainable, could not go to the extremity of professional misconduct.*'

Lionel Read concluded:

> '*The PCC should, in my opinion, review the whole matter in the light of this advice and the draft charges I have settled. They will want to consider whether even those I have suggested should in the event be pressed. A matter of importance must, no doubt, be the attitude and reaction of Percival as the complainant. He might well not wish to pursue the matter on this limited basis.*'

Somehow, what should have remained confidential within the Bar Council became known to Percival. Despite the heavy hint from Lionel Read that, viewed objectively, there were no grounds for criticism, the Bar Council chose, on pragmatic grounds, to pursue the summary charge of 'a failure to comply with the ethics and etiquette of the profession'.

Percival was outraged. He instructed solicitors, who launched unprecedented legal proceedings for judicial review against the Bar Council. Those proceedings claimed that the Bar Council was compelled to pursue a charge of professional misconduct against me.

The proceedings meandered slowly through the courts. The Bar Council, while resisting the application, omitted to take the obvious point that the application was well out of time. Strategically, given that a former law officer was challenging the way in which the Bar Council was dealing with his complaint, the most appropriate way to respond was to encourage the court to conclude, as it ultimately held, that it was for the Bar Council in the exercise of its discretion to interpret and to apply its own disciplinary code and procedures. This was the thrust of the Bar Council case presented with his usual brilliance by Sydney Kentridge QC.

I was not a party to the Divisional Court proceedings, accepting advice that I should remain as far removed as possible from them. What I could not have anticipated was the extent to which I should be named, and shamed, during the proceedings by the press. Disciplinary proceedings were at that time invariably anonymous; and even in cases that resulted in a sentence of disbarment, when a challenge was made before judges as

Visitors to the Inns of Court, those cases were always reported, if a law report was appropriate at all, anonymously.

By contrast, when Percival's challenge to the Bar Council was before the Divisional Court, Lord Justice Tasker Watkins went out of his way to emphasise his own view of my lack of deference to a Silk of almost twenty years my senior, a former law officer and (he might, in honesty, have added) a prominent Freemason. The case predictably achieved widespread publicity in the national press, both during the hearing and when the reserved judgment was published in December 1989.[21] Following the publication of the judgment, my solicitor, Stuart Benson, courteously asked the law reporter why the case was not being reported anonymously, in accordance with precedent. 'On the express instructions of Tasker Watkins LJ' was the unexpected answer.

Once the judgment of the Divisional Court had been published, almost two years after the presentation of Percival's complaint, arrangements were made for a disciplinary hearing. The supervising judge directed:

> *'The case can be properly dealt with without oral evidence on either side. It is directed that witnesses' evidence take the form of written statements and that there be no cross-examination. After service of the papers on the Tribunal beforehand, the matter can be put adequately by counsel by way of submissions at a hearing lasting one day.'*

The hearing took place on Saturday 28 April 1990. It was exceptionally difficult to find a High Court judge who did not know both Percival and me. The hearing took place in the Parliament Chamber of the Inner Temple. Before it began, Percival came in and insisted that, as Treasurer, he was entitled to be present. While his application was rejected, it had the effect of unnerving everyone: both because it was unexpected (the privacy of the proceedings had been emphasised at the previous Directions hearing) and because of the sustained tenacity with which it was pressed, by the Treasurer of the Inn in which the hearing was taking place.

---

21   R v. General Council of the Bar ex parte Percival [1991] 1 QB 212

The start of the hearing was necessarily delayed. By lunchtime, all submissions had been completed; and the tribunal was left to deliberate. Everyone expected a conclusion early in the afternoon. The adjournment, however, dragged on. At about 7.30 p.m. we were asked to return. The tribunal had been unable to reach a decision on which they agreed. The chairman announced that they would reconvene five days later.

The chairman then handed down a twelve-page typed document entitled 'Reasons for Findings'. He stated that the tribunal intended that I should read the document, but that no other step was being taken. No sanction was being applied. Objectively, this course had been adopted to draw a line under a highly publicised dispute between a former law officer, who was the current Treasurer of the Inner Temple, and the Bar Council; and that this was thought the best method of doing so. As in the Great Fire of London, the effective means of controlling the spread of the fire was the wholesale destruction of streets in the path of the fire, to create a firebreak. What the firebreak did to me was irrelevant.

My immediate reaction was that the decision of the tribunal had to be challenged. My advisers persuaded me to reflect; and I took the opportunity to discuss the outcome with Lord Justice Parker, then Treasurer of my Inn. The Treasurer offered me wise advice. I knew that my name had been held back from consideration for election to the Bench of the Inn while the proceedings were current. The Treasurer assured me that if I decided not to appeal, he was able to guarantee my election to the Bench. Such an election would dispel any continuing gossip about my integrity. When I told the Treasurer that I did not intend to appeal, he wrote extremely supportively.

'I am sure you are right, and I hope and believe that, the decision once taken, you will feel that a great weight has been lifted off you. I will, as I told you, do my utmost to ensure complete recovery from the effects of the last few years in the shortest time possible. You will no doubt have irritations from time to time – although it is now over thirteen years ago, I occasionally get asked if I was not once rebuked by Tom Denning! It becomes a joke after a bit.'

I had acquired my own mentor in Roger Parker. I embraced the role reversal. My stubborn independence, which had stood me in good stead as a mentor, was replaced by my willingness to become a mentee, and to adopt the wisdom so liberally extended to me. My gratitude to my mentor remains evergreen.

I was benched on 8 July. Within Lincoln's Inn, my rehabilitation was complete. Outside the Inn, rehabilitation was less rapid. The continued animosity of Tasker Watkins behind the scenes persisted.

I wrote to Mr Justice Michael Davies, then in charge of Queen's Bench listing:

'The PCC matter has been concluded; and I do not believe that the outcome has, or ought to have, any impact on the extent to which I can properly discharge any judicial responsibilities which may be requested from me...'

Roger Parker had previously written to me:

'I have seen Michael Davies J and told him that there is in my view no possible reason why you should not now again sit as a deputy. He agreed and considered that Tasker would also. He will be seeing Tasker today or tomorrow. I do not think there will be any hitch but if there is let me know.'

The response from Michael Davies was bleak:

'Further to our correspondence, I have been asked to let you know that it is thought to be better if you did not sit as a deputy High Court judge in the Queen's Bench Division for the time being.'

Roger Parker volunteered his view:

'Michael Davies tells me that despite his own and my representations Tasker-W has decided that for the time being you should not be invited

to sit as a Deputy. I regard this as both unjustified and silly and will do what I can to make him change course. In the meantime, upset as you will surely be, regard it if you can as no more than a bit of silliness and not worthy of more than a minute's thought. That is certainly what it is.'

The shadow was only removed six months later, when the Presiding Judge on my Circuit wrote:

'I am happy to tell you that the informal ban upon your sitting under Section 9 has been lifted. I will make sure that everyone knows.'

In 1994, David Latham, who was chairman of the Professional Standards Committee of the Bar Council while the Percival complaint was proceeding, wrote to me:

'Ever since our days at Queens' I have respected your integrity. Your problem has been that you have asserted fearlessly and openly when others might have been more deviously emollient. I therefore had no difficulty in giving you my support during that dreadful Percival saga. I have always regretted that I felt compelled not to act for you. I have also regretted that it ended, in the public hearing, so sorely. Tasker knows my views about what he did and said. I wish he had the grace to apologise to you.'

David had been in chambers with Tasker Watkins.

Once elected as a Bencher, I was asked to and did represent the Inn as a member of the Bar Council continuously from January 1991 until my appointment as a judge in 1997. Within the Bar Council I was treated as an equal and a respected colleague. No one ever commented on the events of 1987–90.

In November 2000, there was an unexpected sequel. Participating in a judicial visit to the European Court of Justice in Luxembourg, I was invited to the home of a UK judge. Peter Cresswell, who had been chairman of the Bar in 1990, sat next to me on the bus. I had known Peter since he was a first-year lawyer in Queens' in 1962. Peter asked me if I knew what happened at the end of the Divisional Court case. He seemed surprised when I said that I did not. He had attended, as chairman of the Bar, when counsel representing the successful Bar Council applied for the costs of the judicial review proceedings. Percival had dispensed with his own counsel and was appearing in person. In response to the application for costs, Percival rose and indicated the Masonic sign of acute financial distress. Actively embarrassed, Tasker Watkins rose and, without consulting his fellow judge, he muttered 'No order' and stalked out of court.

'NEVER ON SUNDAY'

Deliver us to laws; they send us bound
To rules of reason, holy messengers,
Pulpits and Sundays, sorrow-dogging sin,
Afflictions sorted, anguish of all sizes,
Fine nets and stratagems to catch us in,
Bibles laid open, millions of surprises...
'Sin (I)', George Herbert (1593–1633)

If you are of a certain age, you may remember Melina Mercouri, and the film that made her name. It is a succinct introduction to what became widely known as the Sunday trading saga. This lasted for twelve years: a period that straddled what was going on in the previous three chapters. My initial involvement started in a local campaign on behalf of B&Q (Retail) Ltd of Southampton. An attempt to introduce some sorely needed legislative reform, following a powerful independent report written in 1984 by the then Robin Auld QC, had foundered ignominiously. It was almost as politically damaging for the Thatcher government as the poll tax.

During 1982, a growing number of local authorities were anxious to clamp down on the Sunday trading activities of retailers such as B&Q. The Sunday trading legislation (the Shops Act 1950) was, on any view, not only out of harmony with a secular society, but made a mockery of a contemporary legal code. Contrary to a general belief that the legislation had been passed to regulate Sunday observance and church attendance, the Sunday trading provisions in the 1950 Act (a consolidating measure) had only been adopted by Parliament in the 1936 Shops (Sunday Trading Restriction) Act. The much-criticised collection of permitted sales identified in the 1950 Act owes its form to the debate in Parliament in 1936, though some of them have origins that go back to the Sunday Closing (Shops) Bill of 1905, which did not reach the statute book, and the Shops Act 1911 (which did not deal with Sunday trading). The 1911 Act was introduced to ensure that shop assistants enjoyed at least half a day off work each week; but there was an exception in the case of barbers visiting their customers at home, who enjoyed no such latitude. Some retailers, pointing to the absurd anomalies within the Act – it was lawful to sell a pornographic magazine, but not a Bible – offered to sell a pound of carrots (which was permissible) if the buyer also agreed to buy a piece of furniture such as a wardrobe. My approach to the increasing volume of cases in which I was instructed with Nicholas Davidson to oppose applications by local councils, invoking their prosecutorial powers under Section 222 Local Government Act 1972, was only to take what objectively was a clearly arguable point of law.

Following the grant of an injunction on 25 June 1982, a succession of applications for injunctions followed; and I was instructed in two of them. The outcome in the Court of Appeal[22] on 26 April 1983 was widely reported. Despite a lack of success in the litigation, this was the second Court of Appeal case since taking Silk in which I had appeared before Fred Lawton, and he was clearly happy with his protégé.

The adverse decision of the Court of Appeal was challenged in the House of Lords. Robert Alexander QC, the most persuasive advocate of his generation, was brought in to lead me. His subsequent performance in March 1984 – the last occasion when I was ever led – justified his forensic nickname 'the welded rail'. His argument proceeded smoothly, without any apparent hiccups or joins. Particularly impressive was the formulation of his reply, which had not only fully anticipated everything that our opponents would say, but which he had written out, by hand, before they said it. Bob received a well-deserved letter of congratulation from Lord Templeman: but we still lost.[23]

---

22 Stoke-on-Trent City Council and Wolverhampton Borough Council v. B&Q (Retail) Ltd [1984] Ch 1

23 Stoke-on-Trent City Council v. B&Q (Retail) Ltd [1984] AC 754

The pressure for reform of the Shops Act 1950 was not only a consequence of the illogicality of the existing law: its enforcement by local authorities was imposing a financial burden that impacted adversely on the ability of councils to fund all their other essential services.

I first suggested in March 1986 to our enthusiastic solicitor, Tony Askham, who oversaw everything during the twelve-year saga, that the way these injunctions were interfering with trade on Sundays might be unlawful under European law. I was no European lawyer, so I recommended seeking advice from David Vaughan QC of Brick Court Chambers and his outstanding juniors, Gerald Barling and David Anderson (later Mr Justice Barling and Lord Anderson of Ipswich KC). They persuaded the European Court of Justice in that, relying on established European jurisprudence, the restriction of trade was contrary to Article 177 of the Treaty of Rome.[24] The Torfaen decision actively turned the tide in favour of the retailers; but not until November 1989.

With the passage of time, a highly professional public relations campaign designed to secure a change in the law developed. The focus for the campaign, spearheaded by David Ramsden, was the creation of the Shopping Hours Reform Council, to which several of my individual corporate clients, as well as B&Q, belonged. These included Kingfisher (who had bought Woolworths, and acquired B&Q as part of that deal), Marks & Spencer and Debenhams. Anticipating the potential avenue for success in showing that the domestic legislation had a decisive, and, in European terms, a restrictive and impermissible impact on the freedom of trade enshrined in the Treaty of Rome, a body of expert evidence was assembled to challenge the validity of prosecutions both in the Magistrates' Court and in the Crown Court.

One of the first of these major challenges took place in Bradford Crown Court in May 1990, over five days. The fact that I now remember nothing of it, save that I led both Nicholas Davidson and David Anderson, illustrates the state of mind I was in following the stress of the disciplinary proceedings. Nicholas had written to Maxine and me:

---

24 Torfaen Borough Council v. B&Q Case C-145/88, ECJ

'For more than fifteen years I have enjoyed every minute of your friendship and admire you both. I admire you all the more for the way in which you have borne this misery, a horrible injustice especially given that John is and always has been a model of professional dedication and unstinting service to all clients. I resent the fact that you have been made to suffer. I have been glad to have been working together more this year than recently and that we start up again for Bradford now.'

The proposed change in the law was vigorously opposed, and a 'Keep Sunday Special' campaign was formed to present the case for retaining the status quo. Meanwhile, local councils were becoming more active in their determination to enforce the law. In addition to the prosecution of corporate entities, as well as seeking civil injunctions to restrain Sunday trading, the questionable device of seeking to prosecute individual directors of the corporate entities was adopted by several councils. It was of particular concern to the CEO of one of my corporate clients, because he was worried that the knighthood for which he had been recommended might not materialise.

———

My next foray in the Sunday trading saga began the next month at Eastbourne Magistrates' Court before a then stipendiary magistrate. I luxuriated for five days in the Grand Hotel, Eastbourne, in the suite once occupied by Emperor Haile Selassie when driven out of Abyssinia by Mussolini. It comprised a vast bedroom, the largest bed I have ever occupied (yet the emperor was a particularly small man), and a palatial run of reception rooms in which I held court with my 'team'. My instructions were to ensure that, if possible, no decision adverse to the client's interest was reached. On Day 5, the magistrate sent for counsel: 'This will be a grave disappointment; but I am unable to complete this case. In strict confidence I have received an appointment as a Crown Court judge; and I take it up on Monday. This case will have to be adjourned; and must start again.' I could scarcely contain my glee. I knew that it was highly unlikely to start all over again. The CEO obtained his knighthood.

The opportunity to gain a distinct strategic advantage in this litigation came when Mendip District Council sought a civil injunction to restrain Sunday trading in their area but refused to offer a cross-undertaking in damages if, at trial, it was found that they were not entitled to such relief. Hitherto, the offer of a cross-undertaking had been routine; but in the light of the recent decision in the Torfaen case, there was a real possibility that the local authority might be unsuccessful. With Andrew Collins QC, representing Wickes Building Supplies Ltd in a similar case, I advised that the shops should make a stand. In May 1990, Mr Justice Mervyn Davies had refused to require Kirklees Borough Council (in the Wickes case) to give a cross-undertaking in damages. He was followed by Mr Justice Mummery in the B&Q case; and thereafter, as we told the Court of Appeal, some one hundred interlocutory injunctions had been granted to local authorities without requiring cross-undertakings in damages. In the appeal to the Court of Appeal in April 1991,[25] I led Gerald Barling and Nicholas Davidson. The issue in the Court of Appeal was starkly identified by Dillon LJ:

> *'The issues as to the cross-undertaking are fundamental because the two councils made it plain in the courts below and in argument in this court that they are not prepared to give any cross-undertaking in damages. If therefore this court is of the view that the judges below were wrong to dispense with a cross-undertaking, these appeals must be allowed and the injunctions granted at first instance must be discharged.'*

The result was that the injunctions were discharged; and this was the principal item of news in the national press. For a time, this result halted all applications for an interlocutory injunction by local councils to restrain Sunday trading. The Kirklees case was the subject of a successful appeal to the House of Lords. I had been instructed to appear for B&Q in the House of Lords; but the House ruled that only the Kirklees case would proceed to a full hearing, and that the Attorney General would arrange for Treasury

---

25   Mendip DC v. B&Q plc [1991] 4 All ER 240

Counsel to intervene, to provide the House of Lords with full argument. The balance then swung back in favour of the local authorities.

It was politically obvious that, despite the way in which prosecutions continued to be resisted in Crown and Magistrates' courts, the campaign needed, to be successful, to be pursued by persuading Parliament to alter the law, and not by advocacy before courts that had to apply the existing law. I persuaded my team to adopt that approach by presenting a joint opinion, prepared by and signed by its (by now) five Silk members; and this resulted in a legal review of the draft Sunday Trading Bill published by the government in its White Paper 'The options for reform'. That joint opinion, dated 22 October 1993, was in the result critical in persuading parliamentarians to support our proposed reforms.

Predictably, the Keep Sunday Special campaign presented its own opposition; but the key feature of our approach was that we analysed each aspect of the existing and proposed legislation dispassionately and clinically. The opinion was printed and was presented to every MP and peer.

The government published a Sunday Trading Bill the following month. Its provisions differed in important respects from those in the original draft, which had been annexed to a White Paper. We were forewarned about the appearance of the draft bill, and Tony Askham arranged for the team to go away to a country house hotel in Wales, to prepare a joint response to the provisions in the bill. The hotel was chosen by David Vaughan, as it was close to his own holiday home. On arrival, the team were hijacked by David and persuaded to go to his home for fun and frivolity in the snow. I was the still small voice of both sobriety and duty. I tried unsuccessfully to insist that we spent the afternoon drafting first, and to postpone the fun until later. In the result, most of Saturday was wasted; after a late start on the Sunday morning, we made little progress; and after lunch I left the team, since I had a professional commitment the following day, making it essential to leave Wales with the second opinion no more than a skeleton outline. My departure left a bit of an atmosphere: but the resulting opinion (printed, as its predecessor had been, and similarly distributed) was in the result an impressive document, albeit my contribution was far less than it had been to the initial one. The criticism of the opposition proposals

focused on their lack of clarity; their arbitrariness; the consequential problems of enforcement; and the likelihood of inherent obsolescence as the
legislative provisions necessarily became outdated. The views expressed in
these two opinions carried the day on a free vote in each house; and the
Sunday Trading Act 1994 has stood the test of time.

———

Realistically, the change in so many families' social habits, and the way
in which they now spend their Sundays, was one of the most objectively
profound social changes of my professional lifetime. When students ask
me for details of any leading cases that I undertook, I tend to reply 'Sunday
trading'; and most of them have no idea that it was once a crime for a
shopkeeper to sell other than a very restricted range of goods on a Sunday.

Since 1990, Maxine and I had jointly conducted an antique shop
(Marryat) in Richmond. We named it after Captain Marryat, the famous
sea captain and Victorian author, and his brother Joseph, the first compiler
of a dictionary of ceramics. They are among Maxine's ancestors. Once the
1994 Act became law, the shop opened for trading on Sundays, within the
limited hours permitted. It was, at least to me, a real pain that – in addition to the responsibilities I had as a Silk, Head of Chambers and latterly
a judge – not only was I undertaking most of the necessary book-keeping
relating to the company, plus the labelling and research of the stock that
had been purchased, but the erosion of what might have been a smidgeon
of free time on Sunday by 'duty' in the shop was, for both of us, something
of a disaster.

THE APPELLATE ADVOCATE

*An appeal is when you ask one court to show
its contempt for another court.*
Finley Peter Dunne (1867–1936)

This light-hearted quip by an American journalist has a kernel of truth: the key to a successful appeal is to persuade the appellate court that the court below was manifestly stupid. While this task was relatively simple in the era of judges like Claude Duveen and Bernard Lewis, and if your case was listed before Lord Denning you were likely to win if you could show that the merits were in your favour, the deference now shown to first instance judges, and specifically to jury verdicts in criminal cases, makes it increasingly difficult to succeed on appeal. Despite the existence of the Criminal Cases Review Commission, established to address the notorious miscarriages of justice exemplified by the Guildford Four and the Birmingham Six, similar cases proliferate: and the current scandal of the sub-postmasters, only brought to public attention by the compelling dramatisation of their plight, show how reluctant the CCRC had been to refer such cases to the Court of Appeal when they were first invited to do so.

Nevertheless, during my final years of practice at the Bar, when asked what my chosen speciality was, I was proud to respond: appellate advocacy. I have resisted the temptation to describe, even in summary form, the many cases that I conducted on appeal, frequently in the Court of Appeal and often in the House of Lords, since the purpose of this book is identified in its title. I do, however, offer a few examples of when a throwaway line had an unexpected impact on the outcome of an appeal. I conclude this chapter with a commentary on an ethical problem that baffled the

Court of Appeal; and, as such, perhaps demonstrated that professional ethics has a chameleon quality.

I had represented a third party in a Court of Appeal hearing, having been unsuccessful at first instance, which turned on the construction of the Public Utilities Street Works Act 1950. The outcome of the case in the Court of Appeal is of little interest, save that my clients' and the defendants' arguments on limitation prevailed.

What might justify a modest footnote in the history of appellate advocacy in the late twentieth century is what happened on the evening before the hearing in their Lordships' House. I attended a memorial service for a Richmond neighbour. Immediately ahead of me in the queue was Lord Bridge of Harwich, who was presiding the following day in the appeal against that decision. In small talk, I mentioned that I was looking forward to appearing before him.

'What are you doing?'

'It is a really boring appeal, which turns on the construction of the Public Utilities Street Works Act 1950.'

'Do you find that Act boring?'

I replied truthfully that I did. Before the case was even called on, I knew that I had kicked the loose ball firmly into the back of my own goal. The speech of Lord Bridge on 29 July 1986 was the sole judgment, allowing the appeal.[26]

––––––––

Once, the fishing fleet in Hull had been simply huge. The local economy was built up on fishing; and the trawlermen of Hull, who went in search of their declining harvest in the perilous waters of the North Sea, were, despite their hardship and valour, facing an inevitable decline. The government took steps to write off the fishing fleet. Generous terms were offered to trawler owners to decommission their vessels; and these included financial compensation to trawlermen who would lose their livelihood. The owners

––––––––

26 Yorkshire Electricity Board v. British Telecom, P. Igoe & Son (Third Party) [1986] 2 All ER 961

happily pocketed the sums proffered by the government, and discussed with their lawyers how they could avoid passing on to the erstwhile employees the sums that reflected that redundancy. The owners struck gold.

It was traditional in the fishing fleet to engage fishermen on short-term contracts, of up to six months' duration. When one contract ended, and the fishermen were still at sea, another automatically came into being. If, however, the contract ended while the trawlerman was in port, he waited for a few days or weeks until a vessel was available for him, and then embarked, armed with a new contract.

The owners purported to defeat the trawlermen's claims by pointing out that no redundancy payment was due where the worker was employed for six months or less. That this was morally reprehensible – the compensation pocketed by the owners included redundancy payments for the trawlermen – was not the point. Could an argument be sustained that, in reality, the trawlermen were engaged on contracts that subsisted for many years?

That was the issue that I met head-on in the Court of Appeal. There was a moment in the appeal when I realised that I had overplayed my hand.

Lord Justice Mustill asked me if I could think of an example of a contract whereby a servant remained in employment but was obliged to do nothing.

Without hesitation, I replied: 'Certainly, My Lord. "They also serve who only stand and wait".'

'Yes,' said Mustill. 'Shakespeare?'

'Milton, on his blindness,' I smugly replied.

'Are you sure?'

Even more smugly, I reproduced the whole poem, with its concluding line, 'They also serve who only stand and wait'. Mustill was not happy; and despite his subsequent friendliness towards me, I am sure this was the turning point of the unsuccessful appeal.[27]

Stung, I pursued a petition for leave to appeal to the House of Lords. Normally, such an oral hearing would have lasted ten minutes. This one began at 10.30. My panel comprised Lord Bridge, Lord Brandon and

---

27   Hellyer Brothers Ltd v. McLeod and Others *The Times*, 28 February 1987

Lord Templeman. They were notorious for their disagreements, and their mutual antipathy. At 1.15, I was still on my feet.

Brandon was wholly persuaded and was encouraging me to continue. In exasperation – with his fellow Law Lords, and not with me – he almost shouted: 'Can't you persuade their Lordships, Mr Samuels?'

Lamely, I acknowledged that I was repeating the same argument; and reluctantly sat down.

———

I end with my final case in the Court of Appeal: Vernon v. Vernon. This case, or rather its companion, raised ethical issues that the Court of Appeal found it impossible to address with a single approach. If the judiciary cannot provide a single answer to an ethical conundrum, who can?

My involvement related solely to contested residence proceedings. They began with a family tragedy. Mr and Mrs Vernon had two small children, whom they entrusted to a nanny. The nanny, driving the family car, drove into a river, and both children drowned. The father rushed to the scene. He had a pre-existing psychiatric illness that he claimed was exacerbated by the post-traumatic stress disorder experienced after witnessing his children's deaths.

Subsequently, three more children were born. Protracted proceedings for damages were maintained by the father. When I represented Mr Vernon in the Court of Appeal, a substantial award had already been made in his favour; but an appeal was in progress.

Mr Vernon wanted two of his children to live with him; and claimed, when I represented him in the Court of Appeal, that he was now mentally fit. However, in the personal injury claim, his case was that he remained psychiatrically disabled, and would permanently remain so. The same expert witnesses who had declared that the father was now able to resume childcare had given evidence in the previous personal injury litigation that the father was permanently incapacitated by mental illness. I held a joint consultation with both counsel representing the father in his personal injury claim. I said that Mr Vernon should be advised that the expert medical reports prepared for the care proceedings, and which had been advanced by precisely the same experts, but which had reached differing opinions to those expressed for the assessment of damages, should be disclosed. If the client declined to do so, counsel should withdraw, since they would be professionally embarrassed. Leading counsel disagreed, and took the view that the reports were covered by legal professional privilege.

Mr Vernon had been awarded damages on the basis that he would never work again. Before the Court of Appeal delivered their reserved judgment, an 'anonymous source' sent them the medical reports that had been deployed in the contested care proceedings. There is little doubt that it was the mother, or perhaps her solicitors. This created a division of view in the Court of Appeal.[28]

Lord Justice Stuart-Smith decided that Mr Vernon's counsel should have advised him that these medical reports should be disclosed; and, if he declined to do so, they should have withdrawn from his case. Lord Justice Evans said the opposite: the documents were privileged, and counsel was under no duty to advise their disclosure. Lord Justice Thorpe, agreeing with Stuart-Smith, went further: it was the duty of counsel to provide this information to those representing the insurers, and to the judge.

Which judgment is correct? How do those students or pupils, assimilating the professional ethics of their role, find guidance in these divided views? And – a personal footnote – my ethical stance seems to have precisely mirrored that of Stuart-Smith. So much for being accused, in 1990, of failing to maintain the ethics of my profession!

---

28   Vernon v. Bosley (No 2) [1997] 1 All ER 614

A MISCELLANY OF MURDERS

An honourable murderer, if you will;
For nought did I in hate, but all in honour.
Shakespeare, *Othello*: Act V, Scene 2

It is a truism that when, on social occasions, non-lawyers meet lawyers whose work brings them into the criminal courts, they routinely enquire: 'How can you represent someone you believe to be guilty?' The response of Dr Samuel Johnson to a similar question has rarely been bettered: 'A lawyer has no business with the justice or injustice of the cause which he undertakes, unless his client asks his opinion, and then he is bound to give it honestly. The justice or injustice of the cause is to be decided by the judge.' In the case of a criminal prosecution the decision is, of course, that of the jury. Similar fascination pervades conversations about those who have killed another human being. Realistically, most of those who have done so have been in the wrong place at the wrong time; or have reacted, perhaps under the influence of drink or drugs, when, with ordinary sobriety, nothing so terrible would have happened.

The relevance of this chapter is that in my limited experience of murderers prior to my subsequent role as a member of the Parole Board, each one helped me learn something about an individual who had taken a life, and so contributed to my education. In time, that knowledge developed my thinking about judicial monitoring and supervision.

Even from the limited experience of the novice barrister in 1966, my first experience of a murderer was remarkable. A reader who has started this book in the middle is invited to refer to what I said about the Thai student in chapter 7, 'First Steps in the Law'.

Fast-forward to 1981. I had just taken Silk. I have described in chapter 11, 'Silk', the sad case of R v. Madhvani, which was my first experience of conducting a murder prosecution. Given that I ended up as a full-time Crown Court judge and was subsequently a judicial member of the Parole Board whose caseload comprised almost exclusively life-sentenced prisoners, that growing experience became valuable in ways I could not have foreseen.

Another case, not routinely to be described as a murder, arose in wardship proceedings. A baby aged about three months had been taken from its pram and swung against a wall, like a rag doll. The baby sustained fatal injury. The only suspects were two children who lived in the same house. One (my client) was aged four; the other was aged about three. Each was represented by an independent guardian, who maintained that, for that child's future welfare, it was essential that the truth should be known in relation to who was responsible for the baby's death. While this, of course, was a family court hearing and not a criminal trial, and neither child was a witness, it was a straightforward cut-throat defence. Both children were represented by leading counsel. The hearing lasted many days. At its conclusion, the wise judge decided not only that it was a joint enterprise, in the traditional sense, but that on the balance of probability each child had picked up the baby, each holding one of its arms and legs, and swung it, between them, against the wall. That is what small children do to their soft toys.

———

John Leggett was what in an earlier legislative regime would have been described as a vagrant. In September 1982 he was one of a group addicted to methylated spirits. They had congregated near Tower Hill; and they had been drinking for days. One of the group engaged in some verbal abuse with Leggett, and he was knocked to the ground. He wanted Leggett's meths; Leggett threw half a bottle of meths over him, struck a match, and the victim was engulfed in flames. At one stage, Leggett was seen to try to quench the flames by urinating over the victim; but a witness heard him say: 'Burn, you bastard, burn!' My junior and I visited Wormwood Scrubs for a consultation. Leggett could remember nothing: he told us he had been drunk for at least a week beforehand. My reaction was to say he had to plead guilty: the evidence of intent to kill was overwhelming. My junior wisely cautioned delay. 'No one pleads in a murder: something may crop up.'

The trial was listed at the Old Bailey. It was a short trial: the summing up began on Day 3 and concluded the next morning. Overnight, the judge prepared a written direction in relation to the issue of provocation (which had not featured in the defence case); but only provided an oral direction in relation to the issue of drink, and the formation of the requisite intent to kill or cause serious harm when intoxicated. The oral direction that the judge gave on the latter aspect was inadequate: and this, together with the prominence afforded to the issue of provocation in the written direction, proved a 'lightbulb moment' for me.

Counsel were not then required to correct any perceived error in the summing up. As soon as the jury retired, I was in the court library; and before the verdict was delivered, I had drafted grounds of appeal. A year later, the verdict was quashed; a verdict of manslaughter was substituted; and a highly delighted Leggett received the news that his sentence had become a determinate one of twelve years, rather than a life sentence with the fifteen-year minimum recommended by the trial judge – equivalent to a thirty-year determinate sentence.

———

The crime of attempted murder is often more heinous than that of murder because it requires a settled intention to kill the victim. In a remarkable case, the victim of this crime died, on the balance of probability, of natural causes; yet my young client was determined to plead guilty to his attempted murder, and there was no basis for advising him to do otherwise.

In March 1988 Mr Barlow, a man aged sixty-eight who lived alone, was found collapsed on the road by Stephen Bishton and his friend Ian Molland. He was heavily intoxicated. They looked after him, and Bishton summoned an ambulance, which took Mr Barlow to hospital. Mr Barlow knew that the two young men lived locally; and mistakenly believed (because Bishton had long hair and was obviously in a relationship with

Molland) that Bishton was a girl. When he left hospital, Mr Barlow sent Bishton and Molland a bunch of flowers and some chocolates and invited them to visit his home for a drink. So unsophisticated were they that they carefully kept his written invitation, and they accepted it.

In unexplained circumstances – and Bishton implied that Molland, who was eighteen months older than him, had suggested the plan – both young men decided to steal what they could from Mr Barlow's home. While they were there, they plied him with alcohol. Then, once their victim was insensible, they ran a bath for him and left him in the bath, to make it appear as if his death, which they both anticipated, had been an accident. Both left the flat, taking Mr Barlow's credit cards, which they used at a cashpoint, and some jewellery.

Mr Barlow was found dead in the bath the following day, and death was certified as due to natural causes. Before Bishton and Molland were apprehended by police, Mr Barlow's body was cremated. When both men were apprehended, both candidly admitted, in response to police questioning, that they had gone to Mr Barlow's flat with the intention of stealing from him, and of killing him so that no identification could take place.

Despite their youth, and the absence of previous convictions, there were no grounds for challenging what each had freely admitted at their interviews; and hence a plea to admitted murder was inevitable. Each young man received a sentence of twelve years' detention.

———

John Rennie, the junior who had persuaded me to undertake the case of Stephen Bishton, continued to influence my acceptance of instructions in criminal cases for which I was probably both temperamentally and professionally unsuited. Meredith and Others was, superficially, a case that hardly justifies a footnote. Aspects of the trial, however, remain as fresh as those vivid days in 1992 when I battled tenaciously on behalf of the client who had been in the wrong place at the wrong time: the car park of a squalid public house, at closing time, where alcohol-fuelled violence among its customers led to the loss of a young life. No weapon was involved: just fists and boots.

Paul Meredith was one of about eleven young people initially arrested for violent disorder. What made his case unusual was that, alone among those arrested and charged, he was informed by the Chief Crown Prosecutor that there was no evidence against him that justified his committal for trial. His complaisant solicitors duly filed their papers. Meredith was plainly a vulnerable young man at the time of his police interview, when he made a series of damaging admissions in relation to his involvement in violent disorder. I asked his solicitor why he had not intervened. 'I thought it would be rude to interrupt' was his candid reply.

All other defendants were committed for trial, facing a charge of murder, as their victim subsequently died. Twelve months later, and on the eve of the joint trial at Stafford Crown Court, advances in DNA profiling placed Meredith close to the victim. Belatedly, a voluntary bill was obtained, joining Meredith as a defendant. I applied to the trial judge for a stay of the indictment, arguing that this amounted to an abuse of process. My arguments, based on the letter from the CPS, the consequential lack of opportunity to investigate a defence, and a legitimate expectation that no criminal proceedings would be pursued, were all swept away.

Two weeks later, the joint trial began. It was the grand opening of the criminal sittings at Stafford. The judge swept into court in his full-bottomed wig, leading a parade of the High Sheriff and assorted flunkies, as the clerk of the court read the verbose commission. A female defendant with a thick Black Country accent memorably called out from the dock, before being asked to plead: 'Gaw blimey, Mr Barker [her defence counsel], why didn't you tell me? I would've worn me bleeding 'at!' Following arraignment, and what was left of the afternoon's proceedings, the judge sent for leading counsel. 'I have been invited to dinner by Mr Barker tonight. I assume that none of you has any objection?' As a former sparring partner of the judge, and a fellow Bencher of Lincoln's Inn, I felt I was entitled to make a modest joke. 'My sole concern is that Mr Barker has not invited me too.' The judge glared at me: I was not and could not possibly be thought of as worthy of entertainment by the Birmingham Bar. 'We shall not, of course, be discussing today's case.'

The next morning, there was a development. Mr Barker rose.

'My Lord, could the indictment be put again to my client?'

'Certainly, Mr Barker.'

The first defendant pleaded not guilty to murder, but guilty to manslaughter. So, in their turn, did every other defendant but one, all of them represented by members of the Birmingham Bar. 'Those pleas will be acceptable to the Crown,' replied the Birmingham prosecutor.

That left Mr Meredith, whom John Rennie had assured me would be inconspicuous as tail-end Charlie in a multi-handed indictment, as the first defendant. The evidence against Meredith comprised specks of blood on his clothing that had apparently come from the deceased, and which recent advances in DNA profiling had identified; and his admission of presence at the scene of the fatal attack, made in response to suggestible questioning by a police inspector. To address this, I had an expert in DNA profiling, who challenged the evidence of the prosecution scientist, but who would, if called, have been the most unimpressive of witnesses; and the powerful evidence of a distinguished psychologist, who confirmed that Meredith's IQ was so low that he would agree with any proposition put to him. Sadly, I could not call him either, as he was committed to another trial.

I had lengthy consultations with each expert. I became, briefly, something of an expert on both DNA and suggestibility. My residual co-defendant was represented by Anthony Hughes QC, also of the Birmingham Bar (later in the Supreme Court as Lord Hughes of Ombersley), who knew, both strategically and tactically, the wisdom of tucking in behind me and keeping a particularly low profile before this judge. This was never more obvious than when I introduced in evidence the letter my solicitors had received from the Chief Crown Prosecutor, expressing his opinion that there was no case for Meredith to answer.

'That opinion is simply irrelevant,' thundered the judge before the jury. 'Mr Samuels practises in civil courts, not criminal courts, otherwise he would know that.'

My point, of course, was that if a senior lawyer had concluded that there was no evidence suggesting Meredith was guilty, how could the jury be sure of it to the criminal standard?

A bad-tempered trial continued with a biased summing up. Waiting for the jury's verdict in the robing room, we were visited by the usher. He announced in stentorian tones: 'Mr Samuels and Mr Rennie, His Lordship has sent me to inform you that he intends to make a wasted costs order against both of you.'

Icily, I replied: 'Shall we take the jury's verdict first?'

When we returned to court, it was a relief to hear that Meredith was not guilty of murder, albeit (virtually inevitably, given his full admissions in interview) guilty of violent disorder, as was Anthony Hughes's client. Both received custodial sentences at the top of the bracket for this latter offence, but they were not appealable.

The judge called John Rennie and me, plus our hapless solicitor, into his room. Reading from a prepared script, he outlined why he proposed to penalise us in costs. 'The defence case has lasted thirteen and a half days; and if competently conducted it would have lasted no more than ten or eleven days. I propose to order you to pay the extra costs involved.'

I asked for a copy of the paper from which the judge had read.

'You can get it from the shorthand writer tomorrow.'

I said I needed time to respond to the criticism, and would do so the following morning. I spent much of the evening and the early hours of that morning analysing what we had done, and why. I identified the problems of expert evidence, of which the judge would necessarily have been unaware.

After about twenty minutes, the judge gruffly said: 'I shall make no order.'

I was on my high horse. 'It is a matter of immense personal regret that these criticisms should be made. They have been made for the first time in my professional career and Your Lordship has indicated that I am unfamiliar with the practice and procedure of this court. I have prosecuted more cases of murder than I have defended.'

The judge listened to me in angry silence. No one ever threatened me with such an order again. I asked my solicitors to order a transcript of what I had said, to be sent both to the Chairman of the Bar and the President of the Law Society, to illustrate the problem of wasted costs orders being improperly threatened against advocates who were merely performing their professional duty.

There were two consequences. First, for about twelve months thereafter, the normal bonhomie that exists between Benchers of Lincoln's Inn ceased to exist between us. Second, and within recent memory, there was another contretemps. We were both present at a normally well-refreshed dinner after a Council meeting at the Inn. I was offered a lift to Waterloo, which I gladly accepted. Grabbing my coat and what I believed was my briefcase from the upper vestibule, it was only when I was on the train that I realised I had the wrong briefcase. I rang the butler. He put me through to the by now long-retired judge, who was still in the drawing room. He demanded that the briefcase be taken, by minicab, to his home, forthwith. 'There are important materials which I need urgently tomorrow,' he fumed.

Of course I acquiesced – at considerable expense. Meanwhile, I surreptitiously inspected the important contents. They comprised a copy of the previous day's *Times* newspaper, plus a clean pair of underpants.

PRISONERS

I never saw a man who looked
With such a wistful eye
Upon that little tent of blue
Which prisoners call the sky...
Oscar Wilde (1854–1900), *The Ballad of Reading Gaol*

The assessment of future risk is at the heart of everything the Parole Board does. You can never anticipate the future behaviour of an individual; and one who has caused extreme harm in the past, resulting in the death of one or more victims, is more likely to do so in the future. My involvement in Parole Board hearings during the subsequent period of over ten years has lent authenticity to my attempts to introduce reforms to the criminal justice system. Most of the outcomes of these oral hearings must be cloaked in anonymity, as their subjects are entitled to confidentiality; and I have distorted the names of prisoners (save one, since I know that the prisoner is dead). However, the case of Peter Franks is one of the strangest.

The story begins straightforwardly. In 1992, Franks committed an unremarkable robbery, his eleventh conviction, and received a sentence of imprisonment. While serving that sentence, he was so appalled by the way a life-sentenced prisoner was boasting of the way he had killed his victim that he strangled that prisoner. On his first appearance, he pleaded guilty to murder and was sentenced to life imprisonment, with a twelve-year tariff. That tariff expired in January 2005.

Franks's progress in custody was as satisfactory as could have been hoped for. He admitted that his early offending was attributable to drug addiction, from which he remained clear; and he undertook lengthy programmes, with positive reports. By January 2004, he was recommended for a transfer to open conditions: HMP Ford, in Sussex.

For much of his time in prison, Franks formed good relationships with prison officers, and this led to suspicion that he was a 'grass'. A recurrent problem was the bureaucratic requirement that responsibility for the prisoner's resettlement following release was that of the external probation officer, who might be located many hundreds of miles from where the prisoner was detained or the location to which the prisoner wished to be released. In this case, the geographical problems were starkly illustrated: in 2005, Franks was in West Sussex and his external probation officer was based in Carlisle. Contact between them was at best limited, and – in the era before video link – was restricted largely to postal communication. When direct contact occurred, it led to a significant misunderstanding.

Although Franks had been a trusted prisoner, his status led to his being targeted by a corrupt officer. The prison officer was suspended; a disciplinary investigation ensued; and Franks absconded, claiming that he had to do so for his own safety. While he was at liberty for seven weeks, he chose to surrender rather than to expose those with whom he was living to the danger of harbouring an escaped prisoner. When he surrendered himself to a local prison, instead of being charged with any offence, he received a nominal penalty.

A bizarre series of events unfolded. Three separate consignments of toiletries were sent to Franks. All were unsolicited. Franks knew, from his long experience in prison, that any toiletries sent in by post would be confiscated and destroyed. The third of these deliveries was said to contain, within a tube of shaving balm, a quantity of heroin worth £20,000. There was no investigation of the find; and the drugs were handed to police, five months later, for destruction.

The next event was the submission of a letter, apparently signed by Franks, requesting a deferral of his parole review until 2006. Franks denied writing the letter. He was represented by solicitors, who had expected the review to proceed.

Within three months of the apparent discovery of Class A drugs, and Franks's alleged involvement in their introduction, Franks was transferred, by taxi, to a prison with a lower security classification. Our attempts to clarify this anomaly with the security governor ran into the buffers. The panel concluded that the way Franks was dealt with was inconsistent with what might have been expected had Franks been involved in an importation of drugs. We noted that the governor had told the Prisons minister (following correspondence from an MP) that Franks had admitted involvement in drug trafficking; yet the same governor told the Parole Board that Franks denied any involvement. The same governor told the Minister of State that Franks had signed for the receipt of the relevant parcel; yet in his witness statement he said: 'We took control of the parcel before Franks received it, so technically he was never in possession of it.' There were several other material inconsistencies in the evidence of the same governor, and the panel concluded that they could not rely on anything he said.

At the next parole review, all report writers recommended the immediate release of Franks; but the panel decided that he first needed to be tested in open conditions. That recommendation for open conditions was accepted, and Franks was transferred to an open prison. Within weeks of his arrival, he was threatened at knifepoint by two prisoners, and he absconded. He was arrested, and was taken to HMP Shrewsbury, where he remained throughout what turned out to be a lengthy review.

Within HMP Shrewsbury, Franks not only gave no cause for concern but provided an invaluable service to the prison authorities by becoming an informal adviser to and making himself responsible for the welfare of the large community of foreign national prisoners housed there. All staff within the prison, and particularly the seconded probation officer and the chaplain, both of whom had come to know Franks well, actively supported his release; but this was opposed by his external probation officer from Carlisle, who dramatically changed her recommendation following a difficult interview with her, when Franks, in order to maintain his composure in the light of what was objectively a volte-face, concluded the interview. In March 2009, release was directed.

What was the sequel? It would be less than human not to wonder. When such decisions go wrong, the released prisoner may commit a further serious offence; and the Review Committee of the Parole Board conducts a careful after-the-event reconstruction of whether the release decision was a reasonable or even a defensible one, on what had been known at the time. Nothing of that nature happened in this case – or in any other case, high-profile or otherwise, that I undertook during my ten-year tenure. Franks's counsel frequently appeared at subsequent hearings, and I asked her about him.

'He disappeared. A bit like *The Shawshank Redemption*. Franks knew he could keep control of his life so long as he was not controlled by the bureaucracy of the Probation Service.'

———

No case had a more bizarre background than that of Horace Smith (a pseudonym, in the unlikely event that this prisoner, born in July 1936, remains alive). The prisoner was a prematurely elderly bachelor aged forty-eight when he murdered in April 1985, and his parole review hearing began when I joined the Parole Board twenty years later. The facts come from the decision letter:

'On 18 April 1985 you arranged for a young woman to come to your home to act out a film sequence which you had written, and which required her to portray a hanging scene. She was found lifeless and strangled by a rope, surrounded by a quantity of black satin, and signs referring to your pen name as an author, Kit Arden. (Your fiction, which until recently you have continued to produce, refers to young women in situations of acute danger.) Next to your victim's body you left a poem, entitled '10 Little Beauty Queens', which identified young women dying in dramatic circumstances, and concluded with one being hanged. You wrote what appeared to be a confession of responsibility for the death of your victim. On 24 April 1986, following a trial in which you declined to give evidence, you were convicted of murder; and sentenced to life imprisonment with a tariff of fifteen years. That term expired in April 2000. There has never been any suggestion that you had committed any other criminal offence, nor behaved violently. While the circumstances of the index offence are undeniably unusual, there has been no evidential

link between your interest in young women in situations of danger and a sexual element; and the Panel consider, after mature reflection, given your age and the absence of any suggestion of sexual offending during your 27 years in custody, that it would now be appropriate to assume any likelihood that you are or have been at risk of offending sexually. The Panel regards the index offence as a bizarre and still largely unexplained offence of violence.'

An unusual feature of this case was the determination of the local Multi-Agency Public Protection (MAPP) panel, chaired by a senior police officer, not only actively to resist any release of the prisoner, but to campaign for his return to closed conditions. This became clear when a note of those proceedings was disclosed. The chairman of the MAPP panel had written:

'The MAPP do not support the release of (Smith) and in addition, it does not deem a prison with open conditions as the most appropriate environment for (him). DCI [. . .] reported that there appears to be a perception by the named judge chairing the Parole Board that there is confliction and discrepancy between the views of Probation in contrast with those of the Police; namely, that Probation are supporting a long-term release plan with a move towards consideration for Release on Temporary Licence (ROTL), whereas the views of the Police, as evidenced by DCI [. . .]'s report dated October 2006, are that (Smith) poses too great a risk to consider release currently. This is a matter to be addressed prior to the next oral hearing to ensure that all involved agencies are speaking from the same perspective [emphasis added].'

What the senior police officer was proposing was obviously an improper interference with the independence of the Parole Board.

After a lengthy delay, Smith was transferred to another open prison, to facilitate the development of a relationship with his local offender manager. The local MAPP took active steps to block Smith's progress. The panel had required Smith to undertake an appropriate number of ROTLs to approved premises, so that his reaction to those visits could be assessed.

However, the MAPP modified the arrangements for Smith's release on ROTL that the panel had approved, directing that henceforth he would be escorted by a police officer and a community psychiatric nurse.

During these absences, Smith (by then aged seventy-five and having spent twenty-seven years in prison) displayed 'behaviour which raised concerns' (namely 'confusion over money'), waved his walking stick about, and apparently demonstrated 'passive/aggressive behaviour'. An emergency meeting of MAPP countermanded the ROTLs that the panel had requested. Subsequently, overnight ROTLs were belatedly arranged by the prison, and all went well.

With more stringent licence conditions than any member of the panel had known, Smith's release was directed. It would be so interesting to know how he fared in the community; but the absence of any record of subsequent failure suggests that there was no problem.

———

It is probably no more than a coincidence that, having undertaken a Parole Board review in relation to a protected prisoner who had given evidence for the Crown in several cases involving IRA murders in 2006, I appear to have become the 'go-to' panel chair. The first case involved a prisoner who had served his fifteen-year tariff, following his conviction of conspiracy to murder, as a protected prisoner with outstandingly positive reports. His release plan involved his removal from the jurisdiction, with a new identity assisted by surgical modification; and his family members were afforded the same level of careful protection against recognition. My panel colleagues agreed that the least said the better; and the rapidity of the subsequent oral hearing is probably a record.

This understanding may have commended me to the senior probation officer responsible for the small number of prisoners who necessarily had protected status. No case was so memorable as that of the individual whom I first met at a hearing in November 2009. I shall call him Gary Higgs, although that was not the name he then bore; and curiously, in all my subsequent dealings with him, which included changes of name, his prison number remained the same.

The protected witness regime was memorably described by this experienced probation officer as '*One Flew Over the Cuckoo's Nest* meets *Groundhog Day*', a reference to a film portraying life in a psychiatric ward and one where events repeat themselves on a daily basis. The regime offered limited opportunities to work, to exercise or to engage in education; and the picture presented to the panel was of repetitive and purposeless days, with the prisoner enclosed in a small unit where the stress of such artificial living conditions magnified every petty disagreement. At the first hearing, the panel not only agreed with the proposal that Higgs would receive a number of escorted ROTLs accompanied by his police handler, but I also suggested informally to his counsel that he might benefit from participation in one of the distance learning courses available through the Prisoners' Education Trust, of which I was then chairman. That suggestion, of course, played no part in the formal decision of the panel.

Not only did the proposed ROTLs go well but, by the time of the next review, Higgs was not only technically a Category D prisoner, but he had adopted the informal suggestion. The decision letter continued:

> '*Following the last oral hearing you had decided to pursue distance learning qualifications through the Prisoners' Education Trust. That enabled you to obtain the further qualifications mentioned above, including a qualification in construction work in which you had obtained a Distinction. Your own efforts enabled you to plan and develop, with brickwork, paving and block work, a garden area on what had been an unused part of the prison, which was about the size of a small football pitch. You did all the work by hand, mixing the mortar for the brickwork and the paving. That garden area would be a credit to most landscape gardeners. The Panel feel added confidence in your determination to succeed when they reflect on the single-minded approach which you have adopted to the development of this impressive feature.*'

Gary was released. His handlers provided him with accommodation in a university town, where he was in contact with students half his age. Gary, quite a charismatic individual, wanted to make up for lost time. We next met in HMP Winchester, in 2013. He had been recalled, having formed a dysfunctional relationship with a young woman, who complained of domestic violence. Her complaints were dismissed on appeal to the Crown Court, but Gary's lifestyle was objectively risky.

Gary was re-released to approved premises in March 2014, when aged forty-two. The panel identified a release and risk management plan and noted that he had formed what appeared to be a stable and supportive relationship with another young woman. There was no reason to assume that we should ever hear about Gary again. The assumption was wrong. A member of the panel, who had been undertaking duty member responsibilities, told me informally that a female with whom Gary had been associating had been found dead, and that Gary was likely to be charged with manslaughter. It was my colleague's perception, from the gossip she had picked up, that no criticism was being directed towards our panel; and if Gary was charged with a serious offence, let alone convicted of it, the Review Committee of the Parole Board would have invited our comments. We were never asked to comment, from which it is safe to assume that the allegation was never established. But the sequence of events remains puzzling.

It was something of a shock to be dealing in 2010 with a recalled life-sentenced prisoner who had been sentenced to death on 2 April 1965. He had qualified for a death sentence, despite the Murder (Abolition of the Death Penalty) Act 1965, because although the bill was successfully passed on a free vote in 1964, the Act only received royal assent on 8 November 1965.

Michael Copeland – I can identify him without embarrassment, as I know that he is dead – was born in April 1938. At the age of sixteen he was sent to an approved school, and later to borstal training. He absconded and was returned to borstal. He was then called up for National Service and discharged because of a psychopathic personality. Meanwhile, between June 1960 and March 1961, he murdered his three victims. The circumstances of each murder, which remained undetected until he confessed to them, are stark. Copeland had killed at least two male victims because they were gay; and the circumstances of the first and third murders were strikingly similar.

Both Derbyshire victims were found in the same location in Chesterfield, with their vehicles crashed and abandoned against the same lamp post. Between the two murders, Copeland had knifed to death a young man in a wood in Germany. Some three years later he visited the home of the detective inspector who had initially questioned him, and confessed. The confession was later denied.

It strains credibility that a serial killer should have remained undetected, particularly when two of the murders occurred at the same location, and when both were committed by an unsophisticated young man. It is remarkable that, following Copeland's discharge from the army, he was convicted and sentenced to short prison terms for unrelated offending, and was later committed to a mental hospital: all before his admission of the murders in 1963.

He was not charged with these murders until 1964, possibly because his mental state was suspect. When he appeared at Birmingham Assizes in April 1965, he admitted responsibility for each of them, and was duly sentenced to death, albeit his legal advisers and the trial judge must have envisaged that, in the light of the legislation proceeding through Parliament, he would be spared the death penalty.

Copeland was functionally illiterate when he came to prison in 1965. During his incarceration, he was regularly visited by a prison visitor. She encouraged him to learn to read and write; and Copeland made such progress that he eventually obtained an Open University degree. A relationship developed, and Copeland married her in 1991. Copeland was released on life licence in 1997, having been in custody for thirty-three years.

There were inevitably adjustment problems. The relationship caused a major rift between his wife and her children. In November 2001, at a time when Copeland had arranged to be visited in his home by a female escort in the absence of his wife, he was accused by the escort of falsely imprisoning her; and he was recalled to custody. His subsequent release was approved by the Parole Board when the allegation of false imprisonment was abandoned.

Despite his return to his wife's home, the relationship remained strained. Copeland was recommended to undergo spinal surgery: this was unsuccessful, and left him in constant pain and doubly incontinent. His wife found him attempting to take his own life. He had left a suicide note. She turned to his offender manager for guidance. She admitted that she should not have married Copeland. She had felt betrayed by the circumstances of his first recall. She was too proud to admit her mistake to her own family; and she acknowledged that it was at her insistence that her husband had been re-released. While she told the probation officer that she did not suggest that Copeland might harm her, her primary concern was that if she were to end the relationship, he might commit suicide. That was the background to the activation of the re-recall to custody; and Mrs Copeland began divorce proceedings.

Prior to the oral hearing, Mrs Copeland had written three letters to her husband, which formed part of the dossier. In the first she described herself as feeling like Judas, because by confiding in his probation officer and triggering his recall, she had betrayed him. The second letter explained her decision to commence divorce proceedings. In the last letter, Mrs Copeland explained that she could no longer visit her husband while he remained in custody. She agreed to bring the clothing and other items he had requested to the gatehouse of HMP Elmley, but intended to leave them there for him. This she did on her final visit: and, having done so, she collapsed and died from a massive heart attack in the prison car park.

Copeland told the oral hearing that he remained in constant physical pain, and antidepressants gave him no respite. He acknowledged how cantankerous he had become to his wife, and that he had attempted suicide. He felt guilty about the separation between his wife and her children and grandchildren, for which he was responsible. If released, he hoped to move back to the Nottingham area, where he had a brother.

Towards the end of his questioning by the panel, which had expressed its condolences on the recent death of his wife, Copeland was asked how he now felt. There was a lengthy pause before he made any response. Unable to sit or stand without acute discomfort, he shuffled painfully from one foot to the other. Tears began to roll down his cheeks. He remained silent. At last, he spoke. 'I feel terrible in saying this,' he said, 'but while I recognise that I no longer have a wife, I no longer have to worry about her expectations for me, and the friction which this has caused. So this has come as a huge relief.'

It was impossible to direct release in October 2010: there was no release plan. The panel did, however, recommend his transfer to open conditions in Derbyshire. He qualified for a further review the following year. Noting when it was due, I asked the assigned judicial chairman of the next panel to tell me the outcome. He did: Copeland died of natural causes, two days before the hearing was due to take place.

———

During the ten years of my Parole Board membership, I conducted over four hundred cases. Some were straightforward, and quite brief. But even the apparently routine case would identify something unique, emphasising the wisdom of the rubric subsequently adopted by PET as a strapline: *More than just a prisoner*. Norman, a man in his fifties of hitherto exemplary character, developed a mental illness for which he was recommended to undertake psychoanalysis. After extensive treatment, not only did he discover that his extensive treatment was unnecessary, and exacerbating his illness, but that the analyst's motivation was personal gain. He took a fishing knife to his next session and attacked her with it; and pleaded guilty to attempted murder. For over three years, he became a hermit in his cell. He grew his hair down to his waist, and never washed. A prison officer left with him a newspaper article that suggested poetry as a diversion. Norman was hooked. Following his successful participation in a PET-funded access course, his poetry featured in Radio 4 programmes; his morale recovered instantly; he became keen to develop his personal physique as a regular gym participant; and by the time of his Parole Board review (when he was recommended for open conditions) he was smart, short-haired and had a zest for life.

———

Rereading some of my decision letters only emphasises the human history in each of them. It was a privilege not only to participate in this process, and to develop links with colleagues that would have been otherwise impossible, but also to become aware of the extent to which reform of the criminal justice system, and its replacement by a holistic process of judicial monitoring of sentencing, may promote rehabilitation. That is the subject of chapter 19, 'Judicial Monitoring'.

THE BENCH

And then the justice,
In fair round belly with good capon lin'd,
With eyes severe, and beard of formal cut,
Full of wise saws and modern instances;
And so he plays his part.
Shakespeare, *As You Like It*: Act II, Scene 7

Shakespeare's fifth age might conveniently introduce some vignettes from the more than thirty-two years during which I undertook a judicial role or served as a judicial member of the Parole Board. A catalogue of the cases that I had the privilege of trying over that lengthy period must be resisted; some of the episodes, however, illustrate aspects of human life, and they can be included in a garland of assorted blooms.

An early judicial memory, as a newly authorised deputy County Court judge, was to approve the adoption of a child. I had no experience of adoption. The case was listed anonymously. Before the adoptive parents came into my room, I was told that they were Mr and Mrs Samuels. They came in with the baby. 'What's his name?' I asked. 'David' was the serendipitous reply. I often wondered what happened to the other 'David Samuels'.

The start of my role as a part-time judicial officer could no longer be justified today, when such an appointment requires the formal approval of the Judicial Appointments Commission and the completion of a lengthy form that identifies the 'candidate's competencies'. My subsequent appointment to Silk in 1981 required no more than the completion of one sheet of A4, plus the support of a couple of senior members of the Court of Appeal. The outcome of that success was my swift and wholly informal appointment as a deputy High Court judge sitting in both the Family Division and the Queen's Bench Division. Meanwhile, as I was actively encouraged to accept the further appointment of an assistant Recorder, my induction as a criminal judge began in 1983.

As such, I attended the first-ever sentencing conference organised by Lord Justice Tasker Watkins. There were over a hundred participants. We were told to consider a factual scenario, and to offer our views on sentence. More and more lengthy sentences were read out; yet my proposal was for two years' probation. 'Stand up, the man who said probation,' Tasker demanded. While his wartime bravery had resulted in the award of a Victoria Cross, I felt similarly exposed as I justified my proposal. Over the next twenty-seven years I focused on the statutory purposes of sentencing; and concluded that the prospects of successful rehabilitation often trumped the demands of lengthy custodial sentences.

This developing thought owed much to happenstance; and, specifically, the introduction of the requirement periodically to review the progress of those who were subject to a Drug Treatment and Testing Order. This came into force in 2000. I asked my senior probation officer for guidance. 'Just make it up as you go,' he suggested. With the modest advantage of parenthood, and the distant experiences of organising adolescents at school and the members of my platoon, that is what I did. I did, however, investigate what was happening elsewhere; and, thanks to the internet, discovered the practice of other jurisdictions. In time, this settled down as a theory of judicial supervision and monitoring; and an explanation of its parameters is described in the next chapter.

What I do *not* do is revisit the many cases I tried as a part-timer and a full-time judge, or justify my decisions or my sentences. Fortunately, few of these were the subject of alteration or adverse comment in the Court of Appeal. There is a well-known cliché of the three ages of the Circuit Judge: in the early years, the new judge wonders what the Court of Appeal will think about the decision. In the middle years, the judge asserts: 'The Court of Appeal is simply wrong!' In the final stage, the judge may say: 'I don't give a damn about the Court of Appeal!' Save that I retain enormous respect for the individual men and women who sit in that treadmill of a court, I have not only reached that final stage, but have travelled well beyond it. So, snapshots from my judicial experience will feature in what follows; but, save for a couple of well-known trials, there will be no regurgitation of the details of either civil, family or criminal cases.

———

I have no difficulty in identifying Ussama El-Kurd, since he made it known during the lengthy criminal proceedings he faced that he wanted to be known, like T.S. Eliot's Macavity, as 'the Napoleon of crime' – in his case, money-laundering. The following explains what can so unexpectedly go wrong in what objectively should have been an unremarkable Crown Court trial.

For five months between September 1998 and February 1999, I conducted what superficially amounted to a straightforward, if extensive, conspiracy to launder what was said to be the largest quantity of 'dirty' money known to Customs and Excise. One significant problem seemed to lead to another.

After a succession of bail applications, and a deterioration in the mental health of the defendant, I heard a further bail application in December 1997. I could only ensure that El-Kurd was fit to be tried by creating a quasi-freedom for the defendant by requiring, as a bail condition, his continued residence in a private psychiatric hospital. The creation of such a bail condition was itself an exercise in some ingenuity. Once El-Kurd was fit for trial, he remained resident in the private clinic, being escorted to and from court each day by taxi.

Things began to unravel from Day 1 of the trial. El-Kurd was represented by Bob Marshall-Andrews, from my former chambers (4 Paper Buildings). I was determined to maintain good relations with him. On Day 1, just as the jury had been sworn, his mobile phone went off. As he was then an MP, I asked whether it was the prime minister. Without drawing breath, Bob replied: 'It was the Lord Chancellor' (it was well known that there was personal animosity between Bob and Lord Irvine) 'but I have cut him off.'

The opening proceeded. Bob objected vociferously to what was described by the prosecutor, Nigel Peters QC, as an 'Aladdin's cave' of treasure. This was said to be a racist comment, given El-Kurd's ethnic origins. This little spat was the foundation of the first of three applications during the protracted trial to stay further proceedings as an abuse of process, on the grounds of 'prosecutorial bias'.

One month after the trial began, there was an unexpected development. Prosecuting counsel said he needed to see me urgently, and that defence counsel were not at court. I agreed to see counsel, with my clerk and a shorthand writer. I was told that El-Kurd was in hospital with a broken arm, following his arrest the previous night. It transpired that, on his way back to the clinic at which he had to reside, El-Kurd suspected that something was going to happen; and he asked his driver to go to the Temple, where he had a consultation with his counsel. Bob telephoned Nigel Peters and asked him directly whether he knew of any prospective arrest. The answer was 'No'; and this was subsequently explained, given that the arrest had been authorised by the prosecution team, to avoid tipping off El-Kurd, which would have been an offence. Fortunately, I was never asked to decide whether avoiding the commission of a tipping-off offence excused a deliberate lie.

Once I went into court, there was an explosion of anger from Marshall-Andrews, directed towards both the prosecution and me, for 'entertaining' the prosecutor in my room. I explained that I had been told that he was not in the court building, that I had a note of what I had been told, that a shorthand writer was present, and that a transcript of what had occurred could be obtained; and this temporarily pacified him. However, Bob launched a further application to stay further proceedings, on the basis that what had happened amounted to an abuse of process. I ruled that the trial should proceed.

Later, those representing El-Kurd applied for a transcript of the hearing held in my room. The tape recording, which had been sent by post for transcription, became lost, and has never been found.

At the half-term holiday break for the jury, Nigel Peters went to New York, and returned with some Disney characters, with which he decorated the room allocated to the prosecution team and their mass of documentary material. One of the Disney dolls was Aladdin. Bob visited the room and reacted with histrionic fury to its presence. That founded his third application to stay proceedings as an abuse. I declined to give a detailed ruling: I had no reason to add to what I had previously said.

Another problem surfaced in early December. Bob and his junior proposed to withdraw from the trial, as their funding was exhausted. This was presented as a request from the solicitors to cease to act for El-Kurd, which would have the effect of precluding counsel, who only act on the instructions of a solicitor, from continuing with their client's representation. While counsel agreed that they could act *pro bono*, they said they could not professionally do so if they were no longer instructed by a solicitor. A very self-satisfied commercial Silk then appeared for the solicitors and told me that the solicitors were entitled to withdraw, because he had so advised.

I conducted my own research and ruled that the solicitors had agreed an 'entire contract', which meant that they could not terminate their client's retainer. This left El-Kurd represented. Without his continuing representation, the trial might have been aborted.

Over the Christmas holiday break, the second defendant absconded. As with the other six defendants, he was on unconditional bail. A vast amount of incriminating evidence had identified his role in exporting high-value euros to Holland. He rode his motorcycle into the Channel Tunnel, never to be seen again. I discharged the jury from considering his case any further. Today, I should have been authorised to proceed with the trial in his absence.

El-Kurd did not give evidence. I remanded him in custody when the jury were in deliberation: first, because he faced an inevitably substantial sentence if convicted; and second, a co-defendant, Peter McGuinness, a courier of many millions of pounds' worth of currency from Liverpool to London, had absconded during the summing up. Although I sentenced McGuinness, in his absence, to ten years' imprisonment, so far as I was told no step was taken by Customs and Excise to trace him and to enforce that order. About a year later, an officer of Customs and Excise asked me for a replacement warrant, having lost the original. I declined the request, saying that I was *functus*, meaning that my judicial authority was spent.

Following conviction, I sentenced El-Kurd to fourteen years' imprisonment, the statutory maximum. I could not envisage a more serious case. Because the Crown had failed appropriately to pursue confiscation proceedings, I could only fine him. On what I was told, his assets amounted to well over £1 million, so I fined him £1 million, with three years' imprisonment in default.

In July 2000, the Court of Appeal upheld the conviction but reduced the custodial term to twelve years, with the fine and its default term undisturbed, on the basis that laundering the proceeds of criminal conduct is less heinous than laundering the proceeds of drug trafficking.

In November 2003, Mr El-Kurd was once again the subject of an unexpected application. The prison authorities had erroneously released him when he had served less than four years' imprisonment, and had ignored the default term of the consecutive sentence for non-payment of the fine. The reason for the failure by the prison service to calculate sentence expiry correctly was the subject of an extraordinary chapter of errors on their part, including an assumption that for a period of more than two years he had been remanded in custody, when he had been on conditional bail.

Matters did not end there. On 3 May 2006, the House of Lords gave judgment in the similar case of R v. Saik.[29] That decision fatally undermined the way in which the conspiracy indictment against El-Kurd and Others had been drafted, notwithstanding the attempt by Nigel Peters QC before their Lordships to justify his approach. In short, while the House of Lords concluded that reasonable grounds for suspicion are enough for the substantive offence of laundering money, they would not suffice for a conspiracy to commit the offence.

Different solicitors pursued an application to the Criminal Cases Review Commission on behalf of El-Kurd. In 2006, once the CCRC had referred his conviction to the Court of Appeal, El-Kurd was released from the sentence he was then serving, on bail. The Court of Appeal subsequently allowed the reference and quashed the conviction,[30] but directed

29   [2008] UKHL 18
30   R v. El-Kurd and Others [2008] 1 Cr App R 1

a retrial. There never was a retrial. This is because as soon as El-Kurd was released on bail, he started a fresh bureau de change.

Thanks to Google, I discovered that this business was successfully operated between 2006 and 2010, when it was shut down; and El-Kurd was once again arrested. The subsequent press report recorded that El-Kurd was convicted of laundering approximately £169 million of 'criminal cash'. Of course, the law had changed in the interim, as a result of the Proceeds of Crime Act 2000; and it is noteworthy that the judge was able to say 'that volume of money laundering represented the proceeds of drug dealing, extortion, robbery and violence and all the other aspects of major crime', avoiding the need to distinguish between the proceeds of drug trafficking and other criminal conduct. That distinction had bedevilled the deliberations of my jury.

———

No one could have anticipated the application made to me before embarking on one of my next substantial trials. The prosecution, without notice to the defendants, warned me that the police had discovered that a serious attempt was to be made on my life, as the designated trial judge. Bound as I was to take the information seriously, I reported it on the telephone to my Presiding Judge. He was both relaxed and laconic: 'You can try it at the Bailey: you will be quite safe there.' That optimistic note ignored the fact that I did not live in the Central Criminal Court, and travelled to work routinely on public transport. Within days, I was visited at home by a chief superintendent of the Metropolitan Police and his sergeant:

'Please explain what route you take to get to work.'

I described my regular commute, which included walking to and from Richmond and Waterloo stations every day.

'Do you travel the same route, or do you vary it?'

I confirmed that I was normally on autopilot during my commute, and usually caught the same inward and outward trains.

The chief superintendent looked gloomy.

'I don't see how we can protect this gentleman,' he observed.

At that moment, our faithful black labrador was stretched out on the floor in the TV room. With heavy sarcasm, I told the officers: 'If the Metropolitan police can't protect me, I'm sure my dog will.'

For much of the next year I presided in the historic Court 1 of the Old Bailey, but no more dramatic event occurred than the occasion when my silk gown became trapped in the runners of the judicial throne – it was so heavy that it ran on steel rails as one pulled it into the bench – so that when the usher proclaimed 'All rise' as we adjourned for lunch one day, a ripping sound preceded the revelation that my gown was torn from top to bottom. This did little for my dignity, as the judges were obliged to process, wearing wigs and gowns, into the dining room.

The background to this case was a 'carousel fraud'. The facts were specified in a ruling that I gave, and which were adopted verbatim in a subsequent decision of the Court of Appeal.

'In outline, the allegation is that trading entities were created solely for the purpose of dishonestly retaining and reclaiming the VAT element of sales of computer processing units and other computer components which were not made bona fide. The goods were properly imported without having any liability to VAT, it being the intention of those responsible for the importation that the goods would be re-sold to a UK-based trader, thereby attracting a liability to VAT at the standard rate; that the purchaser would account to the importer for the purchase price, inclusive of VAT, but that the importer, instead of accounting to Customs for the VAT element as required, would retain the VAT and 'disappear' before any enforcement action could be taken by the authorities. In the scheme as it developed, the same goods would then be exported without incurring a VAT liability, and the entities to whom the goods were exported would arrange for their reimportation into the United Kingdom for a similar cycle of dishonest sales of the same units without accounting to Customs. Meanwhile, to the extent that the purchaser had expended VAT on the purchase of the goods, it would reclaim that sum as input tax from Customs ... The loss to public funds was some £11 million.'

At the outset of the trial, I was asked to direct twenty-four-hour protection for the prospective jury, such was the alleged reputation of the principal conspirators. I declined, not least because I knew from two of my judicial colleagues who had given a similar direction that their trials had to be aborted when the police providing such protection formed inappropriate relationships with female jurors. Once I had clarified, at the request of leading counsel representing a Mr Stapleton, what my probable approach would be to the inevitable confiscation proceedings, should any defendant plead guilty, the three defendants whom the Crown had identified as the primary conspirators were rearraigned and pleaded guilty; and the trial process, as well as the preservation of the judge's life, was undisturbed.

Following guilty pleas by the principal conspirators (Stapleton, May and Bravard) in September 2001, and the convictions of other defendants at the conclusion of their trial three months later, inevitably I was obliged to consider complex confiscation proceedings. The complications of the Proceeds of Crime Act 1995 were notorious, and that Act was subsequently substantially amended. I had to grapple with the earlier legislation. It was discouraging, at the outset of those proceedings, to be told the significant number of discrete issues that I was required to resolve, and on which there was no prior authority. My reserved decision identified nine such issues. Inevitably, given the sums in question, my decision was appealed. The hearing in the Court of Appeal extended over three days; suffice it to note that the largest confiscation order I made, of £3,264,277 against Raymond May, was undisturbed. That decision was challenged in the House of Lords. Following a further lengthy hearing, judgment was delivered in May 2008. It remains, I believe, the leading authority in confiscation cases. The single speech of Lord Bingham, with whom all members of the Appellate Committee agreed, was that May's appeal was dismissed with costs.[31] His liability thus exceeded, by that date, £4 million inclusive of interest and costs. Sometime later, I spotted a press report of enforcement proceedings against May. This told me that, having served his custodial sentence, plus the default term imposed by me for non-payment of the confiscation sum,

31   [2008] UKHL 28

he had satisfied no part of the Crown's confiscation order: the press report indicated that he had not even paid a nominal £1. The entire confiscation exercise appeared to have been a waste of time and of public money.

––––––––

The case of May and Others was by no means the last of the heavy cases I was asked to try, and for which I developed a certain expertise. Multi-handed money-laundering cases, major drug importation and serious fraud were all part of my staple diet once I had concentrated exclusively on crime, in contrast to the mixed diet of civil and crime I had anticipated when I was first appointed. With hindsight, it was regrettable that my appointment coincided with the introduction of the Woolf reforms, which meant that when I was sitting in civil, I was largely sitting in chambers, case-managing cases I knew would never come to trial. Despite the intel-lectual challenge of these heavy cases – no one should assume that crime is an easy topic – and the moments of levity that occasionally lightened them, I gloss over their now dusty details.

What might, however, be of rather more interest to the general reader is an explanation for my failure to achieve a role within the judicial hierarchy that, with hindsight, might have reflected such organising and administra-tive ability as I had shown earlier in my professional life; or which might have permitted the development of the distinct approach to sentencing reform that I have tried to promote.

I had been sitting happily as a Recorder at what was still then known as Knightsbridge Crown Court, despite its transfer to Blackfriars, for over a month prior to my appointment as a Circuit Judge in mid-March 1997.

For much of the following year I was both fulfilled and happy in my work, and in my relations with colleagues, court staff and all those with whom my work brought me into contact. I had volunteered to run the judges' mess at Knightsbridge (Blackfriars, as it subsequently became), and in that capacity arranged ad hoc judges' dinners, visits by the High Sheriff and other dignitaries, and a succession of court parties. My weekly purchase of cheese from a Richmond deli went down particularly well.

When the newly appointed resident judge went abroad for three months, he left me in charge – a role I happily accepted.

However, from the start of my sittings at the Old Bailey in 2001, events seemed to undermine that hitherto euphoric phase. Whether I would 'fit in' at that court was itself open to question. I knew that I was regarded as 'odd', because I declined to drink alcohol at lunchtime; and I was not an enthusiast for the gossip of the day at teatime. However, what ultimately wrecked my relationship with at least one judicial colleague, and thus terminated any long-term aspiration I may have had to undertake the heavy work of the Old Bailey full-time, occurred entirely adventitiously.

Maxine and I had, since 1990, run the antique shop in Richmond (Marryat) mentioned in chapter 14, 'Never on Sunday'. This included arranging restoration and conservation of customers' own property. For this, the business sourced specialist restorers and conservators. A customer requested the specialist repair of two ceramic items, which were sent to the regular restorer in Stoke-on-Trent for an estimate. The customer declined the estimate; and the restorer claimed to have returned them, with other repaired items. They disappeared. The customer claimed that they were valuable eighteenth-century Meissen; the restorer, who had of course examined them, maintained that they were late nineteenth-century copies, much smaller than the original eighteenth-century version, and of little value. Litigation ensued. It started long before I became a judge, and was still in progress about eight years later. What I did not know was that the son-in-law of the customer was a permanent judge at the Old Bailey, whose wife (a former barrister), had been advising her mother to pursue her claim.

The claim meandered through the County Court and resisted my initial attempts (while still in practice) to negotiate a sensible resolution with the solicitors instructed by the customer. Thereafter she acted in person, assisted by her daughter. Richmond solicitors were instructed by Maxine on behalf of Marryat. What I only discovered late in the day was the family connection to the permanent judge, who had told the Recorder of London that he was not happy about my presence in the court. This only filtered back to me through a casual conversation with a presiding judge, who said that, to maintain a 'happy ship', it would be better if I did not return to the Old Bailey once I had concluded the case of Stapleton and Others.

I was content to accept this; but with the passage of time, it was clear that my card had been marked. Following my approval to conduct serious fraud cases, I had requested an 'attempted murder/murder' authorisation, to accompany the authorisations I held; but was told that, since I would no longer be sitting at the Old Bailey, there was no point in giving me one. Other judges at Blackfriars, junior to me both in seniority and experience, subsequently received that authorisation. On the credit side, I had been elected as a member of the committee of the Council of HM Circuit Judges in 2001 and swiftly became chair of its Criminal sub-committee. This was an increasingly high-profile role, once formal liaison had been established between the committee, ministers and senior officials; and I routinely attended meetings at the Home Office, the Department for Constitutional Affairs and major conferences, as well as responding to multiple consultation papers.

Paradoxically, the fact that I was becoming more widely regarded in the judicial community became a source of friction within the small judicial community of Blackfriars; and when a vacancy for the role of Senior Circuit Judge at Southwark Crown Court arose, I applied for it. I was advised to seek some formal assistance with my application, and with the prospective interview process; and I paid for the coaching. Although I knew there were only a few applicants for the post, I was rejected for interview; and because I knew who the interviewees were, I asked for feedback. I received the following:

'*HH Judge Samuels provided very strong evidence in a range of the criteria, including knowledge and experience, intellectual and analytical ability and decisiveness. However, he provided less evidence in relation to some of the other categories, including communication and listening skills, and understanding people and society.*'

Following a conversation with my then Presiding Judge, who had known me well for most of our practising lives and had expressed surprise that I had not been interviewed, I was asked to agree to my application being reviewed by the Senior Presiding Judge. To maintain objectivity, I was invited to obtain the professional comments of my erstwhile coach. She wrote:

> '... I have reviewed thousands of applications throughout my career. I have been asked to review the application of Judge John Samuels QC who has been rejected for interview on the basis of the quality of the answers of two out of the fourteen criteria, these areas being:
>
> • Communication and listening skills
> • Understanding people in society
>
> I have studied these areas and find nothing in his answers which would preclude him for interview. To the contrary, I found the following to be positive indicators for his candidacy for interview...
> It is difficult to understand how his answers would preclude him from interview, rather that they would invite further exploration which is precisely what interviews are about.'

My Presider told me that he had forwarded these comments to the Senior Presiding Judge 'with a long covering letter expressing my own (uncomplimentary) views on self-assessments'.

By the end of the summer of 2005, I had decided to invest my hopes on the development of a community court for Greater London; and the then developing plans for a major event to discuss the formation of such a court made that a sensible aspiration. Since the cases I tended to try were lengthy, I thought I was duty-bound to offer a long notice period. Had the proposal for a community court for Greater London come into being, inevitably this needed development over a lengthy timescale.

My departure from Blackfriars was by no means the conclusion of a judicial role. For the following four years I sat as a deputy at Kingston Crown Court, and this was the happiest of times. My work was challenging; the staff were supportive; and lunchtimes were invariably clubbable. So, long after these events, the echo of 'if only', mentioned at the outset of chapter 12, 'Temptation', inevitably bubbles up: had I stayed put in 4 Paper Buildings, the horror of the Percival saga would never have happened, and my judicial progression would have looked very different. Whether in the long term I should have made a fundamental difference to the lives of others is a question that is not for me to answer.

———

No one who was even vaguely aware of the extent to which miscarriages of justice could occur within the criminal justice system in early 2024 could have ignored the existence of the widening scandal, created by the Post Office, in their prosecution of hundreds of sub-postmasters, alleged to have stolen substantial sums, and of falsifying their accounts. Since this topic is subject to an ongoing public inquiry, I merely adopt it as an introduction to a source of immense personal satisfaction, namely my involvement, since about 2016, with Inside Justice.

This organisation, a spin-off from the prison newspaper *Inside Time*, was founded by the charismatic Louise Shorter. I met her by chance. Within weeks I was a member of its Advisory Panel, comprising not only leading Silks and lawyers with formidable expertise in challenging convictions in the Court of Appeal Criminal Division, but independent forensic scientists of international renown. Many have become personal friends. I had long been aware of the potential for miscarriages of justice. In May 2018 I pointed out, in a lecture to the annual conference of the British Academy of Forensic Science,[32] how far this stain had lain on the criminal justice system since the notorious convictions of the 1970s and 1980s.

Despite the creation of the Criminal Cases Review Commission (CCRC) following the recommendation of the Royal Commission on Criminal Justice, many believe that the CCRC could realistically be more proactive in relation to its reference of cases to the Court of Appeal. While my lecture neither embraced nor rejected that proposition, it explained why it did not. First, I suggested that judicial conservatism tends to mirror

———

32   'The Politics of Wrongful Conviction': BAFS, 5 May 2018

that of public opinion. In 1974, the very suggestion that police officers might fabricate evidence was something the man in the street regarded as unimaginable. The driver for the political acceptance that police officers could and did lie was the development of forensic science.

Second, a police force depleted of essential funding cannot be expected to train disclosure officers effectively to provide material that may undermine the prosecution case, or may assist the defence. Those disclosure omissions, so highlighted in the Post Office prosecutions, have been echoed for many years in cases considered by the CCRC, including applications by sub-postmasters, and the notorious recent case of Andrew Malkinson.

Third, I drew attention to what I described as 'the sacrosanctity of the jury verdict'. While in my experience most jurors are highly conscientious in their attempts to reach a proper verdict, they give no reasons for their decisions; and the margin of appreciation afforded by the Court of Appeal to their verdicts is often very wide.

Finally, I drew attention in that lecture to the imbalance between the statutory duty of the Court of Appeal to allow an appeal when the court considers the conviction unsafe[33] and the statutory responsibility of the CCRC only to refer a case to the Court of Appeal when it considers there is a real possibility that the conviction would not be upheld were a reference to be made.[34]

The lecture concluded with the trite observation that judges are human; and it is a human characteristic to resent criticism. That quality may, and I think does, encourage senior judges, sitting in the Court of Appeal, to avoid criticism of trial judges and what may have gone wrong at first instance unless the error is obvious.

Since joining the advisory panel of Inside Justice, I have been tasked with the drafting of five applications to the CCRC, each of which involved more than a hundred hours of preparation. I also chaired a series of meetings with other bodies and academics designed to persuade the police to adopt a more uniform disclosure regime, following the Supreme Court decision

33 Section 2, Criminal Appeal Act 1968
34 Section 13 (1) Criminal Appeal Act 1995

in Nunn,[35] which happily resulted in the adoption, by the National Police Chiefs' Council, of an agreed and significantly improved disclosure model by all police forces. While I accept why the CCRC decided not to refer two of those cases, three of them remain outstanding; and it is relevant that the first two were murder convictions, in circumstantial cases, in 2008 and 2009 respectively, in each of which the CCRC has to date declined an invitation itself to review the contemporaneous forensic evidence heavily criticised by independent forensic experts who are members of the Inside Justice advisory panel; and in the third case, a conviction in 2018, with a nineteen-year determinate sentence, meanders along, following its submission in 2022. It would give me an immense morale boost to learn that any of these cases have received the result they each so richly deserve.

———

In 2016, the Criminal Justice Alliance kindly presented me with a 'Lifetime Achievement Award': one of those strange glass items you put on a shelf, and whose subtext is: *Now totter off quietly into the sunset.* Over the last eight years, I have happily ignored that recommendation.

---

35   R v. Chief Constable of Suffolk and Another, ex parte Nunn [2014] UKSC 37

JUDICIAL MONITORING

Enthusiasm is the dynamics of your personality.
Without it, whatever abilities you may have lie dormant. A wonderful thing
is this quality called enthusiasm. If you would like to be a power among men,
cultivate enthusiasm. People will like you better for it; and you will make
headway wherever you are.
J. Ogden Armour (1863–1927)
(Found on a prison noticeboard, and repeated *ad nauseam* to
successive iterations of the Pupillage Foundation Scheme)

The second slice of the toastie mentioned in the Preface. A couple of examples will set the scene.

- My court in Blackfriars Crown Court was immense. Normally I was some 50 feet away from those in the glazed dock at the back of the court. The opportunity periodically to review those sentenced to drug treatment and testing orders changed everything. They came into the witness box, a couple of feet away from me. Gradually they opened up, sometimes over months and even years, about what had gone wrong in their lives, and what was beginning to go right. This was outside anything I had experienced, either as an advocate or a judge. Accidentally, I discovered that empathy, plus a willingness to listen, made a difference.

  In time, and with experience in conducting these reviews, I encouraged the practising Bar to learn what this might achieve by offering those sitting in court a quicker listing of their own cases. The primary lesson from the experience was my own. The reviews opened a window into the lives of others, which would normally have remained tightly closed for those of my background – middle-class professional, barrister and judge. It developed my further education.

- No one was more entitled to asylum. Aged ten, he was present when his whole family was horrifically butchered to death in a civil war in Yemen. Somehow, he escaped, and ended up in an expatriate Yemeni community in South Yorkshire. That was the back story in one of my first Parole Board cases. He had formed a relationship with a female Yemeni. She had chosen another partner and left him. This conflicted with their joint culture. He located her, living above a corner shop. By now more sophisticated, he grabbed her mobile phone, to identify her new partner. He had a washing line with him and roughly tied her hands together before scrolling through her text messages. She quickly freed herself and called the police. Charged with false imprisonment, he was committed to the Crown Court, where he promptly pleaded guilty. The judge sentenced him to detention for public protection, with a minimum term of three months. That meant that his release could not be considered by the Parole Board until he had been in custody for three months *and* could demonstrate that he was no longer dangerous.

  Ten months later, we as the panel of the Parole Board first met him. He had no sentence or risk and release plan. He had undertaken nothing in custody: no programmes, no education and no training. He met his external probation officer for the first time that day.

  The panel, which I chaired, undertook some judicial monitoring. We adjourned the case for a month, and told everyone to produce a robust release and resettlement plan. This duly happened. It is tempting to imagine what might have happened to this young man had we *not* released him, and he had joined those *still* serving an indeterminate sentence in 2024, twelve years after this discredited sentence was finally abolished.

As you read this chapter, you may be thinking: how can I apply judicial monitoring? If you are a judge or magistrate, you will have an inquiring mind. Your inquiring mind will encourage you to investigate how monitoring is currently applied by the prison and probation service, by charities engaged with the criminal justice system, and perhaps in other jurisdictions. Get involved. If you are not yet a judicial officer, but might become one, aspire to be appointed, and to apply these ideas within your future role. If you are not involved with the criminal justice system, use your imagination to identify how, as a concerned member of the public, your personal involvement with criminal justice charities can assist those desperate to turn their lives around.

———

Now for my personal journey into judicial monitoring. I stumbled across this concept accidentally. My early reviews showed both progress and promise; and I visited programmes to learn what treatment and support was available through the London Probation Service. Through the internet I discovered the International Association of Drug Treatment Court Professionals (since 2015, the International Association of Treatment Court Professionals, IATCP), then chaired by a Toronto judge, Justice Paul Bentley, whose court was close to the home of my Canadian mother-in-law. He invited me to visit his court. This was a revelation. The progress of those on drug rehabilitation sentences was routinely reviewed at a morning meeting, chaired by the judge, at which representatives of the Probation Service *and* the defence cooperated in identifying the most appropriate path for the offender; and later each offender's treatment pathway was considered by the judge with *all* offenders present. This reinforced the message of a shared optimism to support offenders, coupled with the imposition of sanctions if the offender failed to comply.

I already had links with the New York-based Center for Justice Innovation, whose recently established community courts were making such positive improvements. The Red Hook Community Justice Center was one of its pioneering initiatives; and a joint visit there by David Blunkett, then Home Secretary, and Lord Woolf, Lord Chief Justice, encouraged them to promote the creation of a similar court in England.

The North Liverpool Community Justice Centre opened in September 2005. I was asked to assist the recruitment process. It took the department some years to acknowledge that this role was more suited to a Circuit Judge than a district judge. Belatedly, Judge David Fletcher was appointed as the judge in charge, and he became a colleague and friend in the cause of promoting the problem-solving court concept.

My friendship with Paul Bentley deepened, and I joined the board of the International Association to represent England and Wales. I doubted whether I could do much to promote the concept of the problem-solving court while still a full-time Circuit Judge, whose reviews of those subject to community orders had to be squeezed into Friday morning sittings before 10.30, to avoid interfering with ongoing trials.

By early 2005, I had embraced the concept of the problem-solving court as an effective way of securing compliance with community orders. My enthusiasm was enhanced by a visit to Glasgow, when I was welcomed to the newly established drug court by the sheriffs who ran it. A plan to develop a specialist community court, with Crown Court jurisdiction, for Greater London was my next step. I had pioneered liaison between the Crown Court judiciary and senior officials, as well as ministers, both in the Home Office and the Department for Constitutional Affairs; and I discussed my proposal with all concerned. I knew from Maxine, a senior magistrate on the Richmond Bench, that Richmond Magistrates' Court was due for closure; and this would be an excellent venue, given its transport links, for the kind of specialist community court I had in mind. In July 2005, I wrote:

'*The appropriate use of the DTTO has made a positive impact on low-level acquisitive offending to fund an entrenched drug addiction. The key component of this order is the regular review of the offender's progress by the sentencer. Where continuity of such judicial supervision of the order can be achieved, a correlative increase in satisfactory outcomes is achievable.*

The role of the specialist review court envisaged for Greater London demands a close partnership with London Probation Area. Greater London needs a specialist drug court with Crown Court jurisdiction, as well as at the level of the Magistrates' Court. A unified Greater London court responsible for the supervision of those convicted of drug-related offences should have a pyramidal structure, with at its apex sentencers in an identified Crown Court. An analogy is provided by the Family Courts: cases which begin in the magistrates' court, depending on their complexity, can be transferred either to the local County Court or to the Principal Registry, to be heard by a High Court judge.'

What was not explicit, but was explained to Lord Justice Thomas, the Senior Presiding Judge who supported the concept, was that if the proposal was approved, I wanted to lead it.

With Paul Bentley, I planned an invitation-only event in Lincoln's Inn, to which everyone who might help the introduction of the problem-solving court would be invited. Its potential success was enhanced when Lord Falconer, as Lord Chancellor, agreed to preside; and both Lord Phillips, Lord Chief Justice, and Sir Mark Potter, President of the Family Division, agreed to attend. Ten days before the event was due to take place, I received the devastating news that Paul Bentley had been admitted to hospital. Cancellation was not an option. My friends at the Center for Justice Innovation swiftly arranged for Judge Robert Keating, founding judge of the prototype problem-solving court, to attend. Bob Keating was simply magnificent! Introduced to the gathering by Charlie Falconer, he wowed his audience: Lord Phillips, in thanking him, declared himself entirely won over by the concept; and participation in a related event at 10 Downing Street the following day, plus a full page of publicity in the *Guardian*, concluded this triumphant visit spectacularly.

Increasingly convinced of a need to modify the traditional approach of the sentencer – detached, by the system, from what subsequently happens to those who have been sentenced – my enthusiasm encouraged optimism. The problem-solving model was gaining traction. I was asked to elaborate my proposals in a further paper, 'A Community Court for Greater London – how would it work?'

I received a generous valedictory when I retired, which included a comment from my friend Judge Richard Walker:

'*To me one of the most striking aspects of John's approach to the work of the Crown Court is his commitment to constructive sentencing wherever that is possible. He has proved particularly successful in reviewing offenders sentenced to drug treatment and testing orders. To many judges, including me, the desire to make such orders is sadly not matched by the experience of seeing offenders completing orders successfully. John Samuels, by contrast, has a significant success rate with such offenders. It is a notable judicial achievement which must say a great deal about his personal qualities.*'

I replied:

'*Judge Walker has been kind enough to say that I have found it possible to develop the operation of sentencer supervision. Judges, speaking generally, and the Bar are fascinated by the trial process. Because of the complexity of sentencing, it is necessary that judges get their sentence structure right. But far too little attention is paid to sentence outcomes. Outcomes are particularly critical when we have a prison population which, speaking frankly, is going through the roof. I believe that the way forward is for sentencers to become more involved in sentence supervision so that they can persuade, cajole and encourage those who are the primary responsibility of the Probation Service to turn away from the cycle of reoffending which has been well described as the revolving door. That, in part, is what I intend to do.*'

Following my retirement as a full-timer, I received a kind letter from Charlie Falconer. He included his thanks for my work in the field of community justice and added:

'*I understand you are in discussions with Lord Justice Thomas and my officials about your proposal for a Greater London Community Court and I greatly look forward to hearing the results.*' He wrote a personal postscript: '*I am very hopeful that your scheme for a London Community Court can proceed.*'

My enthusiasm, coupled with international conversations through my new membership of the IADTCP, encouraged exploration of drug courts and their initiatives elsewhere. I travelled overseas: to Vancouver and Dublin (2006); to Washington (2007) and St Louis (2008) – the latter to participate in conferences of the National Association of Drug Court Professionals; and in 2009 to open a drug court in Ghent, and to visit the drug court in Bergen, Norway, run by Ingunn Seim, a staunch ally in promoting the judicial monitoring concept.

Despite international evidence of the success of the problem-solving approach, the subsequent lack of enthusiasm for the concept was disappointing. The proposal for a Greater London community court hit the buffers – the Richmond Magistrates' Court was earmarked for closure and sale. Senior judiciary were reluctant to adopt a proposal that might further erode the limited resources government was prepared to grant to the criminal justice system generally. I therefore focused on my continuing trial work, sitting as a deputy Circuit Judge in retirement at Kingston Crown Court, as well as a growing load of Parole Board hearings. I still conducted reviews of those subject to some community orders.

When my age stopped my sittings in the Crown Court, I was free not only to undertake an increased workload of Parole Board case management and oral hearings, but to engage with think tanks and charities who were keen to pursue a problem-solving agenda. In 2015, despite my long-retired status, I was flattered to be included in a working group, at the invitation of the Lord Chief Justice, to plan the introduction of pilot Crown Courts that would apply a problem-solving and reviewing role.

In March 2016, I drafted a paper for that working group – 'Primary Criteria for the Problem-solving Court' – that included the key features previously explained. It was adopted by the group. In July 2016, Michael Gove, then Lord Chancellor, announced at a meeting of the All-Party Parliamentary Group on Penal Affairs – to the astonishment of its chair, Lord Ramsbotham, and me (we had both for so long advocated this reform, but had heard nothing) – that five pilot Crown courts would be established to promote the work proposed by the working group. Michael Gove lost office in a reshuffle the next day.

The new Lord Chancellor, Liz Truss, told me that she was sympathetic to the problem-solving court approach. Shortly afterwards I was contacted out of the blue by Jonathan Aitken, who knew of my interest, and who invited me to join him in writing an appropriately targeted pamphlet. 'What happened to the Rehabilitation Revolution?' was published in September 2017. By this time, my thinking in relation to judicial supervision and monitoring had embraced those in custody, as well as those serving their sentence in the community.

Our paper explained that sentences tended to be passed in what could be described as the 'snapshot moment' – the moment when the court identifies the penal consequences that flow from the conviction, and then moves on to the next case. We suggested that the detachment of the sentencer from any further involvement in the reform and rehabilitation of offenders was at odds with one of the statutory purposes of sentencing, namely the reform and rehabilitation of offenders. We recommended that twenty-first-century judges should be required to play a supervisory role in the sentence plan of those whom they had sent to prison. Custodial sentence plans and their annual reviews were spotted as infrequently as the Loch Ness monster; and we recommended that the sentencing court should be required periodically to review whether the custodial sentence might require modification.

The promotion of problem-solving courts would help achieve a more effective criminal justice system. We drew attention to the jurisdiction exercised by the French *Juge d'Application des Peines*, who reviews whether the prisoner's progress in custody qualifies for early release. We cited 'The JAP: lessons for England and Wales', a paper written by Professors Martine Herzog-Evans and Nicola Padfield while I was chair of the Criminal Justice Alliance in 2015.

In summary, the paper recommended that sentencers, both full-time judges and lay magistrates, should play a full role in enabling those who genuinely wish to do so to change their habits, to desist from offending, and to lead useful, pro-social and law-abiding lives.

In the following years, my enthusiasm for judicial monitoring and supervision was channelled through engagement with those prisoners and prisons who invited me to do so. My time on the Parole Board had ended in 2015; I had ceased to chair Prisoners' Education Trust in 2012 but had become their President; and had picked up a number of related roles (chair of the Criminal Justice Alliance; vice-president of Unlock, of the Association of Members of Independent Monitoring Boards, and of Tempus Novo; and Patron of the Prisoners' Advice Service and of Revolving Doors).

My engagement with Nottingham Law School actively included the topic of judicial monitoring and supervision; and from about 2016 onwards I accepted invitations to hold discussion groups with those in HMP Send and HMP Coldingley. The latter continued, only interrupted by the Covid pandemic, monthly; and in June 2023 the group was joined by the constituency MP, Michael Gove. Michael Gove then invited the Lord Chancellor, Alex Chalk MP, to visit my group; and he expressed specific interest in the topic of judicial monitoring that it involved. I was delighted when, at the Lord Chancellor's initiative, I explained the judicial monitoring concept to the Prisons and Probation minister, Rt Hon Edward Argar MP, on 24 April 2024.

My perception is that, over the twenty years or so that I have propounded the need for judicial monitoring, many of the judiciary have approved it: with the caveat that time and money will need to be devoted to its implementation. This misunderstands the proposal. Without prescribing the way in which judicial officers might undertake a supervisory role – that is for each of them to identify personally – my proposal is that it would be a fundamental obligation for each judicial officer to accept a continuing responsibility for the rehabilitation of those whom they had sentenced. Criminological research confirms that when individuals perceive that they have been treated with procedural fairness, and more particularly when those by whom they have been sentenced display a continuing interest in their progress, they will respond positively; and the corollary is equally true.[36]

---

36 See 'To be fair: procedural fairness in Courts' published by the Criminal Justice Alliance in October 2014

I held my final monitoring session at HMP Coldingley on 18 April 2024. It was a very moving event: both for me and Maxine and for them – some of them had been regular attenders for up to eight years. All of them signed the leaving cards that they had created for me; and they arranged a small party, including a delicious lemon drizzle cake, which the longest member of the group had baked. Since then, some have followed this up with personal letters. Both they and I were delighted when Lorna Hackett, my friend and colleague, agreed to take on a similar role.

One of my most rewarding monitoring relationships was that which I developed with the Cambridge-based Learning Together programme. Through my visits under its auspices to HMP Warren Hill, I was introduced to a number of those who subsequently became my mentees. The notorious event of 29 November 2019 at Fishmongers' Hall, when, sadly, Usman Khan, a terrorist who had been a graduate of the Learning Together programme, murdered two of its brightest young facilitators, has already featured in chapter 2, 'The Unexpected Mentor'. It was subsequently re-enacted in a sensitive Channel 4 film, *London Bridge: Facing Terror*. At that event, two of my mentees, both convicted murderers, and who had each been in conversation with me, courageously confronted the terrorist. Not only did each of them receive gallantry awards for their exemplary behaviour, but each can properly be described as fully rehabilitated. The success of judicial monitoring could not be more powerfully demonstrated.

ENVOI

Time, like an ever-rolling stream
Bears all its sons away;
They fly forgotten, as a dream
dies at the opening day.
Isaac Watts (1674–1748)

At the memorial service to my good friend General Lord Ramsbotham, in whose footsteps, like the page to King Wenceslaus, I tried to follow as we both pursued the goals of prison reform and prisoner rehabilitation, there was a reading that echoed a piece by Albert Schweitzer, previously recorded by me in a commonplace book:

Not how did he die?
But how did he live?
Not what did he gain?
But what did he give?
These are the things to measure the worth
Of this man as a man, regardless of birth.
Not what was his church? Nor what was his creed?
But had he befriended those really in need?
Not how did the formal obituary run?
But how many were saddened when his life's work was done?

On the same page, I had recorded this from Albert Einstein:

'*A human being is part of the whole, called by us "the universe", a part limited in time and space. He experiences himself, his thoughts and feelings as something separated from the rest, a kind of optical delusion of his consciousness. This delusion is a kind of prison for us, restricting us to our personal desires and affection for a few persons nearest to us. Our task must be to free ourselves from this prison by widening our circles of compassion to embrace all living creatures and the whole of nature in its beauty.*'

Despite my respect for the beliefs of those with deep-seated religious conviction, those two passages represent my settled conclusions.

A similar comforting thought is provided by Herbert Samuel:

'*If there is to be birth, there must be death. Unless there were departures, a time would quickly come when there could be no arrivals since the area of the finite earth would be filled. We can imagine a world in which there was neither birth nor death; but not a world in which there was one without the other.*'

I first drafted this on the Day of Atonement, 2023. To pen such a sentence would have been unthinkable during the lifetime of my parents: while neither of them were observant Jews, their loyalty to the traditions in which they had been brought up, coupled with their personal involvement in the Holocaust, meant that the sanctity of the most solemn day of the Jewish year meant refraining from all activity, other than contemplation of what might have been done rather better in the past twelve months, even if they were strictly not sins. The conventional fasting as well was not, towards the end of their respective lives, obligatory.

It took me many years before I was able to admit that I am an atheist. Confirmed as a liberal Jew, the congregation my parents had joined after the war, I actively acknowledged the ethics exemplified in its teaching, particularly relating to justice; and confidently wrote an essay prior to my confirmation at the age of fifteen entitled 'Why I am a Jew'. The arrival of David and Adam, and the obvious disinclination of Maxine to conform to any routine religious observance, encouraged me to start thinking for myself. A slow progression via humanism meant I agreed with Maxine that any religious ceremony at the time of our marriage was pointless. Periodically, we have attended church services together, for a wedding or a funeral; and on a few occasions I encouraged Maxine to accompany me to a service at the Liberal Jewish Synagogue, of which I remain a member, out of piety to the traditions of my forefathers rather than to any sense of belief. This meant nothing to her, and merely confirmed her loyalty to me as my supportive spouse.

I now find it easy to adopt the similar sentiments said to have been adopted by Albert Einstein:

> '*I am a deeply religious nonbeliever. This is a somewhat new kind of religion. I have never imputed to Nature a purpose or goal, or anything that could be understood as anthropomorphic. What I see in nature is a magnificent structure that we can comprehend only very imperfectly, and that must fill a thinking person with a feeling of humility. This is a genuinely religious feeling that has to do with mysticism. The idea of a personal God is quite alien to me and seems even naive.*'

There is no distinction between that credo and my own.

———

It has frequently puzzled me that great men at the centre of events should find the time to keep a contemporary diary. It would be tempting to identify the first of these as Julius Caesar, whose commentaries on the Gallic, German and British wars may be thought to have set the trend; but Winston Churchill, at the height of the Second World War, appears to have made his own contemporary record, which was subsequently put to good use in his six-volume history of the Second World War. A less worthy example is H.H. Asquith, who, in the desperate years of the First World War, regularly found time to create a record of daily doings in love letters addressed to Venetia Stanley.

Whether I should have emulated these examples is far too late to determine now, albeit my own response to some of the stressful events described in this memoir might have justified some nightly jottings. The events of 1987–90, when the Percival saga was at its height, exceeded any kind of pressure from what I routinely experienced in my practice at the Bar.

I began a succession of diaries in September 2007. I quote the initial entry:

'Perhaps the hardest task is to start with a blank sheet, in the new book. The analogy with other areas of life is obvious. However, for a retired chap, still sitting in the Crown Court, the privilege of being able to do what objectively feels like justice is its own reward.'

I opened with some thoughts on the El-Kurd case and its sequel; and concluded:

'If I had devoted the same amount of time and energy as I did to this case in creating a drug court and/or a community court system, which I could well have done, it would have made a major difference to re-offending, and to blighted lives.'

What might be of rather more relevance to a wider readership, whose interest may have been piqued by the reference to my belated conversion to atheism, are some press references at the time to galaxies.

'We used to think our Earth was unique in the galaxy: now astronomers suspect that most of the Milky Way's 100 billion stars are host to planets, and that many of these are similar to our World ... A 6-year study suggests that 10% of the Milky Way's stars are likely to have planets in the "Goldilocks zone": the area around a star that is neither too hot nor too cold for surface water to exist ... We can expect hundreds of billions to exist in the Milky Way alone.'

I added:

'This topic has fascinated me for as long as I can remember. Of course I was unaware of the progress of astronomical knowledge, and the extent to

which it is provable that planets capable of sustaining life may exist. But I focus on the enormity of the Milky Way's hundreds of billion stars; recognising that the Universe is expanding; and that beyond the horizon of the identifiable Milky Way lie a potential infinity (or at least an indefinite and large number) of similar Milky Ways in that expanding Universe. If then as is postulated we are contemplating a quantity of stars within our own discernible Milky Way capable of hosting planets similar to our own, and that a proportion of such planets are capable of sustaining those elements from which life evolved, it is only logical to assume that there are multiples of life-potential planets in the Universe beyond the Milky Way.

If then such myriads of planets exist, whose nature can only be guessed at, where then does the image of a God Creator fit in? Even if, which defies all reason, a universal creator brought the whole pattern which I seek to describe into existence, I cannot identify myself with such a creator: my insignificance if not my irrelevance is all too obvious.'

I have devoted no more than a few scattered moments – perhaps in rewarding conversations with friends – to these philosophical questionings. My primary focus has, I think, been to get on with the next task: whether it involves the mundane, or something more elevated. Rather than focusing on issues of faith, religion, or a profound thought process, in my ninth decade I realise that my heritage and my upbringing have combined to foster in me a determination to secure justice: justice for those who have failed to find it, and justice for those who probably do not deserve it anyway. For me, it seems, the pursuit of justice is a substitute for the comfort of a religious faith; but it is none the worse for that.

If the next generation of judges is prepared to consider, at least in outline, the validity of mentoring and monitoring as a potential personal ambition, the obligation to leave the world a little better than I found it may have been achieved.

I do not claim to reflect the requirements of some 'higher authority', however labelled by those who apply a theistic description to a personal creed: I only hope that I have made some difference; and I expect nothing in return save the peace, at the end, of having used my talents as I should.

———

I completed a revision of this chapter on 17 January 2024, when I had every reason to believe that I was in good health. Maxine and I had just returned from a twenty-four-hour visit to our favourite Sussex hotel, to celebrate her birthday. The next day I had the first of several seizures, swiftly diagnosed as a high grade glioma, an incurable brain cancer, and a life expectancy to be measured in months rather than years. Serendipity was off duty that day!

This has not altered my thinking. I have embraced the recommended treatment at the Royal Marsden with enthusiasm, and know that my family, whom I so dearly love, will respect the wishes that I have tried to set out logically in a coherent To Do list. I very much hope to see this book published, and the theme that it embraces, particularly that of judicial monitoring and supervision, brought more actively into being.

ACKNOWLEDGEMENTS

This book looked completely different in its first draft, when it was designed as no more than some family background and bits and pieces from my experiences as a lawyer. I imagined that it would go no further than the archives of my grandchildren. Things changed following a conversation with Jonathan Aitken. His personal experience of the prison system had convinced him of the need for rehabilitation; and we undertook, in an increasingly valuable partnership and friendship, the creation of 'What happened to the Rehabilitation Revolution?', successfully published by the Centre for Social Justice in 2017. Jonathan's skills as a wordsmith encouraged me to think that I too had something to say about the part which judicial monitoring might play in promoting rehabilitation.

Before Covid interrupted everything, at a catch-up lunch with my successors as Chairman of the Criminal Sub-committee of the Council of Circuit Judges, Andrew Goymer mentioned that his daughter Eleanor, formerly with HarperCollins, might be able to help. She has been of formidable assistance and, having read an early draft, introduced me to Chris Wold of Whitefox, her former colleague. Since that introduction, in February 2024, the speed of the subsequent journey has been matched by the pleasure of cooperation with all members of the Whitefox team, particularly Sarah Rouse, the project manager, Drew Cullingham, the structural editor, and Jenni Davis, the copy editor. Jenni identified some detailed nooks and crannies in the historic background which even this old pedant, believing he still had a good memory, had clearly forgotten. She is a formidable researcher. All three have taught me how to accept the constructive criticism which they so appropriately offered.

Early drafts of this book, when it was far more of a personal memoir than a focused attempt to promote judicial monitoring and supervision, was shared with many, whose encouragement and kindly criticism significantly improved the emerging features of the rough-hewn block of granite. Particular thanks are due to Peter Honey; the late Richard Rumary; and the late Paul Heim; as well as my friends and mentees Antonia Benfield; Ellie Brown; Dilpreet Dhanoa; Lorna Hackett; and Rhona Scullion.

The leadership of the Nordic countries generally, in their constructive approach to criminal justice reform, deserves a fan-base of its own. No one however has been of more of a personal inspiration to me in developing an appreciation of what the problem-solving drug court can achieve than my good friend Ingunn Seim of Bergen, Norway. From small beginnings she has transformed the Norwegian Correctional Service; and there is a critical lesson still to be learned within this jurisdiction: what is objectively regarded as fair treatment by those convicted of even the gravest crimes can be transformational in terms of their personal rehabilitation.

With the passage of time, and with increasing exposure to those who know how to write persuasively, I learned from Jonathan Aitken; from my son David; and from my friend Sir Terry Waite. I have tried to adopt their more compelling style in my revision; and, even if I have failed in this, my gratitude to each of them remains profound.

To my delight and having been genuinely flattered by the interest each of them showed in my proposals, I have received unexpectedly positive responses from the two surviving Chief Justices of my personal generation, Lord Phillips of Worth Matravers KG, and Lord Thomas of Cwmgiedd.

So many friends, mentees and acquaintances, having learned of the unexpected news mentioned in my closing chapter, actively encouraged the completion of this book with their supportive messages. Far too numerous to list individually, an alphabetical list must suffice:

Mark Alexander; Tracy Alexander; Lord Anderson of Ipswich KC; Tony Askham; Sir Gerald Barling; Carolyn Bates; Lubia Begum-Rob; Ian Bickers; Professor Tim Bliss FRS; Lord Briggs of Westbourne; CJ Burge; Michael-James Clifton; Jon Collins; Tom Conti; Andrea Coomber KC; Lady (Val) Corbett; Marta Cranstone; Dr Antonia Creak; Andrew Curtis; Nicholas Davidson KC; Simon Davis; Douglas and Elizabeth Day; Geoff Dobson; Kay Donalson; Judge Nick Easterman; Judith Fox; Dr Caroline Friendship; Darryn Frost, QGM; Jane Furniss; Steve Gallant QGM; Maryse Gordon; Gibson Grenfell KC; Mark Harries KC; Michilea Hegarty; Amy Higgins; Col David Hills; His Honour Judge David Hodge KC; Nora Holford; Carol Honey; Sir Deian Hopkin; Christian Jensen; Jennifer Jones KC; Joanne Kane; John Kennedy; Morag King; Nicole Lander; Sophie Lenton; Martine Lignon; His Honour Crawford Lindsay KC; Mark Lister; His Honour Judge Lucraft KC; Dr Amy Ludlow; Malcolm Mackinven; Alexandra Marks; Dr Olivera Martinovic; Gurprit Mattu; Eoin Mclennan-Murray; Jo Millington; Chris Monckton; His Honour David Morris; Ranjit Nankani; Michele O'Leary; Anna Owen; Professor Nicola Padfield; Rev Mark Perry; Kenneth Petersen; Michael Pooles KC; Elizabeth Porter; Nuria Riechenberg; Sam Robins; Jo Robinson; Winston Roddick KC; Joshua Rozenberg KC; Louise Shorter; His Honour David Swift; Professor Denise Syndercombe-Court; Christina Tolvas-Vincent; Ryan Walker; Rev Derek and Ven Sheila Watson; Christian Weaver and Virginia Westmacott.

It is conventional even in a first book to pay tribute to a devoted spouse; and as the traditionalist I am I do so without reservation. As the mother of my sons, I owe her everything. But the tribute to her is primarily as my own mentor. Innumerable drafts of these chapters were thrust at her. She would read them; and then, gnomically, would reply "OK". The flash of those brilliant blue eyes told me all I needed to know.